SPIRALLING
TO
THE LIGHT

REVISED EDITION
BRENDA Christa FLEMING

Copyright © 2018. Revised Edition 2025.

BRENDA CHRISTA FLEMING

Dedicated To My Beloved Brother Colin
'A man among men'

ACKNOWLEDGEMENTS

I wish to express gratitude to:

Great Universal Spirit.

Guardian Spirit, Quan Yin, God & Goddess of Compassion, Enlightened Masters, Archangels, Spiritual Guides, Highest Divine Self.

I am indebted to these guides, whose presence provides universal knowledge, ancient wisdom, insights, understanding, and healing guidance, and expands my spiritual growth.

I wish to thank the Enlightened Beings and the Light Workers who work to awaken and align humanity with the Divine Power within us.

I acknowledge and credit the authors I have quoted in words and meditations for their wisdom, comfort, and inspiration. I thank the publishers and authors who allowed their copyrighted work to embellish my words. Throughout this spiritual journey, their written words, ancient wisdom, Reiki, tarot, rune readings, and Spirit Oracle cards have inspired, guided, and validated my path.

Special mention:

Alexis Cartwright *"Transference Healing Animal Magic"* Copyright © 2005 Transference Healing Pty. Ltd., ISBN 0-9750628-2-4 www.transferencehealing.com[1]

Alexis Cartwright *"Beyond Doorways The Mysteries Revealed"* Copyright 2007 Transference Healing Pty. Ltd., ISBN 978-0-9750628-1-4 www.transferencehealing.com[2]

Ciro Marchetti *"Gateway to the Divine Tarot"* Copyright © 2009 Llewellyn Publications

Dorothy May *"Archetypal Reiki"* Journey Editions 2000

Helena Petrovna Blavatsky, *"The Voice of the Silence",* A Verbatim Reproduction of the original edition of 1889

Maria Letizia Renzulli © *"Zen Runes"* © Element Books Limited 1998

The Kryon Writings-*"Lifting The Veil"-* Book 11 Copyright © 2007 Lee Carroll www.kryon.com[3]

The Theosophical Society Printed Brochures. www.austheos.org.au[4]

Toni Carmine Salerno *"Spirit Oracle Cards"* Copyright © 2005 Published by Blue Angel Gallery, Australia www.tonicarminesalerno.com[5]

I have endeavoured to use 'Fair Use' only when including' copyright' material. I trust that the Universe guided me and that the work incorporated was given at the event time, that it dropped into my lap, that it jumped off the shelf, so to speak.

In the manner of tarot cards, runes, and Oracle cards, I have transcribed/ interpreted them to give relevance to the event. I undertook an intensive search to show whether previously published material in this book required permission to reprint. I apologise for any errors. I will make additions and corrections in later editions. Thank you.

---

1. http://www.transferencehealing.com

2. http://www.transferencehealing.com

3. http://www.kryon.com

4. http://www.austheos.org.au

5. http://www.tonicarminesalerno.com

'For Those Who Know
No Proof is Necessary
For those who do not believe
No amount of proof is Enough.'

Adapted from the quote by St. Thomas Aquinas.

INTRODUCTION

With the risk of being labelled eccentric or emotionally unstable, I wrote this book. When we lose a loved one, close friend, or relative, many people sense, feel, see, smell or hear the 'presence of the departed.' This phenomenon is often attributed to imagination or emotional stress and isn't openly discussed. We are tapping into abilities of which little is known. The mainstream population does not want to hear or believe such things, let alone accept that they happen. In this book, I attempt to describe what can and does happen to many people when a loved one dies. We are not stressed to the point of insanity. This ability is a gift, and when embraced, it brings great joy and the true meaning of life. This is a journal detailing events as they unfolded following the death of my brother. I found myself engulfed in what I can only describe as a 'Black Tunnel of Grief,' a period of intense emotional pain. During that time, Spirit appeared to me on numerous occasions. When I emerged four and a half years later, I was guided to journey in Warragul, Victoria, Australia, in 2000.

Life is a series of stories. Some say, 'let the story go,' not believing the tale serves them. When we tune in to our inner voice and listen, heeding our intuition, the story teaches us a lesson. Otherwise, the scenario replays itself in life again and again until we get it, and only then does healing occur. I believe my past is part of who I have become, downloaded in a whim: a song, a word, an aroma, a thought, an association, or a smile. In my life, the death of my brother was so painful that it became life-changing. The events following his death culminated in a moment that served as my 'wake-up call,' a profound realisation that brought me to surrender and the point of spiritual awakening.

This is just the start of my healing and spiritual awakening journey. As I step onto the path of self-discovery and acceptance, there's no turning back!

I've divided my life and stories into the seasons of nature.

My Springtime: Babyhood, Childhood, and Teenage Years.

My Summer: Blossoming into a Wife, Motherhood, and a Career.

My Autumn: Loss and Grieving, Retirement. Finding a passion for writing and awakening to spirituality.

My Winter ~ My Yesterdays and My Today.

Now I can look back and reflect on my life from the beginning until now. The stories have woven themselves into the woman I am today. The puzzle pieces have fallen into place, coming together to form a whole. This is the story of My Autumn.

PROLOGUE

Dearest Brother

Your death has bestowed upon me a gift far greater than I could ever imagine. Most people spend their lives searching for the greatest gift in existence—the insight to understand the true meaning of life.

In dying, you took me to an enlightened, spiritual, and mystical space. There are no words to convey my gratitude for the life you lived and the love you shared. I will always be grateful for the time we spent together.

When I was a little girl, you were my big brother. Throughout my life, you were always there, caring for and protecting me. You had the answers to all my questions. Now I wonder, who will provide me with the answers to the question of why you are gone?

The pain is overwhelming, unbearable. As I write this letter to you, I now recall all the April Fool's Days of my life. It was your special day to play tricks on your little sister. I can visualise the balsa wood model aeroplanes you built and flew from your bedroom window. Look where that dream took you – soaring above the clouds, a pilot behind the cockpit of your plane.

Your last words to me were: 'I Love You.'

Not a single day has gone by since you died when you haven't been in my thoughts. I will walk hand in hand with your memory. My love for you transcends time and space, and it will continue to guide me through each day of my life.

Goodbye, my brother. I love you with all my heart. You will always be with me until we meet again, your little sister.

Binkie.

COLIN

ngland October 1951

E   Two garden paths encircled the small, green patch of lawn, at the centre of which was a shallow pond filled with lilies, reeds, frogs, tadpoles, and many strange yet wonderful wriggling creatures that kept me delighted. On the left path, a young cherry tree grew. Each spring, a blush of delicate pink cherry blossoms burst forth, followed by an abundance of large, juicy white cherries. Where the two paths merged stood a giant, gnarled old pear tree. I loved climbing trees, often scaling high, supported by the sturdy branches; hidden from view among the leafy boughs, it became my refuge. I sat munching on a juicy pear when I heard a noise and looked down into my brother Colin's upturned face and laughing eyes.

"Mum said tea is ready."

I realise I've been caught. It's impossible to hide from my 14-year-old big brother; he knows my every move.

I've Been Thinking
About My Brother
...and I would love
for him to know
What a great guy
I think he is
I would love for you
to know something, Brother...
I think you're a pretty wonderful guy.
And I know I don't tell you
often enough, how much
You mean to me, and how much you always have...
But you're someone I dearly love.
I think of you a lot, and one thought
That has crossed my mind so many times
is that...of the millions
of brothers in the world...
I somehow managed to be blessed
with the best one of all.

~ Laurel Atherton Author Copyright © 1989 by Blue Mountain Arts, Inc. All rights

reserved. Reprinted by permission.

THE DAY OF MY BROTHER'S DEATH

Wednesday, 12 January 1994

In October last year, Mum and I visited Colin in the hospital. I was devastated. My tall, handsome brother lay in bed, tired and lethargic, his skin tinged with a yellowish hue.

Hugging my mother, I said...

"Mama, he is not going to make it."

I flew to Melbourne to be by his bedside. Col's daughter, Gail, my niece, was coming in on a flight from Sydney. Neither of us had been in touch for years due to the breakdown of Col's first marriage. We travelled together in the cab, reconnecting during the journey. I noticed a resemblance between us; we share the same facial features, including our noses and eyes. As we talked, I realised we had similar ideals in life.

At Dandenong Hospital, I felt anxious and concerned. Gail hadn't seen her father in ages. Col was moaning and incoherent. The family gathered around his bedside. I leaned closer, whispering, pleading...

"Don't go, Col, please, please don't go. I need you."

I realised he heard me when he tried to lean up to kiss me.

The Priest arrived, stood at the head of the bed, praying and talking about 'the sins of man.' Col appeared agitated and distressed. The Catholic Church had never been a favoured topic for Colin, and he'd had many religious arguments with Mama over the years. It was clear to me that he didn't want the Priest at his dying bedside.

I whispered: "I understand, I understand!!"

My mother glared at me, saying: "Shush! Listen to the Priest!"

Silently, I said, 'I do not want to listen to the Priest!'

Colin called out to his wife; his dying words were her name.

Later that afternoon, I sat with him, the two of us alone in the hospital room. Holding his hand and unwilling to let go, I silently said ...

"I love you, Col."

The absence of his patient guidance and advice, which he willingly and lovingly provided, became a void I never anticipated. I came to realise that no one could replace his special place in my heart, a place now filled with the profound impact of his loss.

Feeling emotionally overwhelmed, I curled up in my seat on the plane as I flew back to Adelaide. Gazing out of the aeroplane window, high above the clouds, a golden glow filled the sky as a magnificent sunset marked the end of the day of my brother's death.

THE 'GIFT'

A few weeks ago, I purchased a small business and needed to return to work the day after my brother's death. I was on my knees loading a crate full of milk into the fridge when I felt it. While yesterday's flight to Melbourne had left me numb, I could not deny this feeling.

It was early, and the shopping centre wasn't open yet, but I felt someone at the counter. Customers wouldn't arrive for two hours, so I kept loading the fridge. The feeling lingered. There was a presence. I glanced up again and saw the pale blue of his shirt. There he was! Standing at the counter, a sight that both startled and comforted me.

"It's you, Col!"

Still on my knees, glancing behind towards the back of the shop, I peered at his trousers inside the kiosk.

Colin had booked a flight to Adelaide to reconcile with his estranged daughter and visit the small business I had purchased, but death claimed him first; he never made that visit.

Yet here he was! Having my brother there in spirit felt deeply comforting and not strange. As I lay in bed that night, I saw him again; this time, he was inside the bedroom, and I heard him say:

"I was so tired!" Then his heavy presence was on the bed between my husband and me.

A MAN AMONG MEN

T*he Funeral*
Monday, 17 January 1994

Overwhelmed by emotions, I fought hard to hold back tears, shaking physically with my teeth chattering as I entered the church. The floodgates unlocked, and I lost the battle. I was grateful for the unwavering presence of my dear husband of 31 years, who held me close, as well as my precious son and daughter, who stood by my side. Their support was my anchor in the storm of grief. My mother stood stronger than I, her faith sustaining her.

A Police escort was necessary for the Funeral cortege as many drivers from Dandenong Taxis, a company Colin had been a part of for many years, formed a Guard of Honour out of respect for him and to celebrate his life. This display of unity in grief from the taxi industry, a community with which Colin had been deeply involved, was a comforting reminder that we were not alone in our loss.

'Members of Dandenong Taxis and the Victorian taxi industry bade a sad farewell to Colin Brown...

The Dandenong chairman and operations manager praised Colin's skills and ability to lead from the front, behind, or within.

Colin held the positions of director, chairman, VTA councillor, and treasurer at various times.'

Paraphrased from VIC Taxi – Industry Digest February 1994

The Eulogy was a moving testament to... *'a man among men'.*

'A professor of life, doctor of humanity, a man who had the foresight to see the green pastures beyond the mountains of uncertainty.'

The words in my head....

My Brother. My Teacher. My Mentor. My Idol.

He was not just a man among men but a significant part of my life, guiding my journey.

The Eulogy continued, telling the story of a significant loss to his wife, mother, and daughter. There was no mention of his sister, and my heart cried out:

"What about me, what about me?"

At that moment, I heard the last words he spoke to me on the phone just six days ago:

"I love you."

The coffin descended below the ground, red roses and petals landing on the lid. A pack of cards followed. My brother was an avid poker player; then, cigarettes accompanied him on his way. My husband, son, daughter, and I stood hugging, numb with grief, and I raised my eyes to see the priest talking to a group of mourners who were laughing!

How could that be? Why on earth are they laughing?

Later, I was to learn that the topic of their conversation and laughter was poker cards and cigarettes. They shared fond memories of my brother, finding comfort in the lighter moments of his life. That knowledge did not erase the sound of their laughter in my ears or the deep hurt I felt. It was a stark reminder of how we all cope with grief.

CHAOS~WAKING, GRIEVING, WORKING

Shortly after we purchased our own small business, Colin died from Liver and Kidney failure aged 56 years old. I entered a long, dark tunnel of grief.

I had resigned from my career at a Swiss Manufacturing Company, having climbed the corporate ladder and risen to become State Sales Manager for South Australia and the Northern Territory. The Food Industry was male-dominated. As a woman in management, I was a trailblazer in the food industry; it was unheard of in the 80s. I loved the challenges of the job and the regular sales conferences, which allowed me to stay in top-tier hotels, including the Hyatt and Ramada in Australia, as well as internationally in Bali and New Zealand. Occasionally, I travelled to the manufacturing plant in Tasmania and often flew to the Head Office in Victoria. The luxury of a Company car – I had it all.

After accepting the promotion, we moved from Sydney to Adelaide, purchased a new home, and settled into a debt-free life. I tossed it aside, mortgaged the house, and cashed some superannuation to buy the business.

Baz and I had dreamt of owning a little business for years. We dived right in after reading an advertisement for an ice cream franchise in the local newspaper. I struggled to manage the business while grieving the loss of my brother. I was merely existing, not living. The physical toll was immense, leaving my body a constant battleground. The small shop, which was supposed to be a dream come true, became a relentless challenge, a constant reminder of my brother's absence.

Working 80 hours a week, the franchise demanded my every waking hour, overwhelming my thinking, my being, physically playing havoc with my body, and back pain was my constant companion.

SPIRALLING TO THE LIGHT

Waking, grieving, working, sleeping; the dream quickly turned into a nightmare. At the end of each week, I felt mentally and physically exhausted. Like a zombie in pilot mode, I constantly pushed myself beyond my physical limits. The sensation of being trapped in this cycle was overwhelming, a weight I carried with me all the time.

The face I showed the world was a smiling mask, but grief and chaos lay beneath. Only my husband could see the truth he shared with me:

"I hear the sadness in your voice and see it in your eyes."

I ventured into a long, dark tunnel leading to the crevices of my soul.

THEOSOPHY-CORE BELIEFS

In 1993, the year before my brother died, I was driving to Victor Harbor in South Australia as part of my job as a sales manager when I tuned into the radio. The program was about 'Theosophy'. I couldn't recall having heard the word before, and it resonated deeply within my soul. I was listening to my core beliefs, my truths... I now know that these truths and understandings are meant to help me prepare for the pathway ahead, bringing my internal and external worlds closer together.

"I believe in the utmost truth. I think everyone living on the little planet we call Earth is ONE. All races, all religions, all creeds, all sexes, we are all EQUAL.

Specific laws govern the Universe, and its forces do not operate from chance; we are all a part of that Universal Law.

I believe God, whoever or whatever one perceives them to be, abides in each of us, and we are all Divine beings."

'Theosophy means 'Wisdom of God'. It is a statement of the modes of action of the Divine Mind.

This understanding is the heritage of every soul, but he will possess it only as he learns to be a brother to all that lives, for:

"Loving action is the Divine Wisdom at work, and whoso acts lovingly, will inevitably come to this Wisdom."

In possession of the Divine Wisdom, they know the truth, which frees men.'

REALITY

Nine months after Col's death, I was struggling to cope. The small business demanded my attention every waking hour. Mentally and physically exhausted, I pushed myself through each day, the grief unbearable, like a tidal wave that knocked me into submission.

Colin was always there for me. Throughout my life, he had been my rock. I never knew my father; he left with another woman soon after my birth. Colin filled the void as a young girl's older brother and surrogate father. He was patient, gentle, kind, and understanding, always ready and willing to listen, providing necessary advice and support.

The video recording in my mind of Col's death and funeral is playing over and over. As the coffin was lowered into the ground, the flowers were placed on top. It's still running as I write these words. It is impossible to come to terms with the fact that I had no control over Col's death. Believing I controlled every facet of my life, I attended grief counselling. I learnt there are several stages of grief. The loss of control was so foreign and not part of my everyday life's agenda. It became the most important lesson I was to learn:

Life cannot be controlled.

'It is as it is, as it was meant to be.'

LONG DARK TUNNEL

I spent the next four and a half years in that long, dark tunnel. Often, alone in the car, riding out the ebb and flow of this grief, music became the catalyst, consuming me, dragging me down, down deeper. My husband and adult children had withdrawn as my grief was too much for them to bear. The mere mention of my brother's name would bring me to my knees and sweep me away, into the tunnel.

Grief-stricken, I spoke to Col many times; he was always there for me. His spirit manifested in dreams, and his presence was palpable. His essence encompassed me.

I was having some extraordinary experiences. One evening, whilst removing makeup before retiring to bed, I looked into the bathroom mirror:

My face gained a different profile. I turned away, then looked back again into the mirror. Unbelievably, my face became his face, until my reflection became his reflection. I was staring into Col's eyes. At first, it shook me, and I asked:

"What is it, Col?"

I heard him speak his wife's name. The following morning, I rang my sister-in-law and asked: "Are you O.K.?" Phone calls between the two of us since Col's death were mentally exhausting, the joint outpouring of grief immeasurable, there were no words to describe it. My sister-in-law told me her close friend had died of breast cancer. I reassured her that Col was there for her, telling her his spirit had appeared in my bathroom mirror.

Sometime later in my dreams...

There was a green grassy slope. Colin stood at a gateway and said he was going on a journey.

UPWARD SPIRIAL

Mama and I visited my sister-in-law in Victoria. I found it difficult to return to Colin's home, where his absence was absolute. Colin's smiling eyes are no longer there to greet me, yet the memory of him is everywhere. They attended Mass together while I stayed behind. Colin's clothes still hung in the wardrobe, and I buried my face in his blue cardigan, drawing in breath, trying to capture his essence. Curling up in his armchair, I sank into the soft brown velour, allowing it to comfort and envelop me.

Suddenly, my head jerked, my neck stretched, and my head physically spiralled upwards. I had never experienced anything like it before and wondered what had happened to me.

The next day, the three of us visited Colin's graveside. The weight of our loss hung heavily in the air, a palpable reminder of the void left by his absence.

It was a revelation to discover the cremated remains of my father in the 'Boronia Wall'. The connection between Colin and my father, who never knew each other as adults, was a mystery waiting to be unravelled. Both were born in England and now share a final resting place in the Springvale Botanical Crematorium in Victoria, Australia. How ironic, fate deals strange cards! That is another story.

MYSTICS & METAPHYSICAL

I was not only immersed in the mysterious realm of metaphysical experiences; spirit was influencing my mother's life in strange and wonderful ways. When I was a child, the metaphysical fascinated Mama. Later in her life, after returning to the Catholic Church, she denied it, saying:

"It's the work of the devil!"

Mama enjoyed visiting clairvoyants and mediums, which kept our family get-togethers interesting. For fun, she also read palms, the Tarot, and tea leaves.

Often, when she shared stories with family and friends, I felt shivers running up and down my spine. We had a 'Dream Book' similar to a well-worn old black Bible, which we consulted religiously after each dream. In 1997, I sought the help of a clairvoyant in Adelaide, hoping to connect with my late brother. However, the session took an unexpected turn when the clairvoyant revealed: "Your Mother has a sister in England."

I replied that she only had an elder brother who had passed over.

"There is a relative in England doing the family tree."

After I visited the clairvoyant, Mama and I discussed the possibility of her having a sister in England. With my encouragement, she endeavoured to trace her mother's side of the family by writing a letter to:

The Town Clerk, The Town Hall, St. Ives, Cornwall, England.

"Information seeking long-lost relatives."

Then something incredible happened. In the twist of fate, the letter landed on the desk of someone who knew the family well. Mama received a return letter from her mother's sister, Dorothy, who had just happened to be doing the family tree. It was a revelation that would change everything. Dorothy, the key figure the clairvoyant had alluded to, was finally within our reach. Or was she?

My mother's mother, Bessie, married James Joseph Cleary, and they had two children, Michael and Eileen Cleary, my mother and my uncle Mick. The marriage was unhappy. When Mama was two and Mick was just four, Bessie left, taking the children—a brave move, as women had no rights over their children in 1914. Bessie was forced to work, and later, the children were taken from her. They were returned to their father in the care of Aunt Annie and Aunt Eileen. The children never saw their mother again; she passed away only three years later in July 1917, at the age of 32, from tuberculosis.

After the marriage split, Bessie had another daughter, Dorothy, named after her sister, and also the unknown 'Sister in England,' referred to by the Clairvoyant, and the reason Mama looked for her lost family initially. It was a revelation that added a new layer of mystery to our family history.

On her deathbed, Bessie made a heart-wrenching plea over the radio, hoping to reach her estranged children. Alice (my great-grandmother) not only lost her eldest daughter to tuberculosis but also lost contact with her two small grandchildren, Michael and Eileen.

Mama knew nothing of her mother's side of the family, and discovered Bessie to be the eldest of 14 children. She had inherited many aunts, uncles, and cousins. She was in her late eighties and couldn't face the long trip back to England. The saddest part of this story is that my mother led a lonely life as a child. Two aunts raised her from the post-Victorian era, who were very strict, domineering, and showed no affection. She would have been part of a much larger and caring family, and her Grandmother Alice lived to the grand old age of 92, dying in 1959. My Mother moved to Australia in 1955, knowing nothing of the family she was leaving behind.

In 1998, I rang my mother's Aunt Dorothy in England. In her 90s, she asked, "How and why did we start the search for the family?" I told her I had visited a clairvoyant who advised me that my mother had a sister in England.

Mama was known as 'Little Eileen' because her aunt's name is Eileen. Many years later, at a Spiritual meeting, my mother had placed a piece of jewellery on a tray and was sitting in the audience listening, the Medium said:

"There is someone here saying, dear little Eileen, will you forgive me?"

Mama, recognising 'Little Eileen' and realising it was Bessie reaching out to her, cried out: "Yes, of course I forgive you!"

TAI CHI & REIKI INTRODUCTIONS

It was 1997, and as I strolled through the Central Parklands in Adelaide, South Australia, I was attracted to a group of people doing Tai Chi. Pausing to watch the graceful flowing movements, the peace was palpable, and I recognised how much this was lacking in my own chaotic life. I heard my inner voice say:

'I need that peace in my life!'

Life inevitably moves forward, and my life is about to change, so I enrolled in...

"The Australian Academy of Tai Chi."

By chance, during my working day, I called into "The Do Jo" at Highbury in the northern suburbs of Adelaide, which offers Reiki and Tai Chi classes. I chatted with David, the manager, and resonating with his words, I decided to embark on a Reiki course.

REIKI is: 'Universal Life Force' or 'Universal Life Energy'. The principles are:

"Just for today–Do not worry

Just for Today–Do not anger

Just for today–Honour your parents, teachers, and elders

Just for today–Earn your living honestly

Just for Today- Show gratitude for every living thing."

So SIMPLE and POWERFUL!

I was becoming more adventurous in my spiritual pursuits, willing to try new things, open my mind, and deepen my knowledge. This sense of empowerment and growth fuelled my journey.

My first experience of being encompassed by the Light came about when I received Reiki Level 1 Attunement.

August 16, 1998

I am practising Reiki on one of the other students. He is lying on his stomach, and I am sitting at his head with my hands resting on his shoulder blades. My eyes are closed, and I am relaxed as I listen to peaceful meditation music. Then, I experience the strangest sensation; I feel my hands merging deeply within his body, and a brilliant light fills the room. I hear my inner voice say...

'The sun is shining through the skylight.'

When the session finished, I opened my eyes and looked up at the ceiling, finding no skylight.

I was amazed at how I had been engulfed in a shimmering, bright light, despite there being no skylight. How could that be?

RUNE AWAKENING.

My spiritual unfolding was continuing, and I was enjoying the journey of inner discovery. Everything seemed to be happening in a mysterious natural sequence.

My daughter-in-law gave me a set of Zen Runes in a red velvet pouch for Christmas. Knowing little about runes, I remember they were ancient and dated back to the Vikings. The instructions said: "An inspirational combination of Rune Wisdom and Zen Insight ...found by archaeologists in Scandinavia dating back to the Bronze Age (1300 B.C.E.)".

I learnt from the accompanying book titled "Zen Runes":

'Our first contact with the runes always takes place while walking the path of personal growth and creating a beautiful opportunity to go deeper and further in our inner search. The runes offer an opportunity to look beyond the darkness and into the light. Thus, becoming a reminder of our responsibility to look consciously inside ourselves.'

Text adapted from "Zen Runes" Copyright © Maria Letizia Renzulli

This description aptly reflects my current life situation. On Christmas night, I dreamed of a vast field of white flowers, snowdrops, edged with broad-leaved plants. The gardener was collecting bunches of the red and white flowers to discard. I gathered many of the castoffs. My analysis of this dream was:

'The white flowers are for purity, a new start, the red and white flowers together signify death: the death of an era for me. It is time to move on; the year 1998 is coming to a close. I have emerged from the black tunnel of my grief. I'm conscious of being in light and laughter again. The suffering experienced becomes: 'The Journey.'

I conducted my first rune reading on December 26, 1998, which proved to be a significant event.

1st rune–FREYR'S GEBO-COMMUNION-A GREAT GIFT

"You are ready now to grow through communion. You can be one with the Divine, the All, and have freedom to be one and together and together and one. This partnership is the greatest gift in existence."

2nd rune–FREYR'S WUNJO-JOY, SUCCESS

"This is a wonderful moment in your life. The clouds have lifted, the sky is full of emptiness, the sun is shining, and existence is sharing its gift with you. The old knowledge transforms into understanding, putting you in touch with powerful new energy that lies hidden in the depths of your being. Now you can see the path you should follow, choosing naturally what is best for you. Maybe it is time to drop ambitions, goals, and plans that could slow your journey. You are in touch with existence and with yourself. Trust it and let go! It will soon be time to laugh in a new day's light!"

3rd rune–HAGAL'S ALGIZ-PROTECTION, DEFENCE.

"This is the time of transition. Your process of self-change can be accelerated by shifts and turns, causing your emotions to fluctuate. Don't be influenced by this inner turmoil, as it carries a risk of misusing your protective energy, distorting your reality, or leading you astray. Keep your pace, take your space, and your time. Allow existence to protect and care for you. Pain or joy will pass; don't become identified with either of them. The mediator watches and says:

"Ah-ha... "Pure acceptance, without collapsing into the whirlpool, is advice for this time."

4th rune–FREYR'S ANSUZ–MESSAGES.

"Be open now to receive signs or messages to help you begin new things and experience new paths and connections.

LOKI THE MESSENGER GOD, *related to this rune, can bring you incredible gifts in many forms and guises, so be aware.... Ansu is also an invitation to feel the inexhaustible spring of energy available to you, to come closer to your centre and more deeply in touch with your Buddhahood. After the nourishment of your soul comes the possibility of nourishing others, not out of need but from overflowing. Only then can an equal exchange of energy take place. Be open to receive signals from existence and get ready to express your true self."*

How aptly this reading relates to my life right NOW. Just weeks earlier, we had successfully sold the business. Emerging from the dark tunnel of grief after almost five years, the Runes were indicating that I was ready to walk my spiritual path.

I have endeavoured to contact the Publisher Element Books Ltd., Copyright© 1998, for permission to include the work of: Maria Letizia Renzulli, Copyright ©, to no avail. Element Books Ltd does not appear to have been published since 2010. I trust the Universe guided me thus.

DEATH by FIRE, DEATH of A DREAM

Many years ago, my mother visited a clairvoyant. The clairvoyant asked the gathering to place a piece of jewellery on the tray. When Mama's piece was chosen, the clairvoyant said:

"A person in your life has died by fire."

Mama didn't relate to those words, being unaware that her estranged husband had died in a bushfire.

I didn't know my father as he left soon after I was born. As a small girl growing up, I often wondered about him. When I was 22 years old, I learnt of his death. It was 1966, and I was working as a Legal Secretary for a firm of solicitors and barristers, giving me a better understanding of the procedures necessary to trace missing persons. The last known contact from my father was a letter written twelve years before, from Moe in Victoria, Australia, just after he migrated from the U.K.

I wrote to 'Births, Deaths & Marriages' in Victoria, and on the 4th of September 1966, I received a Death Certificate:

Leonard Arthur Brown 'Burnt to death' 16th January 1962.

I cried for the loss of my Daddy. It was the death of a dream. Now I would never meet him.

In an amazing synchronicity, it was 33 years later, in the new year of 1999, that I was to discover more information about my father's death.

My Mothers' neighbour called with a newspaper she received from a relative in Victoria. The paper was the "Warrandyte Diary," a local community news. Inside were articles recounting the dangers of the bushfire season, and one article in particular detailed the 1962 bushfires in the Warrandyte region. There was a photograph "(Pictures courtesy Warrandyte Historical Society)" with this information:

"Leonard Brown died in this concrete tank in Blooms Road, North Warrandyte on 16th January 1962.

Leonard Brown was part of the North Warrandyte Brigade and was fighting the fire on the corner of Blooms Road and Kangaroo Ground Road. He and his neighbour, Harold Betton, were both killed in the fire. Leonard Brown was sheltering in a concrete tank when his house burned down over the top of him."

There was a graphic photograph of my father's burnt-out home. (Based on research by the late Bruce Bence.) Written and recorded in the local newspaper were the details of my father's death, previously unknown to us.

He died on January 16, 1962, nine days after his 50th birthday. We learned later that he was part of the Volunteer Bush Fire Brigade. He was fighting a fire when the wind changed, cutting him off by fire as he ran back to release his birds from the aviary.

Amazingly enough, the neighbour handed the newspaper to Mama on the 37th Anniversary of her Husband's death.

My soul harboured deep hurt, anger, grief, and resentment towards the father I never knew—the father I never had. Having read the details of my father's death, Mama handed over letters he had written to her forty-five years ago. She had kept them all these years. She never stopped loving him. Sitting reading, then re-reading them, the letters enabled me to 'know' him better. I wrote a letter to my father:

To The Man I Never Knew–My Father.
Dear Father,
Although I never knew you, you have been part of my thoughts throughout my life. As a small girl, I looked up into the faces of men passing in the street, wondering:
'Is that my Daddy?'
At seven, I hid behind the kitchen door, excited & shy about seeing you. I was shattered when I realised it wasn't you! It was Uncle Eddy, your brother.
Now, in the autumn of my life, writing to you, and working with Reiki, connecting with my Highest Self, I have been able to heal the pain and loss of the abandonment. I want you to realise the woman I am when we meet again in the next life, but this life will not be relevant!
I am writing to you to gain a deeper understanding of myself and you.
Your Daughter

There was a TV programme called 'Finding My Family'. As I sat watching, my throat constricted, tears streamed down my face, and I felt the loss and grief as I empathised with the people portrayed in the story. On such an occasion, two brothers reunited as adults, having been apart all their lives. One spoke of his feelings towards his departed father: *"Part of me but none of me."* That is how you have been to me: Part of me, *but none of me.*

THE HEALING POWER OF REIKI

I deepened my healing journey with Reiki, using this energy to support me as I grew spiritually.

Reiki is a healing and cleansing of the Body, Mind, and spirit.

REIKI helps open the mind to bring about healing deep within the psyche.

REIKI allows you to delve deep into the hidden crevices of your being, bringing the hurt and the pain to the surface and into 'The Light' for healing.

Cradling, nurturing you on your journey.

The Runes I also read at this time shed deeper meaning into my life, and I could think of my father with peace in my heart for the first time.

1st rune- Once again, I draw

FREYR'S GEBO-COMMUNION I took it to mean 'Communion with my father.'

2nd rune –

HAGAL'S PERTH–INITIATION INTO MYSTERY

"Like the Phoenix consumed in its fire and reborn from the ashes, you may shortly have to face the unknown, some hidden secrets. Your inner eagle is ready to soar free and high, using its eyes to see all around widely from above. As the phoenix radically transforms, I'm reborn."

How apt I should draw this Rune about fire and ashes and rebirth.

During a Reiki healing session, I received an insight:

'Loki the Messenger God', related to the Rune *(in my first reading), can bring you incredible gifts in many forms and guises, so be aware...*

The newspaper article detailing my father's death, and the letters my mother had kept for 45 years, were the gifts from *'LOKI the Messenger God.'* The information they contained worked swiftly to perform a catharsis on my soul.

SPIRALLING TO THE LIGHT

REIKI enabled the buried hurt, anger, and resentment to surface and lift away as the chains were released. I was no longer the little girl looking for her Daddy!' My Eagle Soared, forgiveness and peace followed.

DREAMS, SPIRITUAL INSIGHTS

My healing journey continued in 1999, marked by vivid dreams that provided spiritual insights. I would have loved to consult Mama's old Black Dream book, but it was long gone. In a dream, I was a child again, crying and calling out for Mummy. There were floods, with water everywhere. Wearing a white shirt, Colin appeared at the bedroom door and asked if I was okay. I awoke feeling confused, surprised to see no water, realising that his spirit had manifested. Throughout my life, I have experienced recurring dreams of drowning.

Reflecting on this dream took me back in time...

I had a serious car accident late in 1977. Returning from work, driving too fast as I did back then to pick the kids up from school and kindergarten, I rolled the car, flipping it over on Powderworks Road, Mona Vale, N.S.W., Australia. Climbing out through the shattered windscreen, I was lucky to walk away unscathed. The insurance company wrote off the car, and over the next month, I realised how fortunate I was to be alive. This accident was to change the course of my life, and shortly afterwards, while away on Christmas holidays camping at Park Beach Caravan Park in Coffs Harbour, we spotted a motorhome. In 1977, there were plenty of

Volkswagen Combi vans in Australia, but very few motorhomes were available. The owners of this motorhome had imported it from Europe.

My husband, Baz, and I decided to sell everything and, with our two small children aged 7 and 5, travel the world! After returning home to Elanora Heights on the Northern Beaches of Sydney, we put our house on the market and sold it to the first buyer. The house had tripled in value over the past seven years. We sold every piece of furniture, both cars, and kept only a few children's toys and items of sentimental value. Our possessions fit into five wooden tea chests for storage with Mama.

A few relatives and friends were shocked by this decision. By May 1978, we accepted the first "cancelled" tour package that the travel agent offered us. We flew from Sydney, stopping in Adelaide on our way to Perth, where we boarded the small Russian cruise ship 'Turkmenia', which was heading for Singapore. Upon arriving at Fremantle Dock in Western Australia to board the vessel, our first impressions were:

"It doesn't look much bigger than a Sydney Harbour ferry!!"

1978 was still a romantic, nostalgic era when ships departed from harbours adorned with streamers. Cousins living in Perth came to see us off, and, as is the custom, we tossed out the traditional 'paper streamer', each of us holding onto an end until the final link from ship to shore was severed. We were off on an unknown adventure!

We were aboard the ship for five glorious days. Upon our arrival in Singapore, the weather was stifling. It felt like we had stepped into an oven as we disembarked from the ship. The travel agent had booked a flight from Singapore to London on Thai International. Once in London, we purchased a new motorhome, the Bedford Advantura, which was equipped with two double beds: one over the cab for the children and the other serving as a dining table that could be lowered. It had a kitchen, a shower, and a toilet—everything necessary for a great holiday.

For nearly two years, we loved travelling around Britain, Europe, and Scandinavia, using the money we had received from selling our belongings.

Where is this leading? I am sharing this story with you because it prompted me to reminisce about Wales. We crossed the border from England into Wales, travelling through the county of Hereford, driving alongside a river:

Shivers ran up and down my spine, and a recurring nightmare I'd experienced throughout my life flashed before my eyes. It was this river! I know with spine-tingling certainty that I drowned here!

Years later, a clairvoyant confirmed that I had drowned in a previous lifetime, and I wept as she spoke these words.

The vivid dreams continued, and it felt as if my psychic senses were awakening. It was May in Adelaide, South Australia, when winter's cold, icy fingers made their arrival. The chill seeps into my arthritic bones and settles within my lungs. I woke up suffering from bronchitis.

Baz asked: "How are you?"

"I had a dreadful dream. I dreamt a ship sank."

We received news that the 'Sun Vista' had sunk in the Straits of Malacca off Penang five days later.

1st July. Dear Auntie Joyce, my mother's brother's wife, visited me in a dream. She arrived by ferry and showed me a book she was reading. This made sense since she was an avid reader when she was alive. In the dream, Auntie Joyce called out to her daughters, Tess, Tina, and Annie, to come before the ferry departed. They came running, including Tina, who had been disabled after contracting polio as a baby.

I said: "Slow down, slow down, there's plenty of time."

We sat chatting, experiencing, and exchanging so much joy and love.

Next, Baz's parents, Alby and Muriel, who had passed over some years before, arrived in my dreams. They came for a visit and sat awhile, smiling. I looked into their blue eyes and decided Baz had Muriel's eyes. Muriel was affectionately known as Molly. At the breakfast table the next morning, I told Baz, "Your parents came for a visit last night, and you have your mother's eyes."

Uncle Mick was in my dreams tonight. It is July 23, 1999. I called him 'Dadda Mick', as he was the closest person I had to a father. He passed away from a stroke in 1994, the same year my brother died. We sat together before he passed, and although he couldn't talk much due to the stroke, tears streamed from his eyes as we reminisced and remembered. Colin was like a son to Uncle Mick, who helped fill the void left by the father who had walked away. In my dream, Dadda Mick looked so frail. I tucked him into bed and kissed him on the forehead.

SPIRALLING TO THE LIGHT

On the last day of July, I had a strange, symbolic dream. Baz and I were walking along a grassy slope towards crystal-clear blue water, and there were rocks scattered along the sandy bottom. The water felt strangely buoyant as we waded into it. On the horizon were two symbols: A bridge and the Star of David. After leaving the water, we walked uphill to another landmark: a cross, and then stood gazing out over the bay towards Melbourne.

Synopsis: *The difference between a dream and spirit manifesting: Dreams fade and are forgotten. When Spirit manifests, the memory of the 'dream' imprints on your soul, the core of your being, and is never forgotten. I understood that wading into buoyant water symbolised the beginning of a new life situation- a spiritual refreshment. The rocks represented obstacles yet to be to overcome before the uphill walk indicating it would not always be easy– The bridge symbolised the connection and transition to The Star of David – the close relationship between humanity and the Divine – 'As Above so Below' to finally the Cross on the Hill – Symbol of Eternal Life.*

EXPANDED CONSCIOUSNESS~
White Pulsating Light

New Year, New Century 2000

Life went on. There were times when the grief still hit me like a giant wave, but I realised I had to learn to live without my brother. It was a great relief now that the business had been sold. I felt like I had been released from prison, and the weight had lifted from my shoulders. Baz and I had bought a Winnebago and planned to escape to our first motorhome rally in Warragul, Victoria. The gathering of 1,000 motorhomes, representing various makes, models, shapes, and sizes. Free spirits and retirees travelling around Australia. As we entered, someone gave us an information bag. The following five days were filled with entertainment and activities.

A lecture listed on the calendar of events sounded interesting...

'Morning tea with a Medium.'

The Medium was a popular Clairvoyant from Queensland.

Glenys shared her spiritual journey, followed by a question-and-answer session. At the end of the lecture, she invited everyone to a guided meditation the following morning, Sunday, April 30.

Suddenly, the suggested venue for meditation became unavailable due to complaints from people disapproving of the 'nature' of the gathering. The weather was freezing, and a bleak, overcast sky threatened rain. The new location for the meditation was a tin shed. A biting, icy wind howled around my face as I set up my camp chair in the circle. Snuggling into the warmth of my red ski jacket, I watched as others arrived to join the circle. I meditated for the first time in a 'Spiritual Circle'.

Listening to haunting music, the Medium said:

"Take a deep breath, relax in the chair, and think of a departed loved one."

As I thought of Colin, tears welled up in my eyes. I became aware that my closed eyelids fluttered, my fingers twitched, my hands and feet felt heavy, and my heartbeat pounded loudly in my eardrums. Then, something unbelievable occurred. I was being inflated from within, blown up like a balloon. Although I knew I was sitting in the camp chair, I felt myself expanding. My throat constricted as the tears flowed.

The medium led me through a gateway into a garden filled with tall, ancient trees and vibrant wildflowers. Strolling along a winding path, I arrived at a lakeside. My brother Colin stood beside a rowboat, smiling.

Col and I sat facing each other as he rowed across the lake. Getting out of the small boat on the opposite shore, I was engulfed in shimmering, radiant, iridescent white light. Instantly, my departed ancestors embraced me. The outpouring of love was palpable. Surrounded by that love and absorbing it, my thoughts flew to my present family on earth, sending feelings of deep love to them. Happy, blissful tears flowed down my face.

I relived the first time my brother took me flying in his light Beechcraft aeroplane from Moorabbin Airport in Victoria. I was wearing my favourite red dress. As he introduced me to his friends, I realised how proud he was of me, his little sister. We soared high above the earth together, hovering below the clouds, watching tiny cars travelling along the motorway.

I was nervous as we approached landing, and the palms of my hands were sweaty. Colin said:

"Could be bumpy on landing."

I realised that the meditation had ended when I saw Colin's silhouetted figure surrounded by a golden halo of light, turning and walking off into the distance.

Glenys was encouraging me to return to the present, to this space, this time. I found it difficult to come back; I wanted to remain in this joyous place. The group was invited to share their experiences. With blissful tears streaming down my face, I dabbed my eyes with a soggy tissue. My throat still felt constricted, and I couldn't utter a word. Glenys gestured for me to stay back.

"Do you do this often?" she asked me.

I was confused,

"Do what?"

"Sit in a Spiritual Circle."

"No, this is the first time."

White pulsating light surrounded you, and there was a tall man. "Has your husband passed over?" she questioned.

"It was my brother."

"He merged with you," she told me.

When I returned to Adelaide, I searched the spiritual bookshops, looking for answers to my questions:

'What happened that day?' 'Why did it happen?'

I was disappointed. I did not understand the statement...

'An Expanded State of Consciousness.'

THIRD EYE CHAKRA
April 15, 2001

My life changed forever that day in Warragul at the Motor Home Rally. I devoted the next twelve months to 'find myself'. I joined the Psychic Club of Australia and meditated frequently, hoping to recapture the expanded state I had experienced in the Guided Meditation Circle of Light.

Whilst meditating, I feel a distinct pressure in the 3rd eye region.

Thinking I had left my glasses on, I reached up to take them off, only to realise that I wasn't wearing them. The pressure between my eyes was intense during meditation. I received an insight, a 'knowing'; an inner voice spoke of my Third Eye being open. My brain was filled with colours not yet invented - the brightest, deepest iridescent purples and vibrant, luscious greens flooding my senses - and an inner sense of peace enveloped me.

The 'Third Eye is about Intuition, Inner Vision, Knowledge, and Knowing.

My mind is open to a new vision. My awareness expanded through my Higher Self.

That night, following the mediation, I had a dream...

I was visiting an unfamiliar place, a home unit. The electricity had failed. I glanced out the window; Colin was waiting for me on a flight of stairs. I called out in excitement, and he came into the lounge room. We hugged, and he sat in a large, old-style armchair. I perched close to him on the armrest, while his wife sat at his feet on one side. My daughter, Naomi, was sitting on the floor on the other side of him, and there was a man I didn't know also present. He jokingly asked, "Why did Col have three birds with him?" Col laughed. As Col left, I caressed the outlines of his face, and he walked away with his wife.

As I woke, I recognised I was lucid dreaming.

(Lucid dreaming is the ability to be in the dream, awake, aware.)

I was delighted; I realised I was the portal. Col had been with me so that he could be with his wife. Later in the day, I called my sister-in-law to let her know.

It had been seven years since Colin died. Tonight, his spirit revisited, connecting us all through the power of Love.

DIVINE REALISATION
Body, Mind & Spirit Festival
June 3, 2001

It was that time of year again when I looked forward to attending the Body, Mind & Spirit Festival in Adelaide. At a Reiki workshop, I spoke with Mark Calvert, a Master Reiki teacher from the UK. He invited me to a Meditation Evening. It had been three years since I received my Reiki Level 1 Attunements. Maybe it was time to step up.

I enjoy workshops at Body, Mind, and Spirit Festivals; I laughingly refer to myself as a 'workshop junkie.' At a workshop, I realised that I regularly practise hypnotherapy on myself. I feel it has enhanced my life, taught me to focus on positive thoughts, recognise negative attitudes, and allowed me to turn them around. I learnt...

The quality of our thoughts affects the quality of our lives. We are what we think.

The next workshop I attended was entitled:

'Crystal Workshop,' 'How to Read Your Body,'

I visualised myself as stressed, with shallow breathing, then holding my breath, and I experienced a painful sensation in the right side of my lower back. In contrast, I visualised myself as calm, breathing deeply into my belly, grounded and balanced, with my feet apart. The pain disappeared. There was a fantastic difference in just a few minutes.

The next Workshop ~ *'Angel Meditation'* suggested:

"Your problems will 'lift' when you hand them over to the Universe." Hallelujah!

I attended the Meditation Evening led and guided by Mark Calvert, entitled:

'Divine Realisation Meditation'

Mark guided me to breathe slowly and deeply, down into my belly, my core, and my Hara (navel), then to breathe out through my Heart Chakra. Called forth Archangel Raphael, I focused on opening the Crown Chakra, my eyes flickering and my heart pounding. Sitting motionless, I listened to Mark's voice. I was bathed in the deepest purple, then brilliant, iridescent white light engulfed me, shattering the vision behind my closed eyelids. Closing the Crown Chakra and opening the Base Chakra, Mark gradually guided me back, grounding me in this time and space.

I found myself in a room full of people and realised I had been transported to another realm with ease.

KUNDALINI

After this meditation, I went home and struggled to sleep. Shifting to the second bedroom by myself, I had a vivid dream.

My dream is so absolute. I encountered a large, spoked wheel contraption in the middle of the road. Unable to drive around it, I went onto it. Immediately, the windscreen shattered, the noise piercing my consciousness. I knew, felt, and was aware of 'good and evil' forces, as well as light and dark, throughout the dream.

Mama was there, dressed in a brown nun's habit, in the old traditional style, with the habit framing her face. I said to her:

"I've been so worried about you, I've been away for so long."

She replied, "I have been perfectly all right, no need to worry."

Then I was 'told: "Your initiation is complete."

It was 4.29 am when I returned to bed, snuggling up to the warmth of Baz.

At 5:30 a.m., I awoke with the word 'Kundalini' circling in my brain.

I had not heard this word before.

Later that morning, while standing in the shower with water cascading over my body, I became disoriented. Feeling faint, I dropped to my hands and knees, my head tucked under, attempting to regain my balance. My lip curled up into a snarl. Feeling frightened, I said:

"Go away, go away! In the name of the Father, the Son, and the Holy Ghost."

The experience was unpleasant and disquieting. I walked into the main bathroom to put on makeup before heading to work— the bathroom where I often catch the scent of my brother. On the bench is a perfectly shaped seashell filled with potpourri. A pink, heart-shaped piece fell to the floor. The message I received from my inner voice was: 'Sending you Love'

Later, while driving to work, my daughter called. I could tell by her opening words that she was distressed. Naomi breeds dogs; she has always adored animals, and dogs are part of her family.

At 6 am during feeding, there had been a dogfight, and Naomi had been seriously bitten on her left arm. I realised earlier in the shower that I had foreseen the attack of the snarling dogs when I felt faint and my lip curled into a snarl.

Two days later, I spoke to Mark about the symbolic dream and this incident. He gave me some advice.

"You are a Priestess! There is a need for you to face the dark side and to acknowledge it.

Your Kundalini has awakened."

Kundalini-pronounced: Koondaleeni "Energy of Awakening"

VEGETARIAN

June 17 and 18, 2001

I had arranged with Mark to receive my Reiki Level 2 Attunements. It was a mystical and uplifting experience. Relaxing with my eyes closed, I sank into a deep meditation. Vibrant purple and green colours spiralled, swirled, and circled in my mind. With acute hearing, I heard Mark say:

"There is profound presence."

The power of Reiki attunements continued to unfold in unexpected ways in my life. My husband, Baz, was angry with me for going off and doing my own thing. To get back in his good books, I prepared his favourite meal: rack of lamb.

As he yelled at me across the table, I could feel his anger coming at me like spears. I cut a small piece of meat from the lamb chop and popped it into my mouth. Urgh! It tasted awful, like a kidney. I spat it out. Cold shudders rippled down my spine, and I visualised myself as a cannibal in a past life, tearing at flesh. The next morning, when I opened the freezer door, I was repulsed by the sight of dead meat and made a conscious decision to become a vegetarian. I had previously enjoyed steak and the occasional Big Mac, but after becoming attuned to a higher level of Reiki, I no longer wanted to eat animal meat. Becoming a vegetarian overnight felt like a natural evolution.

Reiki provides: *'Cleansing of Spirit-Purity of Mind.'*

The Healing Art of Reiki ~ The Awareness Institute ~

"The Healing Art of Reiki teaches us to work in balance and harmony with the Universal Life Force, allowing energy to flow through us and be of unconditional benefit to self, others, animals, and our environment."

Reiki is more than just a therapeutic tool; it serves as a pathway to self-empowerment, a spiritual journey that encourages us to become deeply centred in our hearts. Through practising Reiki, we cultivate a stronger connection with our true nature. Love and joy radiate from within, allowing others to connect with their love and healing, nurturing a deeper awareness of being and a bond with the All That Is in a profound space of unconditional love.

ANGELS & the ART of LOVE

I continued my spiritual growth by attending another workshop with Mark Calvert, titled 'Angels and the Art of Love.' The guided meditations into the angelic dimensions were sublime and helped me discover deep peace and a new connection to my Divinity.

I trance into deep meditation, acutely aware of my surroundings.

Powerful energy engulfs me, and I am physically shaking.

An incredible, shimmering white light overwhelms me, and my entire being transcends into love.

From a distance, I could hear Mark's voice, urging me to return to this time and this space. In a euphoric state, I found it challenging. Mark placed his hands on my feet to physically ground me, and then on my shoulders. Gradually, I returned to my consciousness, tears of pure joy streaming down my face!

THE COSMIC CONSCIOUSNESS WORKSHOP

The following month, I attended:

The Cosmic Consciousness Workshop.

This workshop profoundly impacted my psyche. I learned about the different levels of consciousness, realising I had conducted my life by grasping and desiring material wealth, believing that possessions bring happiness.

Due to the immense impact these teachings have had on me, inspiring and encouraging me to incorporate them into my daily meditation and Tai Chi practice, I have included them in a separate section at the end of this book, entitled 'Meditations & Teachings.'

Enjoy!

SHAMANIC CONNECTIONS

I started a thirty-day meditation in late June 2001. Entering my sacred sanctuary, I lit candles, burned incense, and played soft meditative music. At the end of the meditation on July 30, 2001, I watched SBS TV.

'Discovery Program-Ancient Shamanic Healers.'

I discovered that ancient Shamans communicated with Spirits in the Orkney Islands, Scapa Flow, off the far North Coast of Scotland, where my life began. I strongly resonated with them. I have been in touch with my brother's spirit for the past seven years.

My parents were both in the Navy during World War II, stationed at the British Naval Base, Flotta, Scapa Flow, in the Orkney Islands. On the 24th of May 1941, the Destroyer HMS 'Hood', the pride of the British Naval Fleet, departed to confront the German enemy but was torpedoed by the German Battleship Cruiser the 'Bismarck'. Only three people from the 1,421 seamen on board survived. My parents were to lose many friends on that fateful day.

Before Colin died, he visited the Orkney Islands on holiday. He presented me with a 'Shamanic Celtic Symbol', my most treasured possession, which I never remove from my neck. After the Discovery Program, I wrote in my Journal:

There is a distinct connection; my life began in the Orkney Islands. This is an 'ancient sacred place' for communing with 'Spirit.'

RUNE VALIDATIONS & PREDICTIONS

I was receiving messages from Spirit in many different ways.

I sat with the Runes – 'The Oracle for Spiritual Process.'

Each time I drew three runes, their wisdom served as a guiding light, clarifying my position on this journey and signalling the start of a new cycle.

'It is time to care for the planted seed for the flowers and fruit to blossom and grow to complete the cycle. Be patient, give yourself time. You have done your work honestly, now allow existence to nourish you. Understand that delays can be helpful; watch, see, understand, and reconsider obstacles. All inconveniences are helpful reminders to look more closely at your path. All potentiality is now available, so use it creatively in the world of matter or inner peace. The perfect balance, the natural Buddhahood, is at hand. Looking into your heart, you should discover the work you must complete.'

My daughter's company offered her a promotion that required her to relocate to Sydney with her husband. Searching online for a spacious property that would accommodate their dogs and horse, they found themselves pressed for time before she was set to start her new position. The current house needed renovations before it could go on the market, and it felt like one massive rush. I decided to 'read' the Runes. Amidst the chaos of leaving, I was anxious and apprehensive about her.

The Rune Predictions:

Is this the right time for you to go? Take your time, don't rush. Just be. Perhaps you're becoming too serious and identifying too closely with your actions; it's time for a good belly laugh. If you still feel uncertain, take another Rune.

I drew a Master Rune:

Laughter. Live, Love, and Laugh. Enjoy yourself; it's later than you think.
The third was also a Master Rune - Laughter reversed, saying...

This Rune reminds you that it can easily turn your tears into laughter. It's up to you: do you want to cry or laugh? Unreleased Pain. Un cried Tears. What a Drama!!

Oh no! The reading...

Yes, I Cry.

INITIATION by FIRE

In October, my daughter and son-in-law moved into their new property in the picturesque Southern Highlands of Sydney. The garden was a well-established showpiece, with archways of Wisteria adorning the pathways, and shrubs and flowering bushes requiring little attention, which suited them, as they had little time for gardening. There was plenty of room for the dogs and horses. On Christmas night, my daughter rang. Bushfires were raging towards them, and she was sitting on the roof of their home, the only place to receive mobile phone signals. The bushfires had cut phone and electrical lines, and there was no power. The generator pump from the dam was inoperable, and the sprinklers on the roof were not working. I was reminded of my father's death in a bushfire.

The chaotic turmoil of my mind kept me awake all night. I meditated, calling forth Archangel Michael to protect them, passing the chaos and trauma up to the Universe. I had not heard from them the following day, Boxing Day. Television reports on the bushfire only fuel fear; I couldn't watch or listen to them. I continue to meditate, refrain from talking to anyone, and walk in the garden, playing music to soothe my aching soul.

Late in the afternoon, Andrew's mum rings, crying with relief, telling us they were all right. The bushfires swept in on three sides, and, releasing the horses, they took the dogs inside the home. They stood side by side to fight the oncoming blaze, unable to see their hands in front of their faces because of the dense smoke, ashes, and embers as the fire raged around them. The hair on their arms, eyebrows, and lashes was singed off as they fought hard with the little resources they had. Andrew and Naomi realised they shouldn't have stayed when a line of trees exploded near the house. The volunteer bushfire brigade could not reach them; they were fighting to save the house for an elderly couple next door. A battle they lost. All the surrounding homes in the area were on fire. The bushfire raged up the gully, the flames parting at the dam. The house was in line with the dam and was saved. They were lucky to be alive. The picturesque gardens no longer existed. They had owned the home for just 10 weeks.

The previous owners arrived the following day to view the damage. The woman cried, gazing at the garden she had so lovingly tended, which was now a blackened wasteland.

I desperately need to be with my daughter, hug her, but she flatly refused, saying....

"Mum, don't come, you don't need to see this!"

My daughter is a strong Leo woman. When I protested, she remained adamant. NO!

The Runes' advice & warning had been:

'Take your time, do not rush.' It is up to you.

Do you want to cry or laugh? What a Drama!!

Yes, I Cry.

REIKI LEVEL 11 ~ ATTUNEMENTS

In November 2001, I became a Reiki II Helper at the mystical OSHO Centre in Unley, SA. Having recently obtained my Reiki Level II attunements, the experience was profound.

In my journal, I wrote about Reiki II's distant healing.

I send distant healing to Mark, working on his heart chakra, which is encompassed by an intense white light pulsating within and around me, my body spiralling, and my heart pounding. I am resonating intensely with the energy, and the chair I sit on is even moving. In a euphoric state, my inner voice says, 'Move on.' The pulsating lessens as I move from chakra to chakra. Towards the end of the session, as I shift my focus to Mark's feet, I am engulfed by a pulsating light, my heart pounding again in my ears. In time, aware of people moving around, say goodbye to Spirit. Silent tears of joy! I am so blessed.

The second distant healing to Mark is a continual series of fast spiralling, balancing, spiralling, balancing, spiralling, balancing. Towards the end of the session, I noticed a distinct sensation in the middle finger of my right hand. It is like I have no hand; it has merged into the ether, and I'm left with just my middle finger. My psychic pencil. Receiving a distant healing from Mark, I feel weightless, mentally levitating, surrounded by 'The Light,' and intense colours.

As I continued my Reiki training, I found peace in my spiritual journey. I was able to send compassion to those expressing feelings of racism, and I found tranquillity in the face of Colin's death. My healing hands on the core of my being, my navel, merged within myself, reminding me of the first time I experienced this sensation during my Reiki 1 training. I was surrounded by iridescent purple and pale lilac mists, feeling completely at peace.

Namaste, I have merged with my own 'Higher Self'.

Following, I received a Reiki Level II certificate.

MASTER REIKI ATTUNEMENT.

Mark and I travelled to Victor Harbor, a southern coastal town on the Fleurieu Peninsula south of Adelaide, South Australia. The drive was a pleasant hour spent chatting, with sunny blue skies, lovely views, and calm water. We spent the day on Granite Island as part of my training for the Master Reiki Certificate. Meditating, Mark talked of the 'Serpent of Fire' Master Symbol used in Reiki. Red is not usually the colour I see when meditating. As Mark spoke, I became engulfed in a brilliant, deep red, vast river of flowing Lava.

Saturday 5th January at Thebarton cottage, meditating, giving and receiving Reiki Master Symbols. The last sacred ceremony complete: Mark asked:

"What Do You Want to Manifest?" I replied:

"To 'cross over' to be with Spirit."

I sat motionless, meditating, my heart pounding in my ears and beating in my chest, swept away by deep violet and vivid green swirling and spiralling colours filling my mind.

I was in the boat with my brother again, crossing over to the other side. As I stepped onto the shore, brilliant, iridescent, translucent 'Light' surrounded me, flooding my senses. Happy beings of 'light' encompassed me, with profound love flowing forth and radiating out. Once more, I felt sensations of expanding, becoming huge. 'Light' exploded into the core of my being. Merging with 'The 'Light,' and encompassed by 'The Light,' I became 'The 'Light!!!' Visualising Buddha being 'One' with Buddha, tears of infinite bliss streamed down my face, and I felt serenely at peace.

I want to stay in this euphoric space...Instinctively, I know I need to slowly, gradually return to this time, finding myself in the Lotus position in Thebarton cottage, my Master teacher saying:

"You know, don't you!"
"Yes, I know" is all I need to reply.
It is the wisdom of knowing. Thank you; I'm profoundly grateful.

We spent the rest of the weekend meditating, giving, and receiving Reiki. Mark taught me the rituals necessary to become a Master Reiki Teacher, and the required symbols for each Attunement—a significant milestone in my quest for spiritual growth and healing.

Transcending in and out of 'The Light'. The end of the weekend left me content and at peace...

INNER PEACE FOR WORLD PEACE

It is the eve of Baz and my 39th wedding anniversary, 14th April 2002. It's the most glorious autumn day in Adelaide, with a cloudless blue sky and a cool breeze. This morning, while I was showering, I realised why I chose Baz to be my lifelong partner:

I always strive to achieve and challenge myself. Throughout our lives, Baz has had a quiet acceptance of life. Money has never been important to him. My inner voice tells me:

'Happiness is contentment.'

We finish work early and enjoy dinner at a restaurant in North Adelaide. There is a public talk at St. Peter's Cathedral entitled:

"Be the Change You Want to See Inner Peace for World Peace." **Swamiji.** The brochure describes Swamiji as:

"One of our time's most outstanding spiritual leaders and a tireless advocate of world peace. Swamiji has dedicated his entire life to serving humanity. You will be inspired and uplifted in his talks." Swamiji.com.au

I introduce Baz to Mark. Baz does not want to be here. He is appeasing my desires on our anniversary! He does not want to know or understand this part of my life.

I sat motionless, inspired and uplifted, meditating, my heart pounding in my ears and thumping in my chest cavity, carried away by deep, vibrant violet and iridescent, vivid green swirling and spiralling around my brain.

WESAK ~ Full Moon in Taurus

April 27 2002, Saturday
I took advantage of every opportunity for spiritual growth and learning that was available to me. This time, I was attending a Wesak celebration.

The "Wesak Ceremony" is a remarkable global cosmic meditation and an extraordinary spiritual ceremony, commemorated during the full moon in Taurus, the year's holiest day. It is the largest and most sacred Full Moon Festival, when humanity receives the highest frequency of 'Light.' It has evolved into much more than the original Festival of the Buddha, which honours Buddha's birth, death, and enlightenment. It is a sacred time of great spiritual renewal and celebration. It is said that from Mt. Kailash, the holy mountain in Western Tibet said to be both the spiritual and energetic core of the Earth, Archangels & Ascended Masters, and other Beings of Light descend to Earth in the Wesak Valley to bless the faithful gathered there, in a transcendental, universal Mass. During this time, the energies of enlightenment and compassion flood the Earth, blessing all beings ready to receive. The sense of awe and wonder during this celebration is truly inspiring.

Mark & I attended the celebrations at a private home in Stonyfell, Adelaide. It is a gathering of 50 people. The hostess, a 'Spiritual Medium,' welcomes and invites us to connect. The sound of a drum grounds me, whilst a Harpist and Flautist carry me away.

While meditating, the now familiar celestial pressure in my third eye is present. Closed eyelids flicker, and intense swirling colours flood my senses.

Arms uplifted, shuddering, I'm transposed into my Ethereal Body. Downloading powerful energy, a burst of iridescent luminous white 'Light' engulfs me.

SPIRALLING TO THE LIGHT

Calling forth Quan Yin, God & Goddess of Compassion. I'm lifted, up, up, up into the stratosphere, spiralling higher than I have ever been before, filled with an incredible peace, and love overwhelms me.

I find it astonishing to be transported to another space surrounded by people.

I'm slowly returning, before grounding the spiralling starts again, transcending me upwards into 'The Light.' I spiral into the vortex, my heart pounding.

'LIGHT, COLOURS, ENERGY.'

Tai Chi and meditation have become integral to my daily life, bringing me peace and contentment. This morning, whilst doing Tai Chi, a white energy field appeared around two small pictures on the lounge room wall. While meditating, the light brightens, becoming a three-dimensional tunnel of 'white light' encircling the pictures, as the palest yellow and green colours move into the same vicinity. As Tai Chi turns me towards the window and lowers my vision, I see the brightest green and purple interspersed. I acknowledge that I "feel" the presence of energy and 'see' the colours.

Sunday, 12 May 2002 – Mother's Day

The light around the pictures this morning is glowing, a 'halo.' As I meditate, deeply intense 'healing' rays of green appear. Spiritual purple and healing green rays cover three-quarters of the entire lounge room wall. A flickering 'white light' appears on the ceiling. My inner voice is saying:

"Reiki Light."

White Light Energy continues, flickering and moving amongst green and purple.

I hold the manifestation of 'light' and colours for minutes before changing my Tai Chi stance. It is a great Mother's Day gift. Thank you.

BODY MIND & SPIRIT FESTIVAL - ADELAIDE

It's that time of year again when I enjoy Body, Mind, and Spirit Festivals, attending workshops on Saturdays and Sundays. One of the 'special' workshops is:

'Connect to your Spirit Guides and Angels'

"A Journey to learn and understand your spiritual contracts, discover any underlying vows and obligations you are yet to dissolve and form a close bond with your spirit guides. Powerful, simple exercises to draw energy working around you."

Sitting in the front row on the aisle. Easily meditating up into 'The Light' feeling the familiar pressure in my third eye, eyelids flickering, a 'Magical Space.' Placing my left hand over my thumping heart, I heard acutely and was fully conscious of the surroundings. Then I became aware that the workshop had ended, and people were beginning to move. Still, I stay in the brilliance of the white light, reluctant to leave. I can't ground myself, preferring to wait. Finding it difficult to focus on returning to this space, I put my head between my knees, but still, my heart pounds in my ears. Someone says:

"Are you O. K?" I hear them call out to someone. Then I am being guided outside. Emphatically, I tell her: 'I did not want to return! It was so beautiful!' She says, stamp your feet and buy a drum. I find Mark at his display stand, excitedly telling him what has occurred.

1st ANNIVERSARY VEGETARIAN

June 16, 2002

Celebrating a year since I became a vegetarian, I love it!

When I first became a vegetarian, it materialised overnight. I lost weight and found myself constantly hungry, so I relied on carbohydrates to satisfy my hunger. This year, I studied nutrition and realised I lacked protein, so I researched all foods containing protein and adopted a balanced diet without added meat or fish (no flesh, no eyes, no bum!). A handful of nuts each day became a great source of protein, and I discovered I was a 'Lacto-Vegetarian' since I still enjoyed cheese. I loved how I cooked, appreciating the colours of the food on my plate.

At the time, I agreed to keep cooking meals for Baz, including steak, sausages, chicken, roast, and fish—the 'normal' meals—to 'keep the peace.'

Some things were worth keeping the peace for.

ATTITUDE

We have been invited to dinner, to a friend of a friend's home, and the main topic of conversation was the refugees from Vietnam. The host said: "Shoot the bastards, or send them all back!"

For too long now, I have had a niggling feeling that I was being compliant by not speaking my feelings. I believe the solution to this problem is changing our attitude towards our fellow human beings. In my heart, I think a shift in philosophy is the answer. The world's issues will shift to focus on compassion and love, rather than hatred and fear. Speaking up, I shared my thoughts...

"They are fellow human beings, women, babies, and little children."

My opinions were not greeted favourably, and a palpable silence fell around the table, accompanied by glares from my husband. As I lay in bed thinking about the preceding night's conversation, I experienced the familiar pressure on my Third Eye; this occurrence only presents itself when I meditate. Tonight, I felt a sense of validation, confirmation that I had made the right decision to express the words from my heart.

Reiki teaches us that 'answers come in different ways.' Today, I read an article in Elohim magazine that confirmed and validated my decision.

"Change in the world will not happen until there is a change in attitude." *WOW!*

I put out a plea to the Universe...

'Please give me the grace and strength of character to reply from my heart to those who are being bigoted and racist.'

OPEN THROAT CHAKRA

July 2002

"*Please help me connect intuitively with the Energy of my Chakras.*"

Whilst meditating and doing Tai Chi, 'Reiki Light' pulses around the peripherals of my vision, up, onto the ceiling, pulsing golden light enters my third eye.

I'm now back at 'Healing the Healers', a Reiki class at the 'Osho Centre' in Unley, S.A. Healers support one another and provide a public service, while people drop in for healing.

Tuning in and connecting with the Chi, I sense an electrical pulse entering the back of my hands as I raise them in a gesture of surrender. My palms are warm and tingling. I feel pain in my throat while meditating. There's an intense, palpable energy as I move my hands to my throat Chakra, my inner voice validating:

I am speaking my truth, being my truth. My throat Chakra is unblocked.
Love and compassion overwhelm me.

PREJUDICE, FEAR, UNCONSCIOUS, UNKNOWING, UNCARING.

N*ew Year's Day 2003*
It is the start of a New Year. I feel a passion in my heart for humanity to come together, showing respect for each other's differences.

ABORIGINE: from Latin aborigine, meaning 'from the beginning'.

Life is enriched when we seek to understand other cultures and their ways of living. Based on our criteria for life, people often 'fall short' and cannot meet 'our standards and our ideals.' So, we judge them.

There is an essential Spiritual Law. '*No Judgment*'

REFUGEE. from the Latin refugium: to 'flee'

A person forced to leave their country to escape war, persecution, or natural disaster. Synonyms for asylum-seeker include displaced person, exile, outcast, and refugee.

We, as Australians living in the 'Lucky Country,' have not experienced it, so we fail to grasp what it means to be a refugee; consequently, too often there is anger, resentment, and fear. Instead, I feel it's important to see ourselves in them! Why did they come? What drove them to leave their homeland? Let's place ourselves in their shoes and strive to understand their emotions and thoughts. We all, as humans, crave love, compassion, understanding, and protection, rather than rejection, scorn, and persecution.

Love Yourself. It is essential to:
Set aside anger, hate, and prejudice.
Endeavour:
To Understand. Be Compassionate
Love.
Release Prejudice and Fear
Change that which needs to change:
Attitude.

The media fosters prejudice and fear. Change generates worry and anxiety. My brother's death taught me that life is ever-changing and nothing stays the same. I have learnt to release my worries and fears to 'The Universe', asking for help when I need it.

Why did your great-great-great-grandparents leave their homeland? Your ancestors departed the land they were born in to improve their lives, seeking freedom and happiness. Their choice is part of you; you carry their DNA.

SPIRITUAL SUPPORT

Mama was elderly at 91. A fall that broke her hip had left her incapacitated. Unable to stay in the unit alone, she had been on waiting lists for ages, and I was at my wits' end trying to find a nursing home, contacting each one to no avail. On the morning of February 1, 2003, I received a phone call. A nursing home in McLaren Vale, south of Adelaide, had a room in the Dementia Secure Section. They assured me she would be at the top of the list when a vacancy became available in the General Ward. Mum was alright with the idea, but I wasn't sure she was fully grasping it. Worried, I listened to my favourite guided meditation, 'Healing Journey,' by Dr. Emmett Miller, and sent my concerns up to the Universe. I fell into a deep sleep and later awoke, perceiving myself as levitating, being held, the full length of my body.

As I wrote these words, I heard the song –

'You Are the Wind Beneath My Wings', I realised, was the message of support. I adore this song and feel Col is here helping me with Mama. I'm at peace about going ahead with the plans.

KARUNA® MASTERS' DEGREE
March 22, 2003

I have been studying Karuna Reiki ® with Reiki Master Mark Calvert. Today is a special day: I received my Master's Degree. I receive powerful Usui and Tibetan Sacred Symbols during the Reiki Attunement Ceremony. The following passage is taken from the Book on Karuna Reiki ®.

"When translated from Sanskrit, Karuna means compassionate action accompanied by wisdom. The combination of the energetic essence of Karuna and Reiki, which is spiritually guided life force energy, births a new, deep, powerful form for our world."

'**Advanced Healing Energy for our Evolving World**' Author **Laurelle Shanti Gaia.**

'Karuna Reiki ®' has its origins in Usui and Tibetan Reiki, having been developed by William Lee Rand and the International Centre for Reiki Training in Michigan, USA.

The Book on Karuna Reiki ® Advanced Healing Energy for Our Evolving World Copyright © Laurelle Shanti Gaia

INSIGHT~MESSAGES

It is August 30th, the eve of my 59th birthday. Confined to bed with a bronchial virus, I observe the spiritual healing colours of purple and green appearing on the bedroom ceiling. On my birthday, I listen to 'The Gift of Reiki.' I practice Reiki on myself, step by step, while listening to this informative cassette tape I bought several years ago.

With my hands resting on my Solar Plexus, I'm enveloped in a radiant golden-yellow light. I experience a feeling of oneness and spiritual integration. The pressure intensifies in my third eye. While standing in meditation, a wave of gentle, clammy heat washes over me, and I receive a message.

'Move above the pain, focus, you can get over this.'

I refocus and push through the feelings of faintness, continuing to practice Tai Chi while glancing at the paperwork I've been working on. There, before me, are words of inspiration to reiterate and confirm...

Excerpts from...... 'TIME'
"Stand before me on the sign of infinity.
All you of the Earth.......
I will give you the key.
And with this knowledge, please realise
that the responsibility of sharing it comes.
I will show you the way.
It's straightforward.......
The quality of your Life is brought about
By the quality of your thinking -
Think about that!......
Realise that the one thing you have absolute control over is your attitude.......
Each life is linked to all life, and your words carry chain reactions.
Like a stone that is thrown into a pond.
If your thinking is in order
Your words will flow directly from the heart
Creating ripples of love.......
It creates an atmosphere of understanding
which leads to caring, which is Love.
Choose your words with care.
Go forth... with Love."
Book & Lyrics, Author David Soames.

Please Google the Poem narrated by Sir Laurence Olivier, as it is inspiring!

INTEGRATION OF DEATH

This year, I have integrated 'death' into my daily living.

"Learning to integrate the notion of death into our hearts enhances our daily living. Enriches appreciation.

Today, 4 October 2003, these words came to me:

"When the body of Brenda Fleming passes from this life ~
It is only the passing of life from a body.
My True Self, my Higher Self, My Spiritual Self, my Divine Self
The one I know in this lifetime will always remain my eternal self.
Now I am at Peace. Know I have ascended from this earthly plane
Into the Divine 'Light'. My journey is complete.
'The Light' I Know and Love
'The Light' that moves me to tears by its sheer translucent energy and love
'The Light' that encompasses me, making my heart beat wildly,
Whilst I sit in motionless meditation.
'The Light' that has given me the insight and understanding of Life."

PLEA TO THE UNIVERSE
New Year, 2004

My request to the Universe is... *"Please help me verbalise the correct positive terms and responses when faced with negative words and actions."*

Reiki connects on a deep emotional, spiritual, and physical level. It then works through the heart centre to co-create the "Spirit of Healing Energy."

When we connect with REIKI, we are connecting to:

Life Force. Life Energy. Our Highest Divine Self. Our God Consciousness. Our Spiritual Awareness. An Ancient practice ~Laying on of Hands with an Intention of Healing.

REIKI brings Relaxation, Deep Calm, Peace...

Embarking on a Reiki journey has led to integration with my Divine 'Higher Self.' The 'knowing' of Oneness. Oneness Within. Oneness with All. As my life unfolds, the emotional and physical pain this body experiences is inconsequential, part of the journey, learning, and growing.

It's February, and I feel fuzzy, overwhelmed by the mass, and low in energy. I need to rise above to light, love, and joy, and to embrace the Life Force and Energy that Reiki offers. I sought help this morning to return to this state and maintain it in my everyday life. Tonight, in my dreams, the spirit of my dear friend Barry Morton visited me. Barry passed away from a massive heart attack in his forties. I didn't have the chance to say goodbye to him.

"I gaze into his eyes, his mischievous smiling face, full of love. Hugging, touching his skin, so special!"

SPIRITUAL LINK

After returning from a motorhome trip to Tasmania in April, our son David and his family came over for dinner. Later, as he walks out the front door carrying his baby son, he confides:

"Last week I smelled Colin!"

This comment from my son amazes me! I have never mentioned to my family that I sense Col's essence. I'm eager to have a chat with my son. How wonderful it is that we share this phenomenon! A 'Spiritual Link' to Col.

REJECTION & ABANDONMENT

My spiritual journey continued, revealing healing in various aspects of my past and ancestral patterns. The fear of rejection and abandonment had deeply rooted itself in my mother's personality due to her separation from her mother as a small child and her husband's desertion. Mum often felt others were talking about her, believing she had upset them or done something wrong. This fear transformed into anger, causing her to become explosive, vindictive, and then contrite, as she said...

"Sorry!"

She tried to manipulate me, relying heavily on my support for her happiness. I have managed to shift the burden of guilt she places on my shoulders by learning that:

'We are the vessels of our happiness, for happiness comes from within our hearts.

We create our happiness and cannot rely on others to give it.'

I meditate, asking for guidance in understanding and forgiveness.

Through my cherished Reiki practice, I allow anger and sadness to surface as part of the healing process. I am filled with love and forgiveness, directing it towards my father.

ARCHETYPAL REIKI

S uzanne, my close friend, has sent me a Book and Cards entitled: 'Archetypal Reiki' by Dorothy May. I've studied the book over the last few days and have attempted to read the cards. Choosing a 'fan' layout, I picked a card at random:

No. 15 TOR II *The Gateway* ~ The cards show:

I show the Willingness to go through the Gateway. I have everything I need for my Journey to the Mountain. I move through the Gateway and give thanks and gratitude for the new opportunity.

This reading is particularly fitting for me at this moment. On July 31, 2004, while using the Archetypal Reiki cards, I received a significant reading that clarifies all aspects of my journey over the past ten years following the death of my beloved brother.

'SPIRIT GUIDES'

1. **The Issue at Hand**: *I draw* JINJA SHINTO.

   The Shrine of the Soul Kami. The Divine Spark in Everything. This is a Commitment to my Spiritual Growth.

2. **My Conscious Desire**: *I draw* HON SHA ZA SHO NEN.
   Service to others. The Buddha in me reaches out to the Buddha in you to promote enlightenment and peace. I bestow the truths of truth upon you. As above–so below. As within, so without.

3. **My Unconscious Desire**: *I draw* THE SOLAR PLEXUS CHAKRA.

This Provides the Empowerment to Act upon our Beliefs and Values.

4. What is my Inner Fulfilment: *I draw* HARTH.

Love and Compassion, Truth, Beauty, Harmony, and Balance. Harth is Universal Love Flowing Unconditionally through the Universe.

5. What My Inner Wisdom Says: *I draw* DAI KO MYO.

I am Awakened Fully. Completely aware that I am a Spiritual Being in Human Form and we are ONE.

6. Where have I been successful?

I draw THE CROWN CHAKRA, *telling me:*

They have given me permission and the ability to know and understand what concerns us. I am open to connecting with my Higher Self. And I am told:

We become Ascended Masters at this Level. We have mastered all of our Karmic Lessons.

7. What Synthesises in my Life, Situation, or Myself Right Now?
I draw THE CAVE.

Passing through the cave and moving through the Torii represents a state change. A change in Consciousness. A Battle with Ego. But it is over, I have won my Soul. Thank you.

Step by step, card by card as this reading unfolds, I realise the significance to my spiritual journey.

8. What needs to be integrated before the New Birth?
I draw REIKI.

Spiritually Directed Healing. I must allow the REIKI ENERGY *to enter my Body, Mind, and Soul to send my CHI to those in need.*

9. Who is helping me at this time in my life?
I draw SEI HEI KI.

The UNIVERSAL ENERGY. The CHI–The GOD WITHIN–MY HIGHEST SELF.

Synopsis:
The issue encourages me to pursue the Shrine of my Soul, the Divine Spark in Everything. This is part of my spiritual growth and will enable me to be of service to others. I have been empowered to act upon my beliefs and values, expressing love, compassion, truth, beauty, harmony, and balance. I am awakened to know myself as a Spiritual Being. I am aligned with my Highest

Self and have mastered all my karmic lessons. The battle with the ego is over, and I have won my Soul.

I am allowing the Spiritual Universal Energy of Reiki to enter my Body, Mind, and Soul, and I am sending out Chi to those in need. I am being assisted by:

The Universal Energy. My Highest Self. God Within.

Thank you, Col, for bringing me to this point of...

'Spiritual Awakening'. This is an excellent read.

I am overwhelmed with gratitude.

HEARTS FROM THE UNIVERSE

September 2004

I'm having difficulties with my job. Still working at midnight and struggling with the computer, I need to print a report. The printer seems to be doing its own thing; a line of hieroglyphics appears along the top of the page. How weird! Right at the end of the hieroglyphics, there's a solitary little heart. Amazing! Whenever I'm stressed with this job, I receive hearts at the top left-hand side of the sheet. Once, I was sent a solitary red heart. I use these special pages to write in my journal.

My daily life is filled with hearts. I spot a pebble shaped like a heart, a leaf in the garden, and a cloud in the sky.

A clear message...

'Love from the Universe.'

PURE THOUGHTS, PURE MIND, PURE BODY.

Since becoming a vegetarian, people often ask...

'Why did you become a vegetarian?'

While pondering this question, I realised I had no thoughts about becoming a vegetarian or any inclination towards it. So, why? I became a vegetarian overnight after receiving Level 2 Reiki.

Today, I opened my little Book:

'As a Man Thinketh' Author James Allen,

The page falls open ... I received the answer and have paraphrased it:

'Changing our diet alone will not help if we do not change our thoughts. When our thoughts are pure, we no longer require impure food.'

'As a Man Thinketh' Author James Allen

RE-INCARNATION & SPIRIT MANIFESTATION

We were privileged to own a magnificent Hungarian Vizsla for seven years. Our daughter Naomi arrived on Christmas morning with Felicity, wearing a big red bow attached to her collar. 'Fe', who was 12 months old, was initially shy and reserved, but it wasn't long before Fe slotted into our lives and captured our hearts. Fe was a 'perfect dog'—affectionate, quiet, a good traveller, and our constant companion on motorhome trips and rallies around Australia. When she turned two, we realised Fe was epileptic. There's not much I don't know about epilepsy, as we had an epileptic Poodle for 18 years. It was fitting we were 'chosen' to be Fe's parents, and I believe Fe to be the reincarnation of poodle Cara's Spirit.

Taking Fe with us to Tasmania, she travelled in the motorhome on board the ferry. On the return trip, the boat was delayed by several hours. She was well overdue for her medication and had lapsed into a coma.

Fe was part of a trial for epilepsy drugs at the University of Sydney. After several days with a vet, she managed to recover to some extent but was still extremely sick. The vet's recommendation was to 'put her down.' I was not ready to give up! I had experienced several of these episodes. During the long trip back home to Adelaide, I didn't think she would survive. She had lost control of her bodily functions, which diminished the quality of life for all three of us as we were in the cramped confines of a motorhome.

Fe survived!

Two months later, after a change in medication, she succumbed to a series of continuous fits, leading to internal bleeding. It was time! We both felt it in our hearts. After making the heart-wrenching decision, we called our local vet, but when we arrived, they told us he was out on an urgent call.

"Could you please come back in two hours?"

As I write these words, my heart feels heavy. We took her home, knowing that we would undertake that final journey once more.

A few days after we said our final goodbyes, Fe's Spirit returned:

5 am.

Something has awoken Baz, and he gets up to shut the bedroom door. I visualise Fe standing outside the bedroom door in the hallway. She is often in my thoughts and always in my heart. Here she is, back home, her Spirit manifesting.

Love is potent, so powerful.

BEGINNINGS & ENDINGS

New Year 2005

I am consulting the Runes. This is the wisdom they impart.

I draw INGUZ **Fertility.** *This Rune is a reminder of your potential, helping you discover your true power. It is time to utilise it to complete unfinished business and projects, clarify the mind, resolve old issues, and eliminate unnecessary influences. Open to the energy of existence, which will help you naturally in all your endeavours. This will be your truth.*

Such an appropriate Rune for the New Year!

Today is January 24, 2005. Mama had a fall at the nursing home, one of many falls lately, as she had been rather unsteady. It looked as though someone had taken a baseball bat to her face. Seeing her brought both Baz and me to tears. The nursing home staff were unsure what had happened, having found her in the bathroom, believing she had hit her head on the basin or toilet. We spent the day sitting together, stroking her face, rubbing her back, and massaging her head. I was in a wheelchair after undergoing a second arthroscopy on my left knee and could barely walk. I was in severe pain, and the wound felt like ground-up glass. When she dozed off, I read. She woke up, looking at my book, and said:

"Just started?" I nodded in agreement. Then Mama told me she loved me and that I was beautiful. I told her I love her, too. She replied, "We love each other," then whispered...

"Colin said... come on, Mumt." I didn't quite hear her, so I smiled and leaned in closer to her mouth as she said:

Colin said, "Come on, Mumt."

When Colin was joking with her, he referred to her as 'Mumt'. I realised my dearest brother was waiting for her, encouraging her.

LOST & NOW FOUND

I received a call from Glenside Hospital, where Mama had been transferred from Flinders Hospital. They advised that Mama was at the Royal Adelaide Hospital undergoing a CT scan because she had experienced a brain seizure during the night.

We have our home on the market, so we visited her during an open house inspection. On the way, I felt trepidation, meditating and asking for guidance, only to be met with a fantastic surprise.

Special Day! On 27 February 2005, I found Mama! I realised she had been lost for many years. Maybe it was the seizure, the change in medication, or both; either way, there was no more dementia! Who knows? I didn't care. The doctors at Glenside Hospital had changed her medication, and Mama was aware, focused, happy, and laughing spontaneously. Mama enjoyed and often recited poetry, always having a wealth of poems to keep the family entertained. We sat holding hands while she recited her favourites.

Starting with......

'The Green Eye of the Little Yellow God,' then

'Albert and the Lion,' 'There are Fairies at the Bottom of the Garden,' finishing with:

Shakespeare's Henry V: 'Once More Unto the Breach, Dear Friends, Once More.'

She seemed to have regained her faith, mentioning Heaven.

She had lost the desire and ability to pray for a long time.

Speaking loudly, she told me....

"I am mad; I have been a cranky old crab!"

I smile, silently agreeing with her.

Talking about heaven, I say, Col and Len (her husband, my father, the man she loved all her life) are waiting. She mentions other departed loved ones, including Joyce, my aunt, who was married to her brother, Michael, and the aunts who raised her. She is lucid, remembering and recounting a great deal.

Mama asked me to speak to my sister-in-law and her mother (both of whom are good Catholics) to pray for her. She also told me not to cry or be unhappy when she passed away.

"You can visit me in Spirit like Col does," I told her.

"Yes, Col will keep me in line!" she laughed.

Mama explains the madness is real, and that she has brain snaps.

My little Binkie (my nickname) with the farthing face, I love you; you are everything to me, and you always have been.

"The people around here in Glenside are caring and loving. I cannot walk, I will not be coming home."

I am euphoric. We haven't held intelligent conversations like this for years.

Reflecting on the tough years, I am amazed by how her personality has changed. I will always treasure this gift. I lost Mama. Today, I found her again.

INSPIRATION

I had always loved to write, and now I receive inspiration and guidance. Sometimes, clear messages come through—this one I sent to a special friend.

This path, this journey, is not a hobby one takes up at whim. It is a commitment—your commitment to yourself, to be, to find the most essential aspect of your life: peace within, and to connect with your higher self. This is Who You Are, not what you do.

The Gift you give yourself -The Greatest Gift of all.

When you find your peace within, you've achieved your ultimate potential. It flows like the tide, ebbing and flowing, waxing and waning like the Moon. It is eternal and will always be available to you.

You only need to meditate, pray, go within, and be at one with your Highest Self. Your gift is the peace, joy, and love that flow from within, enveloping and engulfing you, bringing tears of joy to your eyes.

You will have achieved everything you need to accomplish in life. Material possessions are merely transient matters. Your gift to yourself can never be taken away, for it glows from within and requires only your attention to reignite it.

The greatest gift you can give others is understanding that we are ONE on this little planet, and from here we grasp the true meaning of life.

We are at peace; we become compassionate towards all living beings. 'Light' will shine from within to encompass others and help them along the path of understanding to love, inner blissful joy, and the beauty of all that is.'

Linda faxed me back this reply:

"Thank you, Brenda, I know I have been truly blessed having a friend like you. I have waited a long time for you to come...I saw you coming from afar, and you are beautiful."

Linda.

THE CRASH

As the biting icy winds of May 2005 swept through Adelaide, I needed to connect more deeply with my spiritual self. I was still in pain from the knee arthroscopy and feeling overwhelmed by my incapacitation. I offered a prayer to the universe:

'Please, light my way, direct my feet on my path of truth.'

I played "The Lohan" (an ethereal piece of music for Tai Chi/Qi Gong) while doing Tai Chi, sensing the familiar pressure in my Third eye. The mystical presence of spirit and love flowed through me.

The house had been causing concern for Baz and me, as it had now been on the market for five months, and for no apparent reason, it wasn't selling, despite many people being keen to buy. I surrendered it to the Universe and chose to go with the flow. Hearts just kept popping out of my printer. The Universe is sending me Love! In hindsight, I now understand why the Universe sent me so much Love.

I mentioned that I crashed in May, but that was an understatement! My son's 14-year marriage had ended. I thought it was a 'perfect marriage'; they had two cherished little kids. The week before, while I stood in the kitchen chatting with my daughter-in-law, everything seemed fine on the surface, but my intuitive inner voice warned:

'Do not hurt my son.'

On May 25, 2005, I wrote in my journal.

David. My dearest son, I wish to shield you from this hurt with all my heart and remove your pain. I love you more than you'll ever know. My heart is breaking for you.

Later, while meditating, I received a message:

'This is David's spiritual journey; it will strengthen him.'

Shortly after, I attended a seminar at the Body, Mind & Spirit Festival in Adelaide...

~ Energy Transfer for Enlightenment ~

Receiving Deeksha, the facilitators Lisa & Pasquo Cassetta placed their hands onto my head:

Meditating into 'The Light,' my heart beating wildly, I was filled with joy. Love radiated, and tears of happiness flowed. I felt at peace after the turmoil of the last few weeks. Thank you.

THE U-TURN

July 2005
    Finally, the house, furniture, and possessions were sold.

The nursing home in McLaren Vale, where Mama was before the fall, cannot accept her back as she is now in a wheelchair. The staff at Glenside Hospital found her another nursing home.

Baz and I left in the Winnebago a week ago to work for Diners Club and American Express on our way to Tasmania. We stopped yesterday in Ararat, Victoria. I woke up with a start; it was 5 am. Intuitively, I knew what to expect. My 93-year-old mother hadn't been well, and a phone call at that hour confirmed my worst fears. Mama had a lung infection, and she wasn't expected to survive. It was still dark. I dashed to the Suzuki; Baz had unhitched it from the Winnebago. I was free to make a U-turn back to Adelaide, leaving Baz to follow in the Motor Home at a more leisurely pace.

On the way, I rang the Nursing Home...

"Please get a Priest."

The reply reminded me it was Sunday; it might not be easy. My mother was a strong, determined woman; she had come back from the brink of death before. I was not confident that the Last Rites of the Catholic Church would save her this time.

After an arduous six and a half-hour drive, I walked into the room. I immediately realised she had lost the ability to speak. Her face lit up, and her eyes conveyed everything I needed to know. I was her joy in life; we were relieved that I had made it in time. My mother loved me dearly; I had been her whole life. Not loved as a small child, she had this enormous capacity to love me.

The nursing staff said the local priest visited earlier today. He had administered Extreme Unction, the sacrament of the Catholic Church for the sick and dying.

I sat beside her bed reading a Buddhist-inspired book to comfort me...

'The Tibetan Book of Living & Dying' by Sogyal Rinpoche.

On Monday, July 18, I had an explicit dream...

A winding road around a rocky outcrop abruptly ends. There was a pregnant woman in the dream. The symbolic meaning...

Mama's time is over; her journey has ended. The pregnant woman signifies a rebirth.

Tonight, in my dreams, I gazed into the blue, smiling eyes of my dear friend Barry Morton, who had passed. His spirit is with me, holding my hand.

Tuesday, July 19th, the doctor called in to see Mama and asked me if I was OK with the noises she was making. She was dying of Pneumonia, her chest rattled, and she was breathing noisily.

"Yes, I'm OK," I replied.

I had been giving her Reiki to ease her passing; she was fighting hard, and I knew she feared going to Hell! I allowed her to 'go', assuring her she was heading to a place of light and love where everyone awaited her. Embroiled in the religious dogma of the Catholic Church, she always believed she 'lived in sin' because she married a Protestant in a registry office instead of the Catholic Church. A kind Catholic nun came to relieve me, for which I was very grateful. Mama would have heard her praying, something I was no longer skilled at.

Wednesday, July 20, 2005, dawns.

Reminiscing: I had my first baby on August 20, 1969, my gorgeous baby daughter, Naomi. A month prior, on 20 July 1969, I sat and watched the 'Moon Landing' on TV, with my Chinchilla cat Simon nestled against my pregnant belly. Now it's the same date—thirty-six years later.

At 2:00 p.m., the nursing staff placed Mama on her back, and her breathing became laboured. A nurse put fluffy lambswool socks on her feet. I held her hand, resting my other hand on her chest and neck, and sent her Reiki.

Knowing she would cherish the sound of my voice, I recited the rosary, something I hadn't done in years.

At 2:40 pm, I was by her side, her eyes wide open. With one last gasp, she shuddered and her chest heaved. Mama was gone, passed over into the Light. Her skin was radiant, like that of a porcelain doll. At 93, her life had drawn to a close.

There is a pine forest near my son's place; I take my two grandchildren there to walk and play on the swings, a special spot. The following day, I walk alone to meditate. While doing Tai Chi, a solitary tear rolls down my face. Mama has asked me not to grieve for her. She has witnessed the grief I suffered after Colin's death.

Tuesday, July 26, 2005

The day of Mama's funeral.

Long-stemmed, pale pink roses, Mama's favourite flowers, adorn the coffin.

In the eulogy, I included Mama's favourite Shakespeare sonnet from Henry V, "Once more unto the Breach, Dear Friends Once More."

Finally, I collapsed into bed in the Winnebago. Intense spiritual pressure pressed on my third eye, deep purple and vibrant green swirling around my mind.

My body is being flooded with spiritual healing. Blessed Be.

Days later, Baz and I left our son behind, along with a broken marriage, as we set off once more on our trip to Victoria and Tasmania. This decision has caused me immense grief over the years. The solace I find is:

'This is David's Spiritual journey, all is as it should be.'

The cards I drew sent me a decisive message:

You're on a pilgrimage, seeking your truth, connection, service, action in the world, and empowerment. Be still and know I am with you. The Buddha in me reaches out to the Buddha in you to foster enlightenment and peace. I bestow the truth of truths upon you, as above, so below, as within, so without.

Wow! How perfect! I sent a text to David:

'Reiki Light, Love & Healing.

GLEN INNES N.S.W.

The New England Town of Glen Innes, in the Central Highlands of NSW, Australia, is a Celtic Spiritual Town with a national monument of Standing Stones inspired by the 'Ring of Brodgar' in Scotland's Orkney Islands. The monument is dedicated to acknowledging the Celtic people, past and present, who have contributed to Australian culture from the Celtic Nations of Scotland, Ireland, Cornwall, Wales, the Isle of Man, and Brittany. Each year in the first week of May, Glen Innes hosts 'The Celtic Festival.'

Here I discovered – The number 33, which had been 'my' number since I was 10 years old, is:

A MASTER number in Numerology, 33 is regarded as the most spiritual number, capable of inspiring and guiding others towards spiritual growth. Individuals associated with 33 are known for their compassion, empathy, and dedication to helping others. Thirty-three carries symbolic and esoteric meanings, and 3x3x3 equals 9 for 'Humanity'. On Tynwald Hill, I find a replica of the Excalibur Sword. In 2002, while receiving my Master Reiki Attunement from Mark Calvert, Master Reiki Teacher, he visualised the:

Excalibur Sword. Signifies: Great Knowledge & Wisdom –
Name Brenda - meaning: Sword - I am Brenda, I wield the Sword
I did not realise the significance of his visualisation until today.

After leaving Glen Innes, our motorhome, with Suzuki in tow, encountered a diesel spill, skidded dramatically, and aquaplaned along the road. It was a scary scenario, but I felt an instant sense of 'Spiritual Presence' as pressure in my third eye. The vehicles came back on track. 'The Universe' is protecting us! Thank you.

ASKING FOR GUIDANCE

I have lacked a routine since embarking on this journey and feel like I'm in a state of limbo. I practised Tai Chi Qi Gong this morning and opened the Reiki Book. The page falls open, titled:

'The Living Practice & Creating a Routine.'

"The concept of the Living Practice is that it is always with you."

Thank you. Guidance and Reiki at work. My resolve is to practice Tai Chi Qi Gong daily and do nightly archetypal Reiki. Tonight, draw the card number 20

Spiritual Attainment Mountain.

It reads: *"I have been travelling my path for many years, perhaps many lifetimes. I am nearing a plateau. I have made peace with the external world, I feel ready to go further* (how true!) *I have asked for guidance to take me further along that path.*

My purpose is to ground spiritual travellers to the earth they are a part of. I am the mountain in my core of rock. There seems to be a stable point, a centre of stillness, and it is my axis. I am to be part of those who seek transcendence and guide them towards the winds of change.

(Excerpts from 'Archetypal Reiki' Dorothy May

Thank you for this Reading.

This pathway, my journey, is becoming clearer; it is 'my purpose in Life.' Shortly afterwards, I received a deeper meaning.

We visited St. Lawrence, Queensland, a free motorhome and caravan camp, in early November. During an early morning stroll along the walkway, I paused in the shade of a tall ghost gum, with the plains and mountains behind me—an ideal spot for Tai Chi. While meditating, I felt the faintest movement in my left hand, then in my right, as I held them in a Tai Chi stance. Opening my eyes, I saw a golden-winged butterfly.

BRENDA CHRISTA FLEMING

Butterflies are magical; they remind us that we can be transformed by going within, meditating, praying, and spending time in spiritual stillness. At some point, we will be ready to awaken and be reborn into a completely new way of being, with open eyes to see the wonders of life.

INNER PEACE

I have been writing for many years, calling them 'Jottings'.

These are the jottings for November 10, 2005.

I do not consider myself religious; I am spiritual. When I meditate, I feel at peace, connecting with my highest inner self and becoming one with all that is. I believe that every religion—Christian, Buddhist, Muslim, Jewish, etc.—aspires to... Peace, Love, Unity.

The greater the chance of world peace, the more people in the world awaken to their inner peace.

The balance will shift like a grain of sand, and world peace will become a reality.

SURRENDER IN LOVE

Reiki awakens me to 'where I am and where I have been' and provides answers after the event.

Today, the answers come in the form of a newspaper article.

I have been experiencing 'Reiki', which flickers light and colours when making love with Baz. Feeling total surrender and a connection to spirit, my heart pounds as it does in deep meditation.

We are in Kingaroy, Queensland, the peanut capital of Australia. I am waiting for the washing to finish, and I pick up a newspaper from the shelf in the launderette titled:

'Living Now' dated December 2004, is almost a year old. I read an article... *"Meeting in Love is an opportunity in relationship to surrender to that which you are, higher consciousness, divinity itself, spirit, to honour that in this moment."* It continues...

"Let your spirit meet in love, to move you in love, to ignite the passion, sexual energies, and the grace of the sacred union."

This article validates my feelings. Thank you...

Adapted from the Newspaper 'Living Now December 2004–Article 'Meeting in Love', Author Brenda Sutherland.

RE-INCARNATION ~ THE QUESTION

C hristmas Day, December 2005
A family reunion to celebrate Christmas at the home of my dear cousin Tessa at Valla near Coffs Harbour, NSW, Australia. The weather is gorgeous. I was in the pool, having fun with little Sofie, Tessa's granddaughter. As we spoke to each other, I looked deeply into her eyes. Auntie Joyce's eyes gazed back at me. Two days later, Tess asked:

"Do you think someone can reincarnate?"

"Yes! I know they can!"

I hesitate before telling Tess. She senses my hesitation and says:

'What is it?'

I explain what happened with Sofie. She hugs me, crying with joy, and then confides that she has felt the Spirit of her Mum through little Sofie.

RE-INCARNATION **Synopsis:**

My understanding is that we reincarnate into our Soul Family, bearing the imprint of our ancestors into eternity. My Mother's firstborn infant, her son, Cecil (my first brother), died on 25th August 1929 from a brain tumour shortly after birth.

My son, David, was born on 25 August 1971. I believe my brother reincarnated as my son on the same day, 42 years later.

JOURNEY CONTINUES ~

New Year 2006

The Crystal Castle in Mullumbimby, located in the magnificent hinterland of Byron Bay, NSW, is a magical sanctuary featuring tranquil sub-tropical gardens, walkways to the Blessing Buddha, and inspiring spaces for meditation, reflection, and spiritual union. I became aware of entering a peaceful state of consciousness while walking around the Labyrinth, my arms moving as a pendulum, swinging together in perfect rhythm, my whole being in balance and peace. A luminous full moon rose, ending a sublime day.

Following this trip, we visited our daughter and son-in-law's property in Oakdale, NSW, located south of Sydney, at the end of January. I was relaxing and listening to a CD. Evanescence's 'My Immortal.' I changed the words slightly; they became so relevant and meaningful for me that they carried me back to the years I spent in the long, dark tunnel of my grief.

'When I cried, you wiped away all of my tears. When I screamed, you'd fight away all of my fears.'

I notice my brother's essence for a split second, breathing deeply into my core. I miss your patience and love, Col. Thank you for being here today. I continue to receive hearts from the Universe. A tiny silver heart glints from the pages as I open my diary this morning. I wrote... "Namaste, I send you my heart, open with love."

We travel to Adelaide to see our son, David, his new partner, Kerry, our grandchildren, Jorgia and Lachlan, and Kerry's girls, Tayla and Casey, who now affectionately call us 'Nanny' and 'Poppy'. Sitting around the dinner table, Dave, Kez, and the children sang to me...

'You Fill up my Senses.' The John Denver song brought tears to my eyes and will never be the same for me again. Music is so evocative. Thank you.

THE ROAD LESS TRAVELLED

May 2006

We have decided to travel to outback Australia, visiting Coober Pedy, an opal mining town referred to as 'the Opal Capital of the World', where people live underground because of the extreme heat of the surrounding Australian desert. We are also going to Uluru, the Sacred, Spiritual, and Powerful Energetic Centre of Australia, which is said to be the Solar Plexus Chakra of the Earth.

The early morning sun caught a crystal on my key ring, reflecting two hearts onto the passenger door of the Winnebago: one silver heart and one rainbow heart. Once again, the universe is sending me a message of love. Thank you. En route to Uluru, the Red Centre, we visit Kings Canyon, located southwest of Alice Springs, colloquially known as 'The Alice,' and its towering red rock cliffs. Here, we experience a bumpy camel ride through the dust of the dry Todd River.

A luminescent full moon rose over Uluru as the sun's golden rays sank lower in the evening sky. Both the sun and the moon were visible. I lack the words to describe this phenomenon, this sheer beauty. I stood transfixed, my eyes gazing meditatively at the flash in the sky as the sun sank below the horizon, creating a halo of the most transparent colours of lilac and blue surrounding the red ochre of this magical rock.

Baz and I took some time to relax in our camp chairs, enjoying a glass of red wine while admiring the full moon over Uluru, accompanied by one solitary shining star, Venus, before retiring for the night. The next morning, we boarded a small aeroplane to witness the stunning beauty of Uluru and the surrounding desert from above.

Today, May 13th, 2006, we visited the Devil's Marbles Conservation Park in the Northern Territory and stayed for a few days. A wild dingo came by, scavenging for food and skulked away when he saw me. While walking alone among the rocks of the Devil's Marbles, I experienced an incredible peace. Meditating and raising my arms in surrender to the clear, endless blue sky, I felt the encompassing canopy of the Australian outback calling forth Spirit, with the energy so palpable in this ancient land.

There came a time in my life when I encountered metaphorical crossroads, with two roads leading in different directions. I took 'the road less travelled'. This desire, combined with my current need to travel that road, grants me sacred time as I nurture my journey. I had already experienced the rewards: bliss beyond all else, a deep, peaceful joy filled with light, colour, contentment, and divine union with my Highest Self.

It is mid-July 2006 when we arrive in Mareeba, inland from Cairns in far North Queensland. It is 'Rodeo Week,' and the town is buzzing. We woke up to find a swag behind the motorhome with a young Aboriginal couple fast asleep. They had arrived during a wild night of partying, noise, and swearing. When they finally awoke, I greeted them, and we sat on the ground together, chatting and learning about the surrounding area and countryside. They apologised for the noise during the night, asking if I could look after their swag. Anna and Marvin lived out near Chillagoe way. Their presence sparked racist and bigoted comments from many members of the motorhome fraternity. I wondered: 'Why is it that those with racist & bigoted attitudes have the loudest voices?' I didn't reply to their comments and stayed silent in the heat of the moment.

Baz needed to fix a light in the Winnebago. When he finished, a tiny piece of gold wiring lay on the floor in the shape of, guess what, a heart! Climbing into bed, I visualised the heart. Instantly, the familiar pressure in my third eye was present, a spiritual presence flooded my being, and I snuggled into the warmth of the doona. Last week, I received a gash on my leg, and the scab healed into a heart shape. There are so many different ways the Universe sends me hearts and love.

A VISITOR

I had trouble sleeping tonight. Climbing down from the bed above the cab, I entered the ensuite in the motorhome, glancing into the full-length mirror as I walked through the door. Mama stared back at me. I said:

"Hello Mama, I have seen your face before. Your eyes are my eyes, looking back at me in the mirror."

Later, I realised that today marked the first anniversary of 'the U Turn' when I returned to Adelaide to be with Mama in her final days before her death. Mama was visiting, as we had agreed she would.

NEW HOME-NEW START

My *Birthday 31 August 2006*
We were busy moving into our new home. 'Riverbend' in Ballina, located in the Northern Rivers region of New South Wales, is an over-50s gated community offering resort-style living. One of the three bedrooms became my meditation room, a sacred space where I connect with spirit and express gratitude. Unpacking and rediscovering treasured items has been an exciting experience. Two such items were coconut face carvings, which I named 'Yin & Yang.' 'Yin' has a peaceful, serene face, while 'Yang' is laughing. It represents the perfect balance: stillness within, partnered with happiness and contentment. In my new home, I felt 'Spirit' as an intense celestial pressure in my third eye, with swirling colours abundant in their beauty, embracing the sensations and crying with joy. Thank you.

About a week later, I find myself reflecting on hearts. The special potpourri heart went missing during the move, and I feel sad about the loss. Then, lo and behold, I discovered it at the bottom of my bag, together with three tiny silver hearts and the obsidian crystal I often carry.

OBSIDIAN – A grounding stone that promotes positive change, fosters inner growth, encourages fulfilment, enhances introspection, supports practicality and stability, aids in manifestation and psychic development, helps disperse negative energies, and serves as an excellent protection stone. Chakra – Base.

This is an apt description as I enter a new home, area, and stage of my life.

On September 20th, I have a dream... Driving uphill on a rocky road, I reach the end, where two round wire barriers block my way. Then, I find myself walking along a busy highway in Paddington, Sydney, surrounded by people and traffic. I know I need to be at a funeral by 9:30 am. Unsure of which bus to catch, I keep walking, hurrying, and glancing over my shoulder. I enter a convict-built stone building to ask for directions, but it's a considerable distance away. Once back outside on the road, I try to hail a cab; I should be at the funeral, but I'm worried because I'm late.

Synopsis: I am nearing a stage where the uphill battle is nearly over (as indicated by the rocky road and the funeral). However, I am not there yet; there is still plenty of activity and achievements to pursue, and I am seeking direction.

It is late September 2006 when I read a newspaper article from 'Elohim'

'What presses your buttons and causes a reaction?'

It reads:

"When you no longer react to emotional happenings, you will be at peace when your beliefs are based on truth. You know that you have moved into harmony with yourself when you have no reactions of an emotional nature to the negative events in life."

This is my aim!!

REIKI MAGIC & INSIGHTS.

October 2006

We are in Mudgee, the heart of Southern NSW's Hunter Valley Wine region, for a motorhome rally. After the rally, we spent a few days touring and visiting wineries. Wyndham Estate Winery was featuring Puccini's Opera. Storm clouds gathered, and then the heavens opened, pouring rain. It wasn't ideal for sitting outside under the stars watching opera.

Reading 'Good Weekend Magazine,' I noticed Richard Flanagan, the author of 'The Sound of One Hand Clapping,' has launched a new book. When we got home, a book had fallen out of the bookcase. It's 'The Sound of One Hand Clapping,' a message for me to re-read—a powerful book.

Reiki Magic at play again.

On November 1st, I watched a programme on ABC TV about dementia and Alzheimer's. It brought back many memories of the past few years with Mama. As I went to bed, I felt upset and disturbed. Immediately, I laid my head on the pillow, and the familiar pressure of 'spirit' settled into my third eye, providing comfort.

Tess, my dearest cousin, was visiting her daughter in Lismore. Today, we had lunch together at a lovely garden café, reminiscing about our departed mums, and we discovered that our mums' faces were reflected in the mirror. Auntie Joyce comes through for Tess, and Mama for me. As we looked at the reflection, our eyes became their eyes. Our mothers stay with us forever. It's interesting because Tess doesn't believe in this 'stuff.'

CONSCIOUS NOT CAUTIOUS

N*ew Year, 9 January 2007*
I was reading...
"Every day Osho 365 Daily Meditations for the Here and Now."
After reading one of the meditations, I received an insight:
I realised my Life had been Conscious, but not cautious.
I interpret the Author's words. The Author explains that there is a subtle distinction. Consciousness isn't based on fear. Fear comes from caution. We become fearful of not exploring new lifestyles, directions, lands, and ways to channel our energy. Caution prevents us from thoroughly enjoying life. Treading the same path repeatedly, we remain fearful of making a mistake.
"Every day Osho 365 Daily Meditations for the Here and Now."

'SPECIAL DAY.'

I love this little poem and often refer to it, sending it to friends and loved ones on their special birthdays.

'This day is a Special Day–it is Yours
Yesterday slipped away; it cannot be filled with more meaning.
About tomorrow–nothing is known, but this day, today is yours.
Today, you can make someone happy. Today, you can help another,
This day is a Special day–it is Yours'

As taken from: "Practical Meditation Wellbeing Programme with Buddhist Principle Venerable Thubten Lhundrup

I have a morning routine. I anoint my third eye and inner wrists with Meditation Balm. Light incense in the garden, do Tai Chi outside on the grass, wiggling my bare toes into the ground. Then, admire and take in the essence of the flowers and shrubs, weeding and pruning as each weed becomes a negative or angry thought to remove. Planet Earth is our school. Our Life Journey, our lessons. I believe the most important lesson is:

Happiness and contentment come from within our consciousness. External gratification and possessions do not lead to lasting joy. Only by accepting and loving ourselves do we attain inner peace and happiness.

Today, more hearts have been sent from the Universe. As I swim in the pool at 'Riverbend', a flower petal floats up, perfect in the shape of a heart, I scoop it up into the palm of my hand.

WELLNESS FESTIVAL ~ BANGALOW NSW.

E *aster Sunday, 7 April 2007*
     Our close friends from Queensland, who have been visiting us for many years, are visiting today, and I am giving Reiki to Suzanne. After the Healing Session, she said:

"As you placed your hands on my feet, I felt as if I were standing upright, and you were holding me in your hands; it was a strange sensation."

It is Easter Monday, and I have decided to attend the 'Wellness Festival' at Bangalow near Byron Bay. Several workshops look interesting.

I joined a workshop, titled "Circle of Eight," with facilitator June Merevale. My first position in the circle was in the southeast, at New Beginnings. As I have recently moved to this area, it's a coincidence. One space around, entering the East, Jane asks:

"Voice what you feel is true for this position."

In the East, we invoke 'Light,' receiving help from the Archangels. This is easy, I start each day by invoking 'The Light,' and recite the ceremony to the attendees:

I call forth Quan Yin, God & Goddess of Compassion.
I call forth Archangel Michael to protect me on the journey of this lifetime.
I call forth Archangel Gabriel, may I always walk in your Light.
I call forth Archangel Raphael to guide me in Healing Spirit.
I call forth Archangel Ariel for Peace, Joy and Love.
My heart is pounding as I call forth my Highest Divine Self into this sacred 'Circle of Eight.'

A Sublime Experience.

RELAXATION & MEDITATION

I introduced a 'Relaxation & Meditation' class to 'Riverbend', where I live in Ballina. I set up a small altar in the craft room every Monday morning, lighting candles, burning incense, and playing soothing meditation music. I teach the ladies to relax, followed by a guided meditation. There is a loyal following of six to ten ladies. It's a special way to start the week. On September 19, 2007, one of the ladies who attended the relaxation class asked me to give her a Reiki treatment. As I set up the massage table, I find a small white heart hiding in the Reiki paperwork. The Universe is sending me love again.

Jan and I spent two hours together in a peaceful, sacred space. Afterwards, I sent the Universe my gratitude... 'Thank you, I greet you from my Heart!'

A resident of Riverbend was found floating dead in the swimming pool this morning! Ray enjoyed the pool and swam twice daily for his health, as he had diabetes. It was an ideal way to leave this life, doing something he loved. Life is so fragile, and his death reminds me how important it is to live in the present, appreciating life in all its aspects and beauty.

Later, I picked up the book I've been re-reading. An old friend, Annie, gave it to me when I visited her in Grose Vale, Sydney, many years ago, before I embarked on this spiritual journey. Once again, I find 'written script' confirming where I am. This book deepens my understanding of the journey. The page falls open, and the author tells me:

'Wise people can deal with the reality of death, knowing it to be part of life.'
"Awakening the Buddha Within" Copyright © 1997 Lama Surya Das

RIGHT DIRECTION

The year 2007 is coming to a close. I have heard that we tend to overreact most to things that are close to our own identity. I am a fussy, fastidious, analytical, perfection-seeking, critical VIRGO. I'm often my worst enemy. These things I know to be true.

We have been away with our daughter for the long-awaited birth of her first baby. Naomi and Andrew have been married for fifteen years. Months before, Naomi had phoned with the exciting news: "Mum, we're having a baby!"

I thought there were more puppies because Naomi's dogs were her family. She replied

"No, not puppies, Mum, I'm pregnant."

Being at the hospital with Naomi and Andrew for the birth of their baby daughter was very special. Meeting our new little granddaughter, Aleisha, for the first time was truly exciting. New babies bring an abundance of love with them. We spent a lot of time together, just cuddling, and took heaps of photos.

Returning home, the garden needed attention. Baz wanted to pull out the mint growing around the base of the bushes, but I didn't see it as a problem. I loved the aroma and taste of mint, and I wanted to leave it there. As usual, he roped me into something I didn't want to do. Before I knew it, I was tending the garden and pulling weeds. I could barely walk, and both my knees were very painful. The pain became unbearable, so I stopped weeding and came inside to rest. Not long afterwards, Baz came looking for me to find out why I was not still out in the garden. He criticised me for not keeping the garden pruned, and I exploded. Then I realised I should not lose my cool, but criticism is not something I take easily, being a fussy Virgo. Conscious of these shortcomings is a step in the right direction! Yeh!

BODY MIND & SPIRIT ~
CHIROPRACTIC NETWORK

New Year, January 3, 2008.
Another year gone! Time for the 'Wellbeing Festival' at Bangalow near Byron Bay, NSW. I enjoy attending and participating in workshops. I had been studying Sacred Geometry, so I was drawn to the stand featuring graphic art and meditation music. I was also attracted to another stand, Chiropractic Networking. While chatting with the stallholder, I realised he had a workshop in the afternoon.

It was 5 p.m., and most people had left the festival. It had rained heavily all day (a result of a cyclone off the southeast corner of Queensland impacting Byron Bay), and it was getting chilly, yet I felt compelled to stay.

The workshop incorporated both Body and Spirit into Chiropractic work. The practitioner demonstrated on a lady who had been a client of one of his colleagues in Melbourne. It was fascinating to watch, as he tapped parts of her body, withdrawing his hand in a clearing, sweeping manner, her body twitched.

I put up my hand when he asked for another volunteer.

Face down on the massage table, he tapped my body. 'I was being breathed', the deep breathing didn't feel like me doing it. I felt very relaxed and spacey afterwards.

The next morning, at 9:30 a.m., Chant Master Ven. Lobsang Tendar, a Buddhist monk, held an opening Ceremony, blessing the congregation. It was a special way to start the day.

Afterwards, I ran into the doctor and discussed yesterday's session. He mentioned he hadn't met anyone as open as I was.

I picked up information detailing the 'Lotus Temple' at the 'Gaia' stand in Byron Bay. Then I stopped at the Chiropractic Networking stand. While we chatted, the doctor said:

I will show you how to stay safe out there.

I explain:

"I have utmost trust in The Universe; I have no fear. I know I am being guided and protected." He says:

"Most people have a fear."

"Most people are striving, searching for something. I am grateful I have this gift," I reply.

"Even though you are open, when talking, your hands are protective, covering your heart; we would work on that area," said the doctor.

"Yes, I know, I put a shield up, using my hands when someone says something I don't approve of or agree with."

You know it, so we both understand what I'm saying.

I tell him:

Something changed my life. I'm holding back and still have plenty of spiritual work to do!

Then, he says:

The energy rising from your lower body is being restrained, feels dry, and is causing pain in your knees.

Wow! My knees are the most painful part of my body.

The session starts with my face down, my arms resting in a sling beneath the table. He touches the base of my skull, moving his hands over different areas of my body. I can tell he is speaking to people passing by, but I don't find it distracting.

Initially, I was only aware of deep breathing. He says:

Pause between the breaths and focus on micro-movements.

There's a movement in my left breast that I can only describe as wriggly. The more I concentrate, the stronger it becomes. He touches the base of my head, asking me to breathe into that area. My left shoulder drops, relaxes, and jerks. He adjusts my feet, bending my left knee back, and when I return it, a distinctive wave travels from my foot to my hip. This continues for a few minutes. The entire leg feels light, unlike the other, yet still feels heavy and congested. I notice the various movements my body is making—micro-movements, tiny jerks or clicks, followed by a release of tension. There's light behind my eyes, fleeting. A left-to-right movement flows through my body. He asks me to lie on my back. I am open and relaxed. The familiar light pressure on my third eye is there, followed by rapid eyelid movements. Shimmering iridescent LIGHT flickers. Peace... Incredible peace and joy consume me; tears roll down my face and into my ears as I lie on my back in this blissful state.

I am asked to sit up as though sitting on a horse. I don't remember where or if he touches me. Only that...

I enter a spiral, my eyes flickering behind closed lids, my body transcending into another space, rising into the stratosphere, swaying, spiralling, sobbing, flowing with the movements of my body. Incredible! I reach up to the Universe, surrendering. Both hands move into the meditation pose. Then, my prayerful hands go to my Third Eye, my Heart, my Hara.

Repeating this ceremony three times, the spiralling and swaying slow until I sit completely still, experiencing transcendence, total absolute bliss, and peace...

It's impossible to find words to describe the events of today. I felt elated, euphoric. Bliss, sheer bliss...

DEEP MEDITATION ~ 'GOLDEN MEAN RATIO.'

I returned to Bangalow today, January 6, to attend a two-hour workshop on Fractal Implosions.

Teaching the Practical Science of Peak Experience.

I am interested in this work. When practising Tai Chi, I experience the Chi, Prana, or energy as an electrical current, a tingling sensation in my palms, the back of my hands, and fingertips. As I wander around the Expo, I find myself at the display stand. The lecturer is a world leader in Sacred Geometry. His current focus:

The Electrical Nature of Life and Consciousness as Modelled by Fractals: Teaching the Practical Science of Peak Experience.

He says, "I am looking for someone who can meditate deeply!"

Impulsively, I said, "I meditate deeply."

He says, "Okay, let's try it. Give me five minutes to set up my equipment."

I sat by the stand, deep in meditation, seeking protection and guidance.

Where is this gift guiding me?

After untangling wires and electrical cords, I was connected to the monitoring machine with a headband.

"Don't move. Meditate!"

That gets tricky when I meditate; I spiral.

He explains that if I move the monitor, I'll need to reprogram and restart it. I nod; just doing that means we'll have to wait another minute before we can resume.

"Start now!"

I realise I need to focus on not moving.

I focus on my breath, the familiar pressure in my third eye instantly present, my heart pounding, ready to leap out of my chest. In my mind, I visualise spiralling down, down, down, my breath encircling my being. Then, spiralling up, up, up into the stratosphere. Usually, my body physically spirals, so I consciously visualise the motion. Brilliant, luminous, indescribable colours swirl around my mind.

I quietly repeat 'Cho Ku Rei, Cho Ku Rei, Cho Ku Rei,' the Reiki Power Symbol known as 'The Doorway to The Light' to myself.

In the periphery of my vision, 'Light' is flickering, entering through my Crown Chakra. Exploding. Engulfing me. Bliss...

"OK, you can stop now!"

I find it hard to stop so quickly and need to refocus my breathing.

He says...

The results are amazing! It took 8 seconds. As I sat next to you, the waves were tangible. Let's try it again and see what happens!

I repeat the meditation, spending more time with it. Afterwards, I ground myself, reach up, and surrender. My hands are in a prayer gesture at my Third Eye, then they move down to the Core of my Being. Slowly, I return to this time and space.

These are the best results ever! Why do you do this?

I'm holding a promotional brochure, and as I glance down, I realise the words on the pamphlet answer his question...

I do it to access my spirituality, and in doing so, I bring about a state of bliss, joy, love, compassion, and incredible peace. Here we weep for each other's pain; then, feeling each other's heart, we know oneness.

Holding out the brochure, I say to him...

"I resonate with these words on your brochure."

I help carry CDS, books, brochures, and a dodecahedron (a spherical contraption) to the workshop. The recorded results from the experiment will be included in the lecture.

During the workshop, they checked my heart alongside the lady next to me. My heart, described as having 'coherence' with 'empathy' when listening to these words, brings a lump to my throat and tears to my eyes.

He tells the audience:

'Brenda achieved an exceptional result earlier today on the monitor.'

I was asked to describe the experiment:

As I visualise, talking my way through the connection and meditation, incredible 'Light' again enters through my Crown Chakra. My heart pounds, my voice breaks with emotion, and I am close to tears-tears of sheer bliss!

The lady sitting next to me introduced herself as Toni. We met earlier in a workshop on Friday. As we decided to have a cup of tea together, several people approached us while we were chatting. They were curious and asked where I had been trained.

'How do you do it?'

"It's a gift. There was no training," I respond.

I return to the display stand for another chat, knowing that I won't have any trouble describing the spiritual aspects of the experiment. What I will need is the scientific explanation. I hope I have it right:

A fractal is a geometric shape that can split into billions of parts, each of which contains an exact copy of the whole. Thought patterns become fractal. For example, in deep meditation, one enters an enlightened, blissful state, reverently known as Oneness.

As I didn't completely understand the process of all this, I recently googled:

"Every thought or emotion we produce has a specific geometrical pattern. The moment you connect spirit and geometry, you get Sacred Geometry. The connection between mental and emotional balance (unconditional love) is sacred geometry."

During deep meditation, my brain wave patterns were referred to as:

"The Golden Mean Ratio" Perfection, Beauty, Completeness.

I have since learnt:

When meditating at such a deep level, the 'Prana', 'Chi', or flow of energy through the pineal gland is restored at the brain's centre, activating the energy field or 'Light Body' around me. The pineal gland is often referred to as 'the third eye' or the 'all-seeing eye'. It serves as the seat of our soul and the gateway to the universe, acting as the connecting link between the physical and spiritual worlds. When activated, the pineal gland releases "feel-good" chemicals, such as dopamine and serotonin, into the body, aiding in spiritual growth and facilitating a connection to a higher level of consciousness.

'Embracing ONENESS through spiritual growth has the power to transform us, lifting us out of chaos, fear and hatred, and guiding us towards

Light, Love, Laughter, Healing, Joy, Bliss, and Peace. This transformation is not just a possibility, but a hopeful reality that we can all strive for.'
Thank you for this knowledge and the beauty it conveys.

I had received Master Reiki on 6th January 2002, six years to the day. Synchronicity was at play again.
www.merkaba.co.il/homehtm[1]

---

1.   http://www.merkaba.co.il/homehtm

THE WOW! FACTOR

O ur Brain is the GREATEST Computer.
The transformative power of meditation is profound, yielding numerous benefits and positive effects.

To access remote areas of consciousness,

To drop into 'the silence' of the mind is incredible.

When pain becomes too much to endure, physically and emotionally, surrendering oneself to 'Universal Force, Universal Energy by Meditating is the gift.

Thoughts turn inward.

Focus concentrates on breathing.

Pain, anxiety, chaos, and fear subside.

This is the WOW! Factor.

THE FUNCTION

I'm invited to attend a function at a local icon's home in Lennox Head the following day. As a newcomer to the Northern Rivers region, I often do a dry run the day before whenever I'm unsure of my directions, which I should have done on my way home from Bangalow. I hadn't given it any thought, being concerned about getting back to Baz, knowing he would disapprove. Subsequently, I got lost! It turned out alright as I arrived just before the 4-wheel drive vehicles left to go to the property.

The property is perched high on a cliff overlooking the ocean north of Lennox Head. Everywhere I looked, there were crystals, Buddhas, and flowing water features, creating a magical and mystical ambience. Fifteen people arrived, and I recognised a few from the Wellbeing Body Mind and Spirit Expo. We mingled and chatted.

Then a question: 'What is your connection at this event?'

I explained that yesterday I was connected to the 'Heart Bliss Monitor', with the results described as:

"Exceptional, the best received."

"How can you use it? What can you do with it, besides Psychically?"

I'm not sure I mentioned that a phenomenon happens to me, and afterwards, I look for answers.

"What is your birth date?"

"Um! You are a number 3."

Suggestions follow: Healing—guided writing. As a Reiki Master with several years of writing experience, that explanation makes sense.

Bess Downton, a director, editor, and producer based in Los Angeles, will be on site to film the documentary. Incredible local authors, artists, and lecturers are also present:

Jain was a Vedic mathematician and an expert in sacred geometry. Jonathan Quinton, visionary artist and geometric cosmologist, and Seth Zakay, creator of sacred geometry glass creations. As the hours creep on, I enjoy the proceedings, but a concern about Baz lingers in my mind. Finally, at 8 pm, Bess is ready. She apologises:

"Thank you for your patience."

The setting was an ethereal, mystical, almost magical alcove. A glowing golden spherical ball sits behind me to my left, and the camera and microphone are ready to roll.

Focussing on my breath, breathing through my nostrils, taking in cool air and carrying this breath of life down to my navel, I feel the presence of Spirit enter my Third Eye. Then, talking my way through, I demonstrate the Cosmic Consciousness Ceremony, finishing with the words...

"When we are One with our Divine Consciousness, we have achieved the ultimate realisation."

Following the interview, Bess, pleased with the results, hugs me.

"Thank you, that was amazing."

Seth Zakay, who creates the most incredible pieces of Sacred Geometry, along with his partner and their large cross Kelpie/Rhodesian Ridgeback dog, gives me a lift back along the track to my car. As we bump along the uneven road, I switch on my mobile, which rings, and it's Baz. He is furious with me, telling me not to bother coming home! Earlier in the day when filming started, we had switched off our mobile phones (or cell phones, as Americans call them). On my way home, I ask for guidance, knowing I must stay calm.

The magic of the last few days will slip from my grasp. Here we are again, with the old patterns re-emerging. My quest into spirituality, Baz's resentment, and my constant appeasement of his anger to keep the peace—I'm holding myself back. The excruciating pain in my knees, which I now realise comes from this holding pattern. My Reiki Master, Mark Calvert, advised me six years ago.

'Just because you follow your path, he won't leave you!'

I no longer have a choice. 2008 is a year of dedication to spirituality, writing, and my well-being. I can only ask for guidance so that Baz understands. The bonding we had as a couple after 45 years was falling on deaf and angry ears, and he had put up mental barriers. I struggled to accept why someone who loves me was unwilling to comprehend the spirit of who I am. A neighbour today validated the work I do in the village, saying:

"You make us happy!"

If only the man I love could see and appreciate that spirituality is my essence.

It's a complete misunderstanding between two people. His voice is crying out, "I've changed," and he doesn't know where he fits in.

I am conscious, focused, and loving it! There's no going back! The challenge is to bring Baz to an understanding. Words alone cannot convey feelings. Baz only sees me doing things he's no longer a part of, and fears that the path will take me away. I trust that guidance will come. For my understanding and Baz's, I need to draw parallels.

Years ago, when the children were little, it was hard to understand why he went away fishing for a week each year. I resented it. Later in life, I want him to spend time with friends, play tennis, and enjoy himself. I need the same respect and acceptance from Baz.

CRYING OUT FOR GUIDANCE

W hilst doing Tai Chi, I meditated, asking for guidance, and the answer I received was:

'Give Baz Reiki.'

Not wanting to be rejected, I express my inner concern.

'He will accept it.'

That's what I hear. This afternoon, we had a Reiki Healing session. Baz fell into a deep, snoring sleep. That's OK; we have started our journey to understanding.

Jane, a village resident, visits to discuss Reiki. I suggest she stay and that we do Reiki together. There is a significant response; her body makes minor adjustments, jerky little movements, as it re-adjusts and re-aligns Spirit.

As we finish the session, her husband arrives, furious with her for not telling him where she was or what she was doing. Here was yet another angry husband who didn't understand!

During my Tai Chi Meditation, the following day, I received another inner message:

'To Confront Death Brings Joy in Living.'

Deep Wisdom.

BREATH WORK MASTERY

*E*aster: *21 to 24 March 2008*
The Starlight Wellness Festival in Bangalow, NSW, is my favourite time of the year when I connect deeply with Spirit and other souls in sync, drawn together in heart resonance.

'**Breath work Mastery.**' The brochure reads: A conscious, connected body and breath technique that promotes accelerated detoxification in the body. This cleanse extends from the physical into an emotional, mental and/ or spiritual experience. (Alakh Analda www.re-birthing.com.au[1])

I lay with my head towards the centre of the room, instructed to breathe deeply into my body without pause. I become aware of others around me breathing deeply and continuously.

I spiral, my closed eyes rapidly moving; flickering lights appear, repeating REIKI, REIKI, REIKI, then CHO KU REI, CHO KU REI, CHO KU REI to myself. I am transported to the 'LIGHT'. My breathing changes, and I'm conscious of someone placing their hand on my heart, saying:

"Breath into whatever is happening."

The 'Light' is a dazzling white, pulsing with iridescent aqua. I have 'crossed over'; I am with my ancestors. There is gentle pressure as I hold someone's hand. Surrendering to the luminosity, my whole body is supported. Deep within me, a sound emerges, followed by another, louder one, crying out into space. I know that other people make sounds, cry, and call out. My incoherent sound shifts to 'OM', growing quieter until I am still, crying with joy in this blissful state, tears rolling down my face, filling my ears as I lie on my back, heart pounding.

Opening my eyes, then closing them again, I'm conscious of the familiar pressure on my third eye. Spirit is still holding my hands as I spiral again. Then,

---

1.   http://www.rebirthing.com.au/

moving back into this consciousness, I took a long, deep, releasing breath into the core of my body.

Open my smiling eyes, each assistant in the room comes, enquiring "How are you?"

"Beautiful", I reply.

It takes a while to ground myself, even as I sit with my back supported against the wall, still gently spiralling. What a gift! Wow! I'm so glad to be a part of it. This intensive experience took me on an emotional and spiritual journey, and I've transcribed it as it was; there are no other words. Thank you.

I wrap up the day with a Shiatsu massage on the grass. Tomorrow is another day I'm eager for.

MAGIC WAND

The next morning, Toni, her friend Leah, and I stop to chat with ZaKaiRan from the Lotus Temple before heading over to Penny to discuss Pendulums. Penny has a workshop I'm keen on today entitled:

'**Psychic Development.**' A sitting circle is formed, and Penny invites us to breathe in colour. As Penny speaks, her wand is passed around to gauge everyone's reactions. The circle is large, and it takes some time to complete. Reaching for the Wand, I hold it in both hands and place it next to my heart chakra.

At once, I feel pressure in my third eye. My head shakes, pulsing in flickering 'Light.' Iridescent colours swirl behind my closed eyelids. My body vibrates physically. Unconscious of anyone around me, I focused on the effects the wand was having. Incredible!

At the end of the meditation, Penny stands up, coming towards me, saying:

"Didn't you have a great experience? I was watching you, and you won the lottery!"

"Wow! That was incredible, thank you, Penny."

She asks me to describe the effect the wand had on me to the group.

After the session, we chatted holding hands.

"Where did you get your Wand?"

"I had it made by an old man who lived locally, and I have lost touch with him."

I am disappointed. The effects were so powerful for me that I would like to own one.

SPIRALLING, PULSING, SPIRALLING

On Easter Sunday, I attended a workshop on **Lucid Shamanic Dreaming.** The opening breathwork carries me straight into 'Theta,' a deep, trance-like brain wave pattern where I remain with my heart pounding, still totally aware of the presenter talking, engrossed in a blissful state, my head pulsing and spiralling 'The Light.' Powerful. I acknowledge how easily I access this magical, peaceful space, asking for guidance. As the class finishes, a woman introduces herself:

"Hello, my name is Grace. We met at Lennox Head."

"I'm making a film on 'Exceptional Women.' Can I have your contact details?"

I'm a little taken aback, hesitating. She says:

"I will be in touch."

I hope I haven't discouraged her. Toni, Leah & I enjoy a cup of tea together, discussing the workshops. On the walk to the car, we bump into ZaKaiRan from the Lotus Temple, Byron Bay. Patting the top of my head, he says:

"You have a Fibonacci Golden Mean Brain."

"Oh yes! Fabulous things happen when I come to these places!" I reply.

Toni, ZaKaiRan and I have a 'group hug' to finish the day. Words spinning around in my brain...

I am Open to Divine Intervention. I am Open to Divine Assistance. I am open to Divine Healing.

SEVEN GENERATIONS

E aster Monday, I show my pass and a lady at the entrance says:
"At the lecture, you described how you connected with the Light! You are a ray of sunshine!"

Wow! What a great way to start the day.

I attend **'Rites of Passage.'**

The facilitator has worked around the globe offering her services. She is dedicated to making a positive impact on the world. The workshop is thorough and proactive. I partner with and work alongside Sally, helping her heal her broken heart. Sally conducts her life from her Base Chakra. I conduct my life from my Third Eye and Crown Chakras, and it's a revelation to realise this.

Jason McDonald, the psychic medium, is running late, so they will switch to an alternative workshop. By default, I will be in the next seminar.

'How to be More Attractive by Connecting with Spirit.'

Kevin conducts a Guided Meditation

"Connect to your father Spirit."

I mentally back away!

As he talks, I visualise an old photograph of my father holding a large parrot. The picture belonged to my mother; she kept it for 60 years.

Kevin says:

"Visualise your grandfather."

I met my Paternal Grandfather in the UK when I was 10 years old, before leaving for Australia. An ancient, older man with claw-like hands stared at me. I found him to be quite frightening.

"Elevate right hand, our Masculine side. Visualise that hand being held."

We regress seven generations.

"Next, our Feminine side. Visualise the elevated left hand being held."

Mother, Grandmother, great-grandmother, great-great-grandmother, back again, seven generations.

Likewise, both hands. Both Masculine and Feminine are integrated—permission to access love in the temple of our body, to free any genetic programming.

This is significant for me, having experienced the intense hand-holding presence at the 'Breath Work Mastery Workshop' two days ago.

My raised arms are physically vibrating. I am moving into 'The Light,' accessing my Ethereal Body, and becoming 'The Light.'

I experienced this phenomenon years earlier with Mark Calvert in an angel workshop. At the end of the seminar, Mark held both hands to steady and ground me, bringing me back into this space. I covered my heart with my hands, concentrating and feeling the soles of my feet on the floor. My heart was still pounding when Jason McDonald arrived to start the next session.

As I leave, I contemplate how much I enjoyed the four-day weekend. A lady at the front desk says:

I know you from the Bliss Monitor workshop! I attended two more sessions in Queensland, and he spoke about you, saying he had met this incredible woman who meditated.

I left walking on air, feelings of gratitude overwhelming me.

LOVE THE HIGHEST VIBRATION~BLISS

J*une 2008*
  I realise...

Love is the highest vibration of energy that is possible. It is Bliss.
The 'gift' is the ability to access the bliss, love, and peace...
I am Blessed.
Divine Consciousness... I am One with my God
I am One with Gaia
I am One with Humanity
I am the Unified Light
You also are the Unified Light
You are One with Humanity
You are One with Gaia. You are One with your God
We are all Blessed.
'NAMASTE, the God in me sees and honours the God in You.'

THE ALPHA PLAN ~ Early 1990s.

In the early 1990s, I purchased a book titled "The Alpha Plan." It was the first of its kind, resonating within me. I found the book revolutionary. Published in 1989, methods of teaching awareness, meditation, personal growth, holistic therapies, Zen Yoga, and relaxation were rare in the Western World.

In June 2008, I again referred to 'The Alpha Plan.' It has yellowed somewhat over the years! This book helped me better understand the 'biofeedback monitor' to which I was connected.

GOLDEN MEAN RATIO

As I spiral into the vortex, I radiate White Light, the energy of Life, while in a deep meditative state. I'm accessing Theta brain wave patterns and achieving a blissfully relaxed state with heightened senses, including an intense awareness of my beating heart. My body swings like a pendulum, from left to right and then right to left, bringing my brain into a state of total balance.

A relaxed state of consciousness facilitates spiritual insights and promotes healing, increasing one's sensitivity, compassion, love, and attunement with oneself. When simply relaxing, I realise I'm in an 'Alpha' state. The Alpha Plan teaches how to access the Alpha State of awareness, which ranges from 7.5 Hz to 12.5 Hz. Theta at 3 to 6 Hz promotes an even deeper level. I recognise the impact this small book has had on my journey.

I'm dozing, and words drift into my consciousness. I want to capture them before they float away into the ether, so I roll out of bed and throw on a tracksuit when Baz says:

"What are you doing?"

I don't answer, as the spell will be broken. It's tough because he repeats the question, and my mind slips back into Beta. I struggle and try to copy the words onto paper as my beta mind kicks in.

Divine Consciousness:
One with God
One with Gaia
One with Humanity
I am ONE
I am the Unified Light
I AM
It is well with my Soul

RECOGNISING DIVINITY

ugust 7, 2008

A We are in Yeppoon, Queensland, staying at 'The Beachside Caravan Park.' The weather is superb, with blue skies and sunshine every day. I'm on the beach reading 'KRYON Lifting the Veil, Book 11,' a channelling from Kryon referring to those of us who see colours. The colours I see today are magical as the holographic title catches the sun. Vibrant turquoise, intense green, and swirling purple manifest into a shimmering ball of deep golden yellow-orange, forming a horizontal haze behind the Kryon title. My brain plays with it, returning it to a ball, and then a horizontal haze again. I etch it into my memory and my mind's eye.

Tonight, watching the Olympic Opening Ceremony in Beijing on television, the Chinese symbol for 'Harmony' and the White Dove of Peace prevailed, encompassing the countries of the World. 'One World, One Dream'. I see the smiling eyes of the athletes, and I am reminded we are all 'One'. Humans living on this incredible little planet we call Earth desire happiness and love. As the consciousness of this planet moves increasingly into 'The Light', we who are 'aware' individuals, must hold the light higher and higher to encompass more people so they too will have the courage to take up the 'Light'.

"Kryon, what is mastery? I'll tell you what it is, Human Being:

It's when you walk around and you're not afraid of life. It's when you're peaceful when others are not. The situations that would cause drama in others do not in you. It's when the world is in chaos, yet you walk into it and don't feel it. Instead, at some level, you think the wisdom of the ages. You know it doesn't have to affect you, and it doesn't have to touch you. Life is just waiting for you to take the hand of your Higher Self. That has always been the invitation. The Higher-Self and the Human Divine Self connect the two; that is your life's purpose. When you do, you become a lighthouse. It's a powerful thing when you recognise divinity in yourself."

These words resonate deeply with me; I find myself at this exact point in my Journey!

"When the lighthouse strikes its light, it does not measure the storm. It does not judge the storm. It does not say to itself, "I must understand where this is all going" before it shines its light. All it knows is that it was built to endure darkness, mighty wind and the waves that will crash endlessly over its structure. It's not afraid, either. It doesn't know when the storm will end, how powerful it will become, or the reasoning behind its creation. All the lighthouse knows is that it's safe, and that it must shine a light in the darkness to help others find the safety of the harbour. It never questions how it became light but knows who it is and what it's for. It also knows the light it carries is expected, and those in the dark are looking for it. Do you see what I am saying? You knew all this when you came in. Profound, it is! Emotional, it is!"

As I read these words, I find myself fighting back tears. They are truly Profound!

Quoted from Kryon Lifting the Veil–Book 11 Copyright©2007-LeeCarroll

'ORKNEY' My Journey into this lifetime began here, to the North of Mainland Scotland, in a haven, surrounded by Lighthouses, the symbols of hope and guidance. An expanse of calm water called the Scapa Flow, ringed by about 70 Islands and 9 Lighthouses, entwining the Orkney Archipelago and the Sea. The name 'ORKNEY' embraces them all.

I am deeply grateful for this gift of 'Light'.

My destiny 'Shine & Share The Light in Love & Guidance.'

DIVINE LIGHT ~ Insight New Dawning, New Name

October 7, 2008

O   I see evidence of New Dawning across the globe. Topics never discussed previously. The Church and clergy are being exposed for their wrongdoings. Doctors sued for malpractice. Banks, business sectors, and tax havens were exposed. Skeletons in family closets, reuniting members after years of separation, aspects of life emerging, coming to 'The Light'. Nothing heals left in the deep crevices of the soul. The light of GAIA shines brighter into these dark places. So Be It.

I'm at my daughter's and son-in-law's property on the outskirts of Sydney. My Daughter is in America, training for a new job. I am here to help with the dogs and to see my baby granddaughter Aleisha again. Baz has gone fishing at Lake Eucumbene for his annual event with old mates.

I learnt we have a 'spiritual name' and put it out to the Universe, asking: What is my spiritual name?

I awoke this morning with *'Christa, Christa, Christa'* going around in my brain. Is this my spiritual name? It makes sense as my middle name is Christine.

Whilst writing these memoirs, I see pieces of my life falling into place like a jigsaw puzzle. Insights, why something occurred at a particular time. Why do I feel connected to a specific number or flower? How did likes and dislikes come to be, and how have they become significant in this life journey?

2008 is coming to a close. Returning home from our trips this year in the Winnebago, the words flowed as I sat at my computer. Often, I feel the familiar pressure in my third eye, knowing that Spirit is with me, guiding me, and I give gratitude.

Today, 20th November, the day before my dear brother's birthday, I have recollected 1998, ten years ago, the year I started Reiki Level 1, also when I received the Runes from my Daughter-in-Law, becoming familiar with them.

I had recorded the first reading on 26th December 1998.

As I re-read the runes of that day, I realise with clarity, the path they foresaw for me has unfolded and is continuing to unfold.

Joyfully, I give thanks.

SOUND & HEALING NIGHT

*T*uesday, *9 December 2008*

I've heard about the 'Sound & Healing' Lotus Temple in Byron Bay.

Roadworks and heavy traffic delays have made me 10 minutes late, and the session has already begun.

Imagine 40 people in the room, lying on the floor with their heads on cushions, all directed towards a focal point: a column in the centre of the room, exquisitely adorned with rose quartz and selenite crystals, flowers, candles, and burning incense. The essence wafting towards me soothes my senses. Fabrics in pastel colours of the rainbow are artfully draped to cover the high ceiling.

Ethereal music and singing voices greet me.

'I have died and gone to heaven!'

A healer places her hands on my heart, the sides of my face, then moves on. I lift my arms to 'feel' the strong, palpable energy—the pressure of spiritual connection in my third eye. I am aware of deep trance meditation. My hearing is acute. Birds are singing in the trees outside. Illuminating 'Light' floods my senses; I spiral, my hands, arms, and legs jerking.

As the session draws to a close, I find myself grounded back in this time and place, feeling a sense of bliss and tranquillity. It's a moment of calm and relaxation that I wish could last forever, entirely at peace...

REIKI & WRITING

New Year 2009

The start of the New Year is busy. Reiki fills my days with five healing sessions for residents in my village. Relaxing in bed this morning, I give Baz Reiki. Baz has fair skin, making him a good candidate for skin cancers, and he has had several removed.

The Starlight Wellbeing Festival, a yearly event, is on again at Bangalow. This morning's Tibetan Blessing, followed by Chicchan's Crystal Singing Bowls and Meditation, provides a magical way to open the festival.

I'm drawn to Matt Shooting Star, the Flute Man. He asked for a volunteer apprentice during the workshop, so I raised my hand! It feels great to produce notes that resemble a tune as directed by Matt. At the end of the session, he hands me a copy of his CD as a token of appreciation.

'Journey Over Mountains.'

Later, as I listen, the haunting notes of the Native American flute carry me away on a journey into another 'space'. Wow! To play the flute like that!

Over a cup of aromatic chai tea, I sit chatting with Matt about flutes. He teaches me the basics, and I walk away with one tucked under my arm, cradled in a lilac suede pouch. His words:

"Play, just play, play, play!"

Another workshop attracted my attention, titled:

'Spiritual Path of Karmic Tarot.'

Initially, I found it challenging to understand the presenter's words due to his accent. However, I felt a deep connection as he explored the tarot. His description of the magician, who begins life by tossing the cards to determine where it unfolds, resonated with my journey.

Then, when one has attained Oneness, being described as The Fool! I ask, "Why is he the Fool?"

"You are still just Human." Is his reply.

Tarot has captivated me throughout the years. It's not merely a deck of cards but a tool that has been part of my life since childhood, when my mother dabbled in the metaphysical. It serves as a mirror reflecting my inner journey and a guide that helps me navigate life's twists and turns.

The next workshop is fascinating—Vedic **Maths with Jain**. Vedic Maths, an ancient Indian system of mathematics, is not just about numbers, but a way of understanding the universe. Jain's teachings have transformed my perception of mathematics, turning it from a dreaded subject into a fascinating exploration of patterns and relationships. I wish that, as a child, someone had described Maths as Jain does. I'm sure I would have enjoyed Math instead of dreading it. Jain has produced a beautifully handwritten book that talks about his passion, 'The Golden Mean Ratio.'

After the session, I introduced myself and reminded him that we had met a year ago while I was recording the documentary at Lennox Head. He didn't remember until I mentioned I had been connected to the monitor accessing 'The Golden Mean Ratio.'

We talked for a while. He ends by saying:

I'm privileged to meet you again; someone of that level is a gift.

"Yes, I know, the greatest of all gifts," I reply.

As I walk away, I'm humbled by his comments.

It's Tuesday, 20th January, and The Lotus Temple Byron Bay's Sound and Healing night resumed after the Christmas break. The emotive, powerful sounds of a didgeridoo pulsated and vibrated through my body, carrying me away into the stratosphere. I feel blessed.

WHY? ANSWERS VALIDATED

Tess, my cousin, rang. She has been in Coffs Harbour Hospital for nine days on an antibiotic drip. She needs to go to RPA Hospital in Sydney for further tests. The breast cancer she had ten years ago has likely metastasised.

The following morning, Terry, my cousin, Tessa's brother, left a message on my mobile telling me:

Tess has been diagnosed with cancer in the bile duct. Terry worries about his youngest sister, Annie, and how she will cope with the news. He has asked me to call her.

While playing a guided meditation CD entitled 'Zen Garden' for the ladies at 'Riverbend' today, I sensed Colin standing behind me. He placed his hands on my shoulders, and I breathed in his essence. I know his spirit is here to support me during the coming months of Tessa's illness.

Tibetan chanting welcomes us tonight at the Lotus Temple, preparing our senses for meditation. A healer arrives, with wolf-like sounds emanating from his throat as he places his hand on my heart, resonating deeply within me. My body jerks, sinking into the floor before relaxing. I feel his hand on my body for ages, even though he has moved on to another person. The spirit remains. Profound!

Today, I meditated on the question, 'Why?'

"Why does life appear so difficult?"

I reflect on the last few months of my mother's life, wrought with pain from falls. My dear Auntie Joyce, in the final stages of lung cancer, fell and broke her hip. Why did that happen? She didn't need the extra pain and torment: Dadda Mick, the stroke, the subsequent disabilities. My dearest brother, his life snatched away too early. Why is it so hard? I turned to meditation to seek answers to life's challenges. Why does life often seem so difficult? It's a question that led me to a profound realisation; I receive a message when I read...

'The Tibetan Book of Living and Dying.' Sogyal Rinpoche. Taking it from the shelf, a page falls open:

Life's difficulties, the pain, the suffering encountered in our daily living, enable us to move emotionally into an easier acceptance of our ultimate destiny. Death.

Several years back, I did the same thing. The notion of death was always close to my mind. It became my awakening or rebirth, and I came to accept death, moving into a state of sublime joy and fearlessness. Today's lesson confirms this for me.

As I wander through my garden, I do, indeed, confront death daily. Today, a small flower bud; tomorrow, a full bloom. I delight in its purity, enveloped in the fragrant essence. Perfection is ephemeral. Within days, autumn descends upon this little flower's life, vibrant colours fading and turning brown, until the next day, it lies dead. As it falls to the earth, its nutrients are absorbed and recycled, creating a continual cycle of life and death.

February 12, 2009

There have been horrendous bushfires in Victoria, Australia. One hundred eighty-one people are dead, 1000 homes have been lost, over 5000 people are homeless, and up to 1,000,000 wildlife and pets are estimated to have been lost.

Whilst reflecting, I am reminded of the Mayan predictions for 2012, and I tell Baz, 'There will be a changeover of Energy, a subtle shift in 2012.' As the ancient Mayan civilisation predicted, Earth-GAIA is moving from darkness into a more enlightened phase.

The analogy: a set of scales is balanced, with rice on each side. It takes just a single grain placed on one side for the balance to tip, marking the movement of the critical mass. While individuals may think they are alone, they cannot effect change; each of us becoming aware and coming together as 'One' will foster a movement toward a compassionate and caring world, not driven by money. I view the current world economic crisis as part of this movement. The tsunami, the horrific earthquake in Japan, the terrorist bombings in the USA on 9/11, and now the initiation by fire in our ancient land of Australia, with the loss of so many lives. Disasters of such magnitude evoke compassion and care within us, awakening us to what is truly essential in life: not material wealth or possessions—easily lost—but the love and support of our family, friends, neighbours, and community.

References made: Adapted Words and Knowledge from "The Tibetan Book of Living and Dying" Copyright © Rigpa Fellowship 1992 Harper Collins Publishers Inc.

TESS

It's February, and I'm with Tess. Doctors have removed the gallbladder and confirmed that the breast cancer has now metastasised to the bile duct.

Tessa relaxes deeply during the Reiki Healing Session, commenting that it reminds her of the relaxation classes she attended when she had breast cancer.

I call forth my Guides and trance into deep meditation, a rush of energy moving me as a pendulum, backwards and forwards, directing pulsating 'light' into Tessa's solar plexus.

After the session, Tess says:

"I thought you had switched on the light, but when I opened my eyes, it was still dark here!"

"How beautiful," I reply.

I am elated, Tess is moving into 'The Light'. The following day, I gave Tess another Reiki session. She enters into deep relaxation. Afterwards, she says:

"There were two lights, and a misty lilac haze. In the middle of the haze...

She hesitates:

This sounds funny, but there was a green wreath, a circle of green leaves. I had a weird sensation. I knew you removed your hands, but felt they were still there!"

Moved and emotional, I tell her we are calling in High Powers. The spiritual presence remains, even though the person has moved away.'

Later discussing the vision, she says:

"It was a wreath."

A clear message reached my heart: of her impending death.

On Thursday, 12th March, Tess rings with test results: she has stage 4 cancer, the last stage. Cancer has spread throughout her lymph nodes and bile ducts. Opting not to receive chemotherapy, she feels she will not benefit from it, and the doctor has agreed with her. I'm sad, as I am losing my 'sister.' A sense of calm overcomes me, knowing she has made her choice.

In early April, Tess rings again. She has visited an oncologist and undergone additional tests. The oncologist has suggested that chemotherapy may give her 'more time'. So, she has agreed. She has been informed that she can stop if it does not agree with her.

Hindsight:

As I edit this book many years later, the decision to embark on chemotherapy may have given Tess more time. Indeed, I know chemotherapy did not enhance her life; the absolute reverse occurred; it reduced her quality of life, causing her untold pain and discomfort. Her bowel became ulcerated, and she suffered nausea and vomiting. I believe her first intuition not to receive chemotherapy was a wiser choice.

EVALUATING

O ver the past month, I watched two TV shows that highlighted parallels in my life. I have documented both these programmes and their significance. Tonight, the show delved into the Catholic Church and the practice of exorcism.

As I recall, I've been interested in the metaphysical for many years. I look back on my teenage years, kneeling in church at the Latin Benediction, watching the pageantry as the priest swings the 'censer', a ceremonial vessel used to distribute incense. The evocative essence surrounding my senses, the mantra of the Rosary, and my heart pounding loudly in my ears are no longer part of my life.

Baz and I were married in the Catholic Church on Easter Monday, 15 April 1963, when I was 18 years old. The revolutionary Contraceptive Pill was available only to married women. The Church's condemnation and renunciation of it continues to this day. I was a young woman in love, and the proper way to express that love in 1963 was to get married. However, I was not ready to embark on motherhood, so I decided to take the pill. This led to a dilemma: I could not continue attending confession and confess to a sin I didn't believe I was committing. I attended Mass every Sunday at St. Mary's, Miller Street, North Sydney, while my new husband, an Anglican, waited patiently outside reading the Sunday paper or returned to our new little flat at Neutral Bay. I kept attending Mass, avoiding the confessional, knowing that parts were missing and the puzzle was disintegrating. Then life's journey unfolded: mortgages, children, travel, and a career, never looking back at those teenage years.

In 2009, I was 65 years old; some might say I was an old lady. In my heart, I'm still that young teenage girl, and my heart once again pounds in my ears with joy as I sit in silent meditation. Twice a year, I attend the Wellbeing festivals at Bangalow in the magnificent hinterland of Northern NSW. It is here, over the last two years, that I have experienced transcendent spiritual encounters.

I also attended the 'Lotus Temple' in Byron Bay, part of the Academy of Energy Science & Consciousness, each Tuesday night. I feel swept away, connecting with every part of my being to the Divine. The memories of those heart-pounding teenage years have resurfaced.

Back to the Catholic Church and Exorcism. The parallel I drew tonight as I watched the show...

When I received my Reiki Master training, I placed my trust entirely in the Universe, surrendered, and opened myself up spiritually—something I had been reluctant to do until then. I exorcised the fear demons from my childhood, including the Devil and Hellfire damnation instigated by the Catholic Church, replacing them with a loving Divine Connection to my Highest Self, my inner God.

It was 11:30 p.m., and I sat at my computer, writing.

The other programme referred to 'Geometric Patterning,' based on the Fibonacci Theory, the Spiral, the Golden Mean Ratio, and Leonardo da Vinci's 'Perfect Man.' I realise this is the phenomenon I experience in deep meditation: attaining the Golden Mean Ratio, total Joy, Inner Bliss. I don't fully understand it. Future generations will learn considerably more with a click on the internet. My time is running out! Will there be enough years? The days, the weeks, the months, and the years fly by, and I have so much more to do and learn.

The Golden Mean Ratio, as I understand, is...The Vibration of The Golden Mean Ray of Light and Bliss.

The coming together of the Body and Soul in perfect balance and alignment. Spiralling physically while meditating at a deep level activates my DNA, igniting the Pineal and Pituitary glands in the brain, and launching me into an incredible, illuminating Light with an overwhelming feeling of euphoric bliss. The Pineal gland, the size of a grain of rice, sits below the Crown Chakra deep in the middle of the head, and the Pituitary gland sits in the middle of the brow between the eyes, the Third Eye, the Clairvoyant Eye. They are the Gateway, the links to higher consciousness, Intuition, and Knowing.

JOYCE is WAITING, WELCOMING

D ying is lonely! I want to be there for Tess, but can I? The journey is hers alone.

May there be peace within. May you trust that you are exactly where you are meant to be.

May you not forget the infinite possibilities of faith in yourself and others.

May you use the gifts you have received and pass on the love that has been given to you.

May you be content with yourself just the way you are.

Let this knowledge settle into your bones, and allow your soul the freedom to sing, dance, praise and love. It is there for each one of us.

Quoted Verse: St. Teresa of Avila

Driving southward, the landscape changes, reminding me of the distance taken to reach Tessa. She is very ill, Baz and I have driven from Cairns in Northern Queensland to Valla Beach in NSW, a distance of over 2,000 km in the motorhome to be with her. My heart carried an aching weight. Tessa's Indian doctor's words echoed in my mind, urging a release of the burdens she had, a call to let go of the negativity, anger and sadness.

During the Reiki Healing, I stood close, observing her surrender into relaxation. The peaceful expression on her face brought tears to my eyes. When the session was over, her voice imbued with joy, Tess said softly:

"Mum was walking towards me, smiling with outstretched arms, wearing a dress with autumn tones, and her hair was as she wore it in the fifties."

When she spoke of her mother, the vision Tess described painted vivid colours of love and remembrance in my mind. My Auntie Joyce, radiant in her autumn dress, smiled – her essence wrapped around us like a gentle embrace, her spirit lingered as a comforting presence amid impending uncertainty. Tess and I shared sacred moments, tears of joy spilling freely as we talked about Joyce's 'coming through' today — the power and sheer beauty of Reiki were validated in my life once more, serving as a reminder of the bonds that tie us together, even in the face of illness and death.

Today is a lovely autumn day, with clear blue skies and a gentle breeze. I head to the beach, read for a while, then go for a walk. While walking, I feel inspired to practice Tai Chi, my body moving in harmony with the earth beneath my feet. Embracing the solitude, I could almost feel Tess beside me, her laughter mingling with the sound of the surf. I visualised Tess and I on Valla Beach where she lives, realising it is not a path we would tread again together. As I contemplated Tessa's journey, a wave of empathy washed over me. My heart is open and raw, not shying away from the reality of her death. Encompassing everything before me, I felt his presence—my brother. I surrendered to the moment, supported by his love that transcends time and space, accepting the months ahead and embracing a blend of sorrow and peace.

IGNITE YOUR DIVINE VOICE

J *uly 2009*
　　I am attending a workshop at the 'Lotus Temple', Byron Bay...
'Ignite Your Divine Voice. *Create Your Divine Reality Expression and Empowerment–Working with the Throat Chakra.'* Facilitator Lelama.

I need 'guidance in expressing myself.' Aware that I do not always voice my true feelings, now is the time to embrace my Truth, the Truth of who I am. This will be the perfect workshop.

I was surrounded by fellow souls, four men and three women, all open and eager to discover their truths. The air was thick with possibility as we formed a circle on cushions surrounding a central pillar. The altar was adorned with rose quartz and selenite crystals, accompanied by burning incense, candles, and fresh flowers—an enchanting array of colours invites us to connect. Columns stretch up to the ceiling, decorated with flowing, draped fabrics in pastel colours reminiscent of the rainbow. In that shared space, I felt the heartbeat of the Universe, a resonance of energies. Lelama speaks of the 'Golden River' coursing deep into Mother Earth from the Crown Chakra to the Base Chakra, symbolising the flow of divine energy and the connection between the spiritual and physical realms. Saying:

"Permit your Highest Self to communicate in your voice." Lelama encouraged, her words wrapping around me like an assuring hug.

As I meditate deeper into the Golden Grid, I become lost in the flow of sound; a language surges from deep within - 'light language' bubbled forth, my voice resonating with Asian inflexions. I repeat, E'La E'La E'La, euphoria and tears flowing. This newfound voice, this connection with the Spirit of Mama, fills me with delight and a sense of empowerment. The session concludes with a powerful symbol of unity, as we all join hands to form a circle around the central pillar.

Lelama says:

'Let your voices fly,' saying Ha Ha Ha Ha, laughing ecstatically, giving way to 'my voice', moving, dancing, laughing, revelling in the experience. In the embrace of that divine energy, I looked at my companions, laughter escaping our lips as we echoed joyfully through the sacred space. Our hands entwined, we formed a circle of unity, the energy swirling between us as we surrendered to the moment – voices soaring, laughter erupting. Ecstatic, we finished with a group hug. I feel reluctant to let the moment go, for the evening to end. That night, I had a dream:

The dream transports me to a different time, another life. I feel uncomfortable and insecure around strangers, struggling to communicate verbally. Baz walks down an incline towards me. He appears young and good-looking, wearing a priest's collar and a cloak. His hair is darker and slicked back away from his face. I realise he is the master teacher, the shaman. I strive to catch his eye as he stands before the group. At first, his eyes flash by, then lock onto mine. My eyes pleaded, silently communicating with him. As we walk away together through archways, we enter a large open room. I feel we are being watched. Behind one of the decorative screens, I overtly tell him, 'Eyes are watching us.' Then, I cry out loudly:

Ishtar, Ishtar, Ishtar.

I woke myself in the early morning light, loudly calling to 'Ishtar'. This dream, along with the subsequent invocation of Ishtar, marked a significant turning point in my spiritual journey, leading me to a deeper understanding of my past and present. The dream was a bridge to realms unseen, a desire for connection, wisdom and love. A profound experience that opened up new pathways in my spiritual journey.

I Google 'Ishtar' and discover...

'Ishtar is the Ancient Babylonian Goddess of Love and War.'

Words jump from the text. I learn I can invoke Ishtar for many reasons.

"Ishtar soothes with her divine wisdom, love and compassion in times of distress or confusion. She lends her comforting support and allows for opening or clearing the pathway for a new direction." www.orderwhitemoon.org/goddess/Ishtar[1].)

---

1.   http://www.orderwhitemoon.org/goddess/Ishtar

Wow! That was perfect for my dream. While meditating on the dream, I had an insight, realising that in a past life, I was...

Speechless, lost, disempowered, and calling Ishtar for help.

The course I attended last night with Lelama opened, released, and transformed that memory, allowing me in this lifetime to know, love, and embrace my Divinity. It empowered me with a voice to share wisdom in the form of writing a book entitled:

"Spiralling to the Light"

Additionally, providing service fosters compassion for those who seek and need support. Goddess Ishtar and Quan Yin will offer compassionate support as I navigate the journey of grief when Tessa departs from this life.

In my heart, I know there is no death, only the passing of a body. I can face the impending death of my cousin with peace—this peace did not exist when I lost my dearest brother 15 years ago. He has carried me a long way. By accepting the inevitability of Tessa's death, I've learnt that talking honestly and openly together brings quality of life. It's a mix of sadness, tears, laughter, and gratitude for the time we've been given. It's a time for families to gather, express their love for one another, and understand the true meaning of family.

THE LEGACY OF LOVE

September 28, 2009
While in Sydney, visiting Cousin Emma and Matt for the birth of their baby son on the way back up the coast, north of Newcastle, Louise, Tessa's eldest daughter, calls.

Tessa passed away peacefully today at 11:30 am. The circle of life continues; one new baby soul enters the family while another soul departs.

Tess held a small bouquet of African violets, her favourite flowers. I went to her bedside, gently stroked her face, and kissed her goodbye.

Tess was merely a shadow of her vibrant self. Always accepting the inevitability of her death, she inspired those she encountered. May we discover the same strength when our journey comes to an end. Being a close-knit family, this acceptance allowed us to bond closely, enriching our quality of life.

Love was her legacy.

To mourn too long for those we love is self-indulgent. But to honour their memory with a promise to live a little better for having known them, gives purpose to their life and an easier acceptance of their Death.
Sayings of the Buddha

DISCOVERING THE TAROT

My interest in Tarot re-ignited after attending a workshop. Three of us, having had an appeal for Tarot throughout our lives, signed up for the eight-week course.

On a day trip to the 'Crystal Castle' in the magnificent hinterland of Byron Bay, I picked up a pack of Tarot Cards in the bookshop. Entitled:

'Gateway to the Divine Tarot.' Ciro Marchetti.

The designs and colours were fantastic; they called out to my heart and had my name stamped on them! The book entices me to:

'Enter through the portal to a magical world of lost knowledge, detailing past information and future guidance.'

After a few weeks of study, Jane instructed us to read for ourselves. Choosing randomly, I spread the cards across the table. Looking and analysing again, I became emotional as I saw my life laid out before me, step by step.

Mystical, Magical, Tarot.

Reference Gateway to the Divine Tarot © 2009 Ciro Marchetti.

SLEEPLESS NIGHTS

It is 12:30 a.m., and I'm unable to sleep. I am wide awake, feeling hot, cold, and hot again.

Through my earphones, I listen to "Healing Journey" by Dr. Emmett Miller, a soothing meditation tape I've had for years. I usually fall asleep easily. I doze, and then I'm wide awake again. I get up to write, words buzzing and spiralling around in my brain, and finally, I sleep in the second bedroom.

The next day, Baz sulks like a spoiled child. He doesn't want to talk unless necessary, and he doesn't appreciate my sleeping in the other room.

Realisation dawns that that is precisely what he is. I learned that his mother was 39 years old, and both his older brothers had already moved out of their home. Explains a lot, a little spoiled boy to older parents!

WHEN YOUR SOUL IS SINGING

A*pril 2010*
    My life has moved on once again. I have sold the house in 'Riverbend', the over-50s Resort, and settled into a little villa in Ballina.

The Easter Starlight Wellbeing Expo at Bangalow is on Friday. I take my friend Eileen as she has never been there. We arrived to receive the blessing of Ven Lobsang Tendar, the Buddhist monk who attended this Expo. Then, we visit the Crystal Singing Bowls, deciding it's a great way to start the day.

The crystalline sound of the bowls resonates within my being. I go with it, moving up and out into the stratosphere, to 'The Light.' Spirit has settled into my third eye. I feel the familiar pressure, then the expansion. My body vibrates, going into a spiral, then swinging left to right, right to left. Incredible, vibrant colours flood my senses.

There is a Workshop at noon entitled...

'Eagles don't Fly in Flocks.' The brochure reads...

"The true place of self-discovery is in owning your talents and abilities, stepping up and taking your place in the world as a unique and wonderful individual. Own your true magnificence using ancient wisdom tools to clear any blocks and negative limiting belief systems holding you back from finding your path and reaching your true potential."

During the workshop, Paul (the presenter) asks the question:

'What in your life would you change, what is holding you back?

Meditate on it, see that occasion and change it.'

I have a visualisation: Sitting in the computer chair, leaning sideways to reach something on the floor, I feel excruciating pain zigzagging through my left knee, tearing the meniscus.

I realise this marked the beginning of my knee problems. While meditating, I enter an enlightened space filled with light, love, energy, and colour. Paul continues...

'Imagination will take you there! Go inside for the answers. Something is holding you back. You'll know what it is, so tap into your intuition.

'You need to experience the darkness to move into the Light.'

'Stepping off the pathway, moving ahead, flying with your life, when your soul is singing, that is where you are meant to be.'

A powerful Poem by Marianne Williamson...

"Our Greatest Fear" ends the session.

Thank you, Paul, for an 'Inspiring workshop'. www.ancientpathways.com.au[1]

The following day, I am standing on the balcony energised from the sunshine, next session starts titled:

"Urban Shaman Raym." Raym Richards, Shaman, writes a column...

'Living Now', he talks of his experiences. I resonate with much of what he says. He had not been 'spiritual' until his total awakening. Towards the end of the session, Raym invites 'feedback'. I mentioned being connected to the Bliss Monitor here at the Starlight Festival a few years ago, when I accessed expanded states of consciousness. Raym says:

"You were the one!"

After the workshop, I spoke with Raym, who told me how blessed I am.

"I know, I give gratitude daily."

Purchasing his book, 'Alchemy of Crystals', he explains:

'The book will tell you what most people go through to get to where you are.'

Raym has written another book, titled "Spirit Guides." I feel I already have that book in my collection. Later that day, we sat talking; he reiterated how blessed I am; it is a gift.

While drinking Chai Tea, Shaun, a lecture participant, sat with me and exchanged information. Shaun had asked Raym a question...

"Is there any going back?"

Raym replies:

"No, and why would you want to?"

I agree, there is no going back.

Shaun tells me he works with abused children and does 'Polarity Therapy', he walks in the wilderness to access his spirituality. I think immediately of Paul Hoogendyk:

"When your Soul Sings, that is what you should do."

Shaun also writes, hoping to publish the book, which he initially said was for himself, but others encouraged him to share it. So, we had several things in common. He talked of the author James Redfield:

'The Celestine Prophecy.' & 'The Tenth Insight.'

Synchronicity, I tell him I read those books. We agree they had a significant impact on our lives.

I've been unpacking and setting up since moving into our little 'Villa', a quaint and cosy space I now call home. Words are flowing; I run for a piece of paper to jot down the thoughts before they flitter off into the ether. Yesterday, in the shower, my inner voice...

'I am experiencing inner knowing, my eyes open wide with wonder.'

RACIAL INTOLERANCE

My spiritual journey and awakening are having an impact on all areas of my life. I heard a report on the news of young teenagers attacking a person with a Scottish accent, and the victim is now in a coma. It is a repeat of an occurrence where an Irish traveller will never have a quality of life again, having sustained dreadful brain damage due to an attack, and a similar event occurs with a person from India.

As I travel around Australia in the Motor Home, I experience and hear derogatory conversations, bigoted & racial comments. Constant intolerance towards Aboriginals. Sadly, also from relatives, friends, and loved ones. Why is it so? Everyone, except the Aboriginals, came here as an immigrant, migrant, or Free Settler. The Original Boat People were our very own Ancestors. Arriving in boats or planes, sponsored by Government Schemes, others paid their way, as my mother did with two children, wanting to come to the shores of Australia, as it has so much to offer. Why? To seek a better life and raise a family. Many returning to their Mother Country, not feeling welcome, sensing and hearing the racial disquiet that abounds in Australia, and not wishing to partake of it.

I make a pact to speak my truth, realising I can no longer stay silent. I have held back all my life, fearful of offending and castigation, but now I am no longer afraid!

GRACE WITHIN

WESAK, the commencement of the Spiritual Year and Buddha's Birthday, is a time of profound significance. The sheer magnificence of this event fills me with awe and wonder, connecting me to the spiritual journey we all embark on. It's a reminder of the profound beauty and depth of our spiritual growth, inspiring us to continue our journey with renewed vigour.

As I perform Tai Chi in my walled garden this morning, I am enveloped by the swirling colours of the Chakras. This internal transformation, stirred by the meditation, fills me with silent, joyful tears. It is a powerful reminder of the hope and encouragement healing practices bring our spiritual growth. I am truly blessed and grateful for this journey, a feeling that fills my heart with contentment and appreciation.

I picked up a newspaper at The Lotus Temple, entitled NOVA, and have just read an incredible article. The article, entitled "Warrior Spirit, Holistic Healing," is by Chandrika Gibson, ND, a holistic yoga teacher and naturopath. He talks of when one faces a health/life crisis diagnosis and how each of us handles it. Do we follow the traditional accepted pathway of what I call 'the medical roundabout', opting out for drugs and or surgery, or do we stop and reflect, look within?

The words written by Ian Gawler (Meditation and Lifestyle teacher):

"The person who seeks an internal perspective, who enters a battle not to vanquish but to fight with honour and find more of themselves in facing their challenges honestly, gains something meaningful, whether they win or lose; that person finds a sense of grace within themselves." To take responsibility for your Healing through nutrition, exercise, and meditation... Beating cancer (or any other health issue) is not a matter of violently attacking the disease with shock and awe tactics. The disease has manifested in your body, so you are fighting

with yourself. The wiser approach more closely resembles the martial artist's stance, using the forces within to strengthen what is good and diminish what is no longer serving the evolution of the entire being. When the whole being is addressed, the mind, soul, spiritual self, and the physical body, the experience is far more transformational. With this approach to healing, the body's survival is not the only measure of success. Even if the body degenerates (and remember that ultimately it must), the mind can find peace, let go of grievances, and feel expanded. The expanded perception opens new paradigms that help the person feel ready to transform beyond this physical form. That is not a bad way to go out. Not kicking and fighting to hold on to the body and worldly attachments, but content that you took every step to heal yourself, and the inner life has precedence. Self-healing is about the internal transformation that facing one's mortality can bring. We are all handed challenges in this lifetime, it is how we handle those challenges that is important, it is part of the 'Evolution of our Spirit'

It resonates with my 'Knowing', and I cry joyfully as I read it!

I have paraphrased from the article.

Nova Holistic Healing Journal April 2010. Warrior Spirit. Holistic Healing by Chandrika Gibson ND–the above words written by Ian Gawler (meditation & Lifestyle teacher)

ESSENCE of SPIRIT

As I lie prostrate, I feel the presence of the healer before he comes. His hands are 'hot' on my body. 'Tibetan Chanting' vibes resonate deep into my soul. He rocks my torso, my solar plexus. I am aware that my closed eyes are flickering; peripheral light enters. I am spiralling, my body jerking as I enter an 'expanded state of consciousness.' Incredible, illuminating, indescribable 'Light' explodes. I am floating, levitating, again and again spiralling into 'The Light'. Someone places their hands on my chest, my feet. My hearing is acute, I am aware of individual singing voices & sounds, a man nearby snoring, and a bird outside singing. I know the healers have moved on. I still feel the healing hands of Spirit as a warm blanket over me. I am at Peace. The essence of Spirit remains.

Leaving Temple Byron, we agree the energy tonight was very 'soft'. Both Eileen and Lyn received visions of a newborn baby—how interesting—a new start, new beginnings, new consciousness. Both sent the same message.

We've had visitors from South Australia stay with us. After they left, walking into the ensuite, I smelled Colin's essence—also, just a fleeting trace the following day.

Dave, our son, rings. He is excited, standing in a large hole in the ground, ready for their swimming pool. Later that same night, he rings again, distressed having learnt that the guy to install the pool is not arriving on Wednesday as agreed, this is the second time he has cancelled. It upsets Dave, and he asks me to send him strength, so I agree to send him Reiki. As we are about to hang up, he says:

"Oh, talking of Reiki, you know how I 'smell things,' as I was getting into my car the other day, I smelt Nanny Fleming's house, then thought of John, remembered walking upstairs with him into Nanny Fleming's Unit."

(John was Baz's brother who died at the age of 56 from lung cancer.) The title of this chapter 'Essence of Spirit, " is so apt; Dave and I both experience the essence of Spirit.

Hindsight: Editing this book eight years later, I realise that both Eileen and Lyn did move on, with new starts and new beginnings; both now live interstate. Eileen in Queensland, Lyn in Tasmania.

UNWORTHY, ACCEPTANCE, LOVE.

Ocha, a Healer from the Divine University, invites me to a Sound and Healing session on Wednesday, 2nd November. Ocha's voice reverberates, swirls, blends, soothes my psyche. Incredible! Towards the end of the session, the sounds gently massage deep down, deep within. Tears of joy flow as they so often do. The following Wednesday, with eight participants, Ocha guides us in meditation to the centre of Gaia - Mother Earth. Beneath Uluru. Visiting, visualising, and connecting with sacred places. Sounds resonate deep within me. Ocha says...

"Is there a part of your heart you are unworthy of?"

'No, I feel divine love, totally worthy.'

Ocha...

"If there is any part of you which you have not accepted, bring it forward, love and accept."

There is a part of my body, my knees, that I have not loved. I think they are big & fat. Sending love and compassion for all the years my knees suffered rejection, I'm overcome with acceptance and gratitude. A healing! Ocha, inviting a few words of feedback from each of us, I say:

"I am encompassed in a Pillar of Light. Blessed Be, Blessed Be, Blessed Be."

We stamp and pound, grounding energies into Mother Earth, forming a standing circle, whooshing energy through the centre. Hugging, Ocha says to me:

"I see, you're an incredible energy healer."

"Thank you." Namaste.

SHAMANIC CONNECTIONS

I return to the Lotus Temple, another session with Ocha. While waiting, I am sitting on my 'Salubrion' Meditation Stool, which I bought years ago. It is an extension of me these days and attracts interest.

Where did you buy it?

'Through a mail-order magazine, I have not seen another.' It may now be available online!'

Ocha's guided meditation takes us to Mount Kailash, a sacred mountain in the Himalayas, Tibet.

At once, I am transported to the top of the mountain peaks, surrounded by swirling mist, spiralling off into 'The Light.'

Ocha says, *"Let your brows become the oceans."*

Gently, rhythmically balancing back and forth. I become the ocean, the waves rippling to the shore.

Throughout the guided meditation, I stay focused.

Repeating Ocha's words in my mind, experiencing my exquisite colours, purples, lilacs, and greens, swirling around my brain. High in the sky, I see a white Eagle. I am that Eagle, flying, soaring, witnessing, in awe of the magnificent spectrum. Metaphysically, I am given a rock, a crystal of 'Light'

Ocha says, *"Bring the stars into the rock."*

Stars and Light explode in my brain, engulfing my very being. My head moves, pulsing in The Light. I am consciously aware. Letting it happen, going with it. At One with the Universe. At One with All. Ocha sings high-pitched, ethereal sounds. I enter the ice-blue plateau she is describing; the pulsing slows, then stops. I am the pendulum. Side to side, side to side. Side to side...

Returning to my meditation space, I sit in the Lotus position on the meditation stool, knees bent. The physical discomfort is real, my knees are screaming, and I'm not sure how much longer I can endure without stretching. I support them from underneath, providing Reiki Healing, a testament to my dedication to the practice.

Ocha says, "Sit in silent meditation for 10 minutes, asking for guidance on any issue that needs resolving."

Requesting guidance for 'constant painful knees.' I hear:

Just go with it, whatever transpires, accept.'

Under Ocha's guidance, I embark on a journey deep into the Earth to Uluru. As I immerse myself in the meditation, my focus shifts from my knees, and the pain dissipates, leaving me in a state of peace and tranquillity.

'Om Mani Padme Hum' swirls around my brain, repeating, acknowledging a blissful, uplifting meditation.'

Ocha invites feedback on 'guidance.'

I tell her of the message to *'just go with it.'*

Standing, lifting arms at each level...

I demonstrate my daily *'CEREMONY.'*

Lifting arms slightly, hands and fingers pointing to the ground.

UNCONSCIOUS

Grasping at life as it passes quickly, desiring possessions, and material wealth. Unless we awaken, it is a needless pursuit.

Lifting arms to hip level.

CONSCIOUS

Realising life has a deeper meaning – beginning to ask questions – what is my life all about?

Outstretched arms, heart level.

SUB CONSCIOUS

Dwelling in our subconscious is to meditate, become still, aware, and mindful, and go within to tune into our inner being.

Lifting arms to Shoulder height, fingers pointing up.

COSMICALLY CONSCIOUS

Connected to Mother Earth, Gaia, the Cosmos. Tuned into Mother Nature, daily witnessing beauty. It's a profound sense of connection, a feeling of being part of something greater than oneself.

Arms open, fully elevated. Surrendering.

HIGHER CONSCIOUSNESS

A blessed state, being connected, moving away from negativity into acceptance. Compassionate, feeling others' pain.

Arms are fully elevated, and palms are brought together in a prayer posture above the head.

DIVINE CONSCIOUSNESS

True Awakening, filled with the joy of just living. Full to overflowing, giving, connected to your Highest Divine Self. At Peace. You come to know and love yourself. Gain inner knowing and insights. At one with all, your Light shines to all around you. It's a joyous celebration of life, a testament to the beauty of existence.

You have accomplished everything in life that truly matters.

Slowly bring your hands down to your heart, with open palms, and place them on your navel, the centre of your being.

Ocha says, "It's beautiful."

Another woman tells me...

"There is a sense of Shaman surrounding you."

AKASHIC RECORDS

November 21, 2010

Today is my brother's birthday. He would have been 73 years old. Bart Cummings, Horse Trainer, reminds me of Col, who is similar in appearance. It is Melbourne Cup Day, and Bart Cummings is on TV. Baz says:

"Bart Cummings reminds me of Col."

"I agree, I was thinking the same!"

Yesterday, I was checking emails. Ocha has accessed my 'Akashic Records' and channelled information concerning the knee pain I experience. I expressed my gratitude for Wednesday's meditation session, describing how powerful I found it to be. Ocha channelled these sounds for me to tone:

EE A YA YA YA............................ YA

EE A YA YA YA............................ YA

A LA A MA A

EY A LA LA LA MA

"Tone these sounds to lift this from you. Your intention... Release to Source through a rainbow bridge held within your being, to all that is, either within Earth or to Source. A deep Spiritual Connection is being called forth for expression in a book."

Well, I am certainly doing that!

LUCID DREAMING

A wakening to the last day of this year, the dream floods back into my consciousness. Lucid dreaming allows me to step back into the dream, conscious and aware.

I walk into a large room with people, grey walls, and barriers. I sense anger and animosity around me. On the lounge is my brother. I recognised the profile of his face and dark hair, and noticed the shiny black shoes. He wears a white shirt, a black narrow tie, and a grey suit.

When I was a small girl, he invariably persuaded me, with his mischievous smile, to polish his black shoes for him.

'Colin,' I call out, elated. He turns, standing to greet me. His smiling face, outstretched arms embracing me, holding me close and safe. I haven't experienced his spirit to this degree for a while. It is so precise, so black and white. His expression was full of Love. When I need him, he is always here.

As I lie quietly in bed contemplating the dream...

I'm reminded of the poem...

BRENDA CHRISTA FLEMING

'There is no death
Death is nothing at all. I have only slipped away into the next room.
Whatever we were to each other, we are still. Call me by my old name.
Speak to me in the easy way you always used.
Laugh as we always laughed at the little jokes we enjoyed together
Play, smile, think of me and pray for me.
Let my name be the household word that it always was
There is absolutely no unbroken continuity.
Why should I be out of your mind because I am out of your sight?
I am waiting for you, for an interval,
somewhere very near, just around the corner...
All is well.
Nothing is past,
Nothing is lost.
In a brief moment, all will be as before, only better.
Infinitely better and forever.
We will all be one forever.'
Henry Scott Holland - Carmelite Monastery, Tallow, Waterford

BANGALOW STARLIGHT WELLBEING FESTIVAL

January 6, 2011

My favourite time of the year comes round again. The Bangalow Starlight Wellbeing Expo' starts today. I pick up Eileen and Lyn from Riverbend. Lyn has not been there before and doesn't know what to expect. I have printed a program from the website that highlights the seminars.

Raym introduces Chant Master, Tibetan Buddhist Monk Venerable Lobsang Tendar, Festival Blessing.

After that, the three of us head to the Guide Hall to unwind and immerse ourselves in the soothing, tranquil sounds of pure quartz crystal singing bowls with Camilla Nova. We remain in the hall to receive the Oneness Blessing.

The lady walking around asks for our email addresses. She introduces herself as Grace. I recognise her as someone who approached me previously when she mentioned she was writing about 'Extraordinary Women' and wanted to interview me. It honoured and flattered me. I couldn't contact her again because the email address was no longer valid. So here she was again! Hugging, we were delighted to see each other. The three of us share a yummy, delicious vegetarian lunch and chai tea, then we attend an exciting, dynamic hands-on workshop:

'Raghida Sharman' ~ **'Shamanic Journey.'**

Raghida connects with everyone in the circle of 30 people. At one point, a lady breaks down, crying. I can't just stand by and listen; it tugs at my heartstrings. I approach her, giving Reiki and supporting her from behind as she cries her heart out.

The last seminar of the day...

'The Template' - 'Alchemical Ceremonies Using Sacred Geometry to Awaken the Light Body Matrix Activating Our Dormant DNA.'

I connect with this seminar, resonating with the understanding that I have achieved this state of being.

The next day, Lyn and I attended the Tibetan Blessing and Crystal Bowls relaxation session once again, with Chiccan guiding us through a meditation. Lyn was impressed and decided to have a 'Tarot' reading with Chiccan.

Ancient Teachings for Modern Times. Presenter Paul Hoogendyk is at the top of my agenda. Once again, Paul delivers an engaging presentation that involves everyone. He encourages us to 'feel' the energy in the room. It's intense and palpable. With arms raised and open, we walk around the space, connecting with others, smiling, and looking into each other's eyes. Paul prompts: 'Now, look to the floor, bring your hands to your chest, close in, notice any change.'

The change is dramatic. There is a contrast between being open and accepting and closing down while failing to connect with anyone. This is life. People are busy, rushing around and not connecting! I feel sad.

Paul's guided meditation invites us to recall past relationships and instances to cut through the strings of attachment that are no longer needed. I must confront the part of my life when I owned a franchised ice cream business; there's still so much pain and anguish attached to it. Sending Reiki love and healing, releasing.

SPIRIT RE-VISITS

There is currently a threat of flooding. The Northern Rivers, a far north coast area of New South Wales, is cut off by floodwaters, and Ballina is essentially an island.

An incredible day today. Col's Spirit Essence has been in this house since last Saturday, in both bathrooms, although it's more often found in the en-suite. His aroma is intense today. I question why. Over the years, Col usually arrives during times of distress. Then I remember, today is also the day my brother died, 17 years ago.

I picked up Eileen and Lyn from Riverbend to attend the meditation at The Space in the CWA Hall in Ballina. I recently learnt about the session when I met Maria, a facilitator at the Starlight Festival. Upon arrival, we 'blindly' chose a card from the 'Guardian Angel' pack, which felt just right, as I refer to Col as 'My Guardian Angel'. Susan leads a powerful guided meditation, and I find myself 'Spiralling into the Light'.

On 16 January 2011, Friday, my cousins Tina and Ed arrived from Brisbane and decided to stay overnight. On Saturday, Tina and I looked through Col's photo album. I scanned the photos into the computer while Eddy transferred them onto a USB drive. Today, I searched for more images to complete the album and re-read letters, cards, and other documents. The following words are written in Col's funeral booklet, which I have paraphrased. (Author Unknown.)

"I will not be far away, for life goes on, so if you need me, call and I will come. Though you cannot see or touch me, I will be near. And if you listen with your heart, you will hear my love around you, soft and clear. Then, when you must come this way alone, I will greet you with a smile and a Welcome Home."

Oh! How true this has been for me. Col's Spirit always comes when I call his name in anguish. His Spirit has been with me all week. This is the first time I've re-read this passage since his funeral seventeen years ago.

FLOODS-CLEANSING COLLECTIVE SOUL

The floods have been devastating, especially in Queensland, as they have spread across the country through our river systems.

Australia has been experiencing a decade-long drought, and now we have the Flood of the Century!

"The Cleansing of the Collective Soul.

The time for Compassion and Giving."

When people open their hearts, they come together and put aside differences.

Oh! My wish is that they should remain in this mindset.

THE UNKNOWN JOB

Tuesday, 8 March 2011
    I attended a Sound and Healing Session at the stunning Lotus Temple in Byron Bay. Qala, the facilitator, invites those present to stay for supper and continue the conversation.

Qala means "a small seed pearl of wisdom."

Qala takes me into deep meditation, creating a spinning vortex that opens my heart chakra. Deep, brilliant, iridescent colours — green and purple — far more vivid than I see in everyday life, engulf my senses. They swirl in my visual cortex. I transcend through my Crown Chakra, immersed in a delicate pale lilac colour, enthralled by the presence.

Qala speaks with each person individually after the meditation, giving her full attention to addressing everyone.

To me, Qala says:

As I talk with you, counsellors surround me. You meditate. Do you do counselling? You have a job to do, but you don't yet know what it is. You have been preparing for seven years. Karma is clear. Everything is balanced, except for one aspect that is deeply buried. Quan Yin will help you with it. It has to do with your base Chakra, your femininity, your sexuality; they are telling me you need to work with the Christ energy—the Master's Thank You.

My reply,

"I am honoured, thank you."

This is relevant. Qala is the second person to tell me I have a job to do. No, I don't know what it is yet.

I am gently spiralling, acutely aware of Qala talking to others around me. My pounding heart becomes the dominating influence on my focus. Reluctant to leave, slowly bring myself back to this time and space.

I work daily with Quan Yin, the Goddess of Compassion, and the Archangels Michael, Gabriel, Raphael, and Ariel. I call forth my Divine Highest Self, my God within. Since receiving Karuna Reiki attunements, I have become one with the Buddha and resonate profoundly with the Buddha's energy. Quala is telling me I need to connect with the Christ Energy. Last week, while going through my memorabilia, I rediscovered a postcard that I have had for years, depicting the face of Christ on a snow-covered mountainside. Indecipherable for many people, the face 'jumps out' at me. The following day, while meditating, I asked Quan Yin for her help in contacting Christ Energy.

Before me is a cross. I see the cross in front of and within my Third Eye Chakra, taking in and embodying the symbol of Christ.

Namaste.

FAÇADE of LIFE

L ast night, I had a dream, and now, hours later, I recall it.

I am in an open paddock, walking through several buildings as I search for Baz. Many people are sitting in groups. I can't find him, feeling frustrated, as we are performing a play (skit) together. I need to wear a costume, but I can't find it or the location for the skit. I ask several friends where Baz is. My friend Dave says:

'Baz has auditioned and been accepted for many parts; he has fabulous costumes.' No one knows where he is at the moment.

I keep searching, feeling increasingly baffled. I meet Jorgia, my granddaughter. She says:

"Poppy wants to know the name of your book. Feeling anxious, I tell her:

'Spiralling to The Light.' She writes it down.

"Where is Poppy? Have you been talking to him?" she says

"He was on the phone, I told him, you couldn't find the costume."

"Why does he want to know the name of my Book?"

"He is going to talk about it."

"He can't do that!" I woke up!

Insight: At least I will call the book 'Spiralling to The Light', eliminating other titles. The frustration I experience, I suppose, relates to the façade, the play-acting of life. Instead of focusing on what is essential, I get lost in daily activities, like illusory play-acting. The dream tells me to get on with what is necessary.

END of an ERA

Tuesday, 22 March 2011

Lotus Temple, Byron Bay. Qala announces:

"Tonight is the last healing session performed by the Healing Team at the Lotus Temple. We are moving on, but I'm not certain where to go from here. Check the Echo Newspaper for announcements. Please add your name to the email list."

They have removed the crystals from the central column; the decorative hangings have also been taken down from the walls. The delicate, coloured, draped fabric ceiling is all that remains.

I hug both Qala and Ocha as I leave. Ocha says they hope to set up in Temple Byron.

Driving home, I feel a deep emptiness. Unfortunately, this unique and mystical chapter of my life has come to an abrupt end.

THE TEMPLATE CEREMONY.

G *ood Friday, 22 April 2011*
First day of the Starlight Festival, Bangalow. The highlights of my day are:

A café chat lecture by The Buddhist Monk Tendar.

Closing my eyes, I see' Tendar's 'Light Body' as a Halo of 'Golden Light' surrounding his head. After telling him of this, he smiles serenely at me.

Then, Raghida the Shaman delivers a 'Powerful Presentation.' The presentation was a transformative experience...

The guided meditation carried me deeper, further down into a cleansing stream. I swim and wallow in the sensation of the baptismal waters rushing over my body. I walk down through a meadow, reconnecting with my innocence, gazing into my own eyes as I was when I was a child. I receive a gift—a pyramid-shaped crystal quartz, simply beautiful, and I gaze at it in wonder.

Raghida says:

Connect with your totem animal.

In my mind's eye, I see a lion. I look into the lion's eyes.

Raghida asks*:*

"Take the small child into your Heart Chakra. The gift of crystal into your Crown Chakra. The animal is in your Base Chakra, aligning them." *This meditation is compelling. The strength of the lion connects me through my Base Chakra to Gaia, the precious love of this little child, and the Light of the crystal quartz aligns my entire being.*

Tears silently creep down my cheeks, I sit in 'The Light' absorbing the 'bliss,' sheer joy. Namaste Raghida.

Sunday, 24th April. A spiritually enlightening weekend. Eileen and I head to the Bangalow Markets beforehand. It's hectic since the 'Blues Fest' is on at Byron Bay. We browse the stalls, picking up a few small items. I enjoy a delicious falafel wrap for lunch. After that, we make our way into the festival for a 2-hour workshop entitled:

'The Template'.

Giving out hand mirrors ...

Look into your left eye, thank your mother for life, forgiving any transgressions. Now, look into your right eye, thanking your father for life, forgiving any transgressions. Again, look into your left eye for your sisters who have walked your path, thanking and forgiving them. Now, look back into your right eye, acknowledging your brothers who have also walked your path, and thank and forgive them. Finally, into our 'third eye,' back, back, back in time and space. I do not remember where I go; I'm spiralling and vibrating.

The facilitator says, "Put the mirror aside."

"Connect to fire, earth, water, the ether, the sun. Focusing on the elements of each."

The Earth transforms into a large crystal. Sacred geometric shapes symbolise the elements of fire, water, ether, and sun. I focus and spiral into an altered state of consciousness. My head physically spins, and my heart is pounding, pounding, pounding.

I'm blissfully crying. My body is vibrating, pulsing in 'The Light' through my Crown Chakra and pulsating with the spiralling.

⟲⟳

I felt people moving and heard my name being called from afar. Consciously, I knew I needed to return to this reality, put my hand on my heart, slow the vibrations, and realise that people were talking, getting up, and leaving the room. I sat, absorbing, reflecting, and grounding.

I am filled with awe and wonder as I acknowledge the transcendence into another space. It's a mystical, extraordinary experience that leaves me speechless, as no words in the vocabulary can truly capture this phenomenon.

When I crossed over to the other side with my brother, I could only grasp the concept of an *'Expanded State of Consciousness'*. However, I now genuinely understand its profound meaning and transformative power.

MANIPULATION, ANGER

Eileen and I had a long walk back to the car. Before dropping her off, I called home to collect and return the book, 'The Twelfth Insight,' by James Redfield. Baz is in the shower and doesn't know I've come in. After driving Eileen home, I had a quick chat, discussed the weekend, and breezed in happily.

WOW, Baz's anger hits me again. I thought we were done with all this. But no, here he is again, destroying my happiness and not wanting me to be away from him. He manipulates and smothers me if I'm away longer than he expects. I'm not responsible for his happiness; if he's not happy, he's making himself unhappy. When Baz plays tennis and watches sports on TV, I'm glad he's doing what he enjoys. Baz sees my happiness; his eyes fire daggers, destroying my pleasure. I assume we're both in a blissful state of lovemaking and life.

Yesterday I said out loud:

"I have no issues, I am in a perfect place!!"

Boy! That tumbled around me! Life and love are so fragile!

MAMA Re-VISITS

Baz and I have been with Naomi Andrew and Aleisha for a few days, visiting to keep the bonds close with little Aleisha. It is late, 11.30 pm. As I walk along the hall to prepare for bed, the familiar gentle pressure in my third eye, echoing a greeting from Spirit, is present. I pause, a smile creeping onto my lips. As I undress in the dark, lights flicker in the periphery of my vision. The pressure increases, disturbing my field of vision. I snuggle into bed and continue to hold the presence of 'Spirit', asking:

"If I'm meant to know whose spirit I am experiencing, please tell me."

The response came back.

"Mama."

Mama died six years ago – 20th July, tomorrow is the anniversary of her funeral. She is here with me as I asked her to be.

Naomi and Andrew have mentioned a ghost in the house. I discussed it with Naomi the following morning. She says it's a woman, and she's in the hallway. Just as I experienced it, she asked me if I knew who. I relate the story to her; she rejects it. Mum was not one of Naomi's favourite people due to religious brainwashing. I brush it aside, saying:

"Perhaps this is an easy open portal."

She agrees and says no more.

Mama lingers in my thoughts as it is August, my birthday month. When she was alive, she consistently honoured birthdays, making them special.

I'm in the ensuite, coming through the sliding door and stopping in my tracks. I glance out into the summer room. For a blink of an eye, she sits in the chair, turning away from me, a little old lady with silver hair, peacefully gazing out into the walled garden. My heart swells, and just as quickly, she's gone.

That night, Mama's little dog, Pepe, who had passed over, returned in a dream. Baz and I were looking after him. I called out as I left the room and walked downstairs.

"I have forgotten the dog."

Racing back up the stairs into the room, I can see his lead through an alcove, calling to him:

"Pepe, Pepe."

He slides out of the alcove along a short tunnel into my arms, snuggling into me and making little appreciative sounds. The joy of our reunion in the dream was palpable, filling me with warmth and comfort.

Weeks pass, but the images of Mama and Pepe linger, vivid and cherished, a gentle reminder of her love that once again transcends time and space.

CELEBRATING SKIING

Dave, our son, wants to celebrate his 40th Birthday on August 25th, 2011, at The Ski Rider Perisher, NSW, Australia.

For many years, Baz has said he wants to ski once more. I've resisted due to the intense knee pain I experience. It's been a long time, maybe seven years. I wouldn't have skied again had it not been David's 40th. I have trepidation, not wanting to spoil anyone else's holiday if I find it difficult to ski or become injured. I stay positive, asking for Universal Guidance.

Skiing is my passion. I was in my forties when I learnt to ski, and I remember taking the kids on a bus trip to the snow in their early teens. In my mind's eye, I visualise...

As the chairlift ascends to the top of the mountain, I feel the crisp morning air tingling my cheeks; it's the only part of my body not fully covered in ski gear. The sky drapes like a crystal blue mantle above the snow-covered peak. Fluffy white clouds nestle into the rocky outcrop of the blue mountain. When I alight, my skis connect with the pristine, untouched purity of untracked mountaintop snow before the crowds of skiers arrive. I am alone, listening to the sound of silence in the early morning dawn. I feel the adrenaline kick in as I experience the thrill of the descent, my body flowing gracefully, curving and weaving its way back down to the base of this majestic mountain.

Skiing has been a revelation, and I've made a significant decision.

'If I can confidently and lovingly ski as I skied on this holiday, I need not think of knee replacements right now.'

UNIVERSAL BALANCE

Tonight, the Full Moon is in Libra. Perfect Equilibrium. Universal Balance.

I am reading my numerology book and have discovered that adding Baz's birthday and my Birthday dates come to Number 22.

It's a revelation—the most BALANCED number in the Universe.

22 Embodies:

Spiritual Evolution. Worldly Success.

The coming together of two spirits in:

Reason, Intellect, Vision, Feelings, and Skill.

It combines these elements in its Balance.

Each intertwining layer of our lives clicks into place, creating a tapestry crafted from years of love, echoes of laughter and a shared journey. How beautiful!

THROUGH THE DOORWAY

At 'The Space' tonight, a guest speaker discusses Feng Shui, a topic that has never piqued my interest. However, the lecture's theme, 'Clearing things from your life you no longer need,' Strikes a chord. This concept of releasing past traumas and negative energies is a pivotal part of my spiritual journey and personal growth. It's not just about decluttering our physical spaces, but also about decluttering our minds and hearts, making room for new experiences and growth. I am guided to ...

Step through a metaphorical doorway, letting the memories of my childhood home wash over me as I wander from room to room. Each room serves as a portal to the past. I catch glimpses of my younger self, cringing at the taste of cod liver oil forced down my throat.

One day, I spat it onto the lounge chair, leaving a stain on the upholstery. I put that chair at the front door for removal. I also had an unpleasant memory. I had run home from school, desperate to use the toilet. I was 5 or 6 years old. When I reached the kitchen door, I couldn't wait any longer, and with relief, I wet myself. My mother was angry and upset with me. I left those wet knickers at the front door as I went out.

I adore the villa where I live. Each room carries its unique charm, filled with memories and mementos from my life. My friend Eileen's words describing my home:

"Perfect like Brenda."

Thank you, Eileen. Such a lovely compliment!

Over the past few moves, I've had to part with many sentimental items. It's never easy to let go of the jumpers Mama knitted with love. Nevertheless, I took the advice and gathered a whole bag for the charity shop, a small sacrifice for personal growth, releasing the old and making space for new beginnings.

'A SIGNIFICANT DAY'

November 11, 2011

After Baz leaves for tennis, I enter my meditation sanctuary. I plan to enjoy today, as it represents a vibrational, powerful day for spiritual awakening and new beginnings. I will meditate, listen to music, and chant—a perfect day.

In the evening, Eileen and I go to 'A Women's Gathering.' Full Moon in Taurus. Fourteen women attend. There is a heavy cloud and misty rain; unfortunately, the moon is not visible.

The first guest speaker is Eliza (a tarot lady I have met previously), who invites us to draw or choose two cards.

This morning, I drew the 10 of Pentacles, which I read as 'Abundance.'

Now, 3 Pentacles & The Empress.

Eliza agrees with me, describing it as the end of the cycle.

3 Pentacles invites me to 'share my skills with others.'

The Empress, to Love and Nurture.

Synopsis:

I have reached the end of a cycle and am now ready to share my skills with others. Loving, nurturing those seeking and in need.'

How lovely! The tarot reading beautifully validates where I am, leaving me with reassurance and affirmation. It's a comforting reminder that I'm on the right path of abundance and nurturing, guiding my spiritual journey.

The next guest speaker is Rhianna. She has us up dancing and swaying, to release Kundalini. My Kundalini Spirit was released during Reiki Training many years ago. After the dance, she invites us to take a large piece of paper and a crayon and go with the flow. In the semi-dark, I cannot distinguish the colours of the crayons. When I have finished, I shine a light onto the paper. My drawing is of the Kundalini Serpent. I am unsurprised; I have long had a deep inner connection with my Kundalini Spirit. Appropriately, it flowed naturally from my hand onto the paper in the darkness. The colour of the crayon was Red, representing the Base Chakra. Yeh!

The last guest speaker introduces herself as Arabella. We gather, forming a circle. I do not relate to what she is saying; she describes 'demons and terrorists within each of us.'

Following meditation, she suggests we stand up.

Saying 'It has to be genuine to be effective.'

Next! I hear the most blood-curdling scream, physically jumping, trying to dull the sound. I bring my hands up, covering my ears. I am shocked. Arabella invites those present in the circle to scream. I walk out of the circle, separate myself, arms outstretched in surrender to the skies, listening to the screams. In my heart, I'm disappointed. I have spent a magical day quietly meditating, and the grand finale shocks and rocks me to my core. I need to distance myself and be alone.

Walking away, I catch a glimpse of a luminous full moon as the clouds clear. How lovely.

Eileen and I discuss the proceedings on the way home.

"Brenda, there probably were women who needed to vent their feelings."

Eileen brings me back to reality. Selfishly, I am thinking only of my feelings.

At home, I realise I have left my little lantern and candle behind at the Amphitheatre.

The following day, I texted,

"Did you find my lantern & candle?"

Arabella texts back:

"Yes."

We agree to meet for coffee.

Everything that comes into our lives is for a reason. Arabella and I spent two hours over coffee talking. Arabella tells me about her life. She has sad and serious issues going back to her childhood, marriage, children, etc., etc., etc., no wonder she needs to 'scream it out. I deeply connected with her, understanding her need to release the pain.

She says:

"When I saw the lantern and candle, I thought she was gone, but she has left her 'Light' behind."

Beautiful words. Thanking her, we hug. Leaving, I reflect on the conversation, realising again how blessed my life has always been and is now.

THE PENDULUM

Last week, I misplaced my prescription glasses. Baz and I searched high and low in the house, the cars, and the caravan, but couldn't find them. I'm struggling to see with old glasses, which are cheap ones from the chemist. Listening to my inner voice, I hear a suggestion:

"Use your Pendulum."

I purchased a Star Tetrahedron Amethyst Crystal pendulum years ago, along with a book titled "Pendulum Magic for Beginners." Richard Webster.

Sitting quietly in my Sanctuary, I hold the pendulum in my right hand, using my 'psychic pencil finger,' and thumb:

Calling in my guides, my Highest Divine Self, say:

'I have lost my glasses, I need help.'

Asking questions:

"Are my glasses in the House?" The pendulum tells me a definite no!

"Are my glasses in the car?" A very definite YES!

During lunch, I tell Baz about the 'pendulum.' He says:

"I have looked in the car!" I say, "I have too!"

After lunch, I searched the car again. I had already looked on the floor, under the seats, on the sides of the seats, in the glove box, and under the glove box. There is an open compartment in the console, and at first glance, it appears empty. However, as I feel around, I discover them. Not visible when peering into the space, they sit toward the back. I feel emotional as I walk into the house. It's incredible to use my little pendulum to access information from my Highest Self. This experience has given me a great deal of confidence, as the answers I received were overwhelmingly positive, validating the questions I asked.

MYSTICAL, MAGICAL, JOTTINGS

This morning, in a 'dream state,' I found myself among many teachers and healers. As we descended into the Earth's bowl, winding ever down, a sense of unity and purpose filled the air. Despite the darkness and mist that obscured our vision, we were all united by a shared mission.

There are seven teachers, young, perhaps in their twenties. I vaguely recognise the leader, who is dressed in a pale blue jacket with buttons and a pocket on the chest. The teachers' jackets are a deeper blue. The lecture is titled "Ancient Wisdom." As I listen to the words, I instinctively know these teachings, this wisdom. The feelings conveyed among the crowd are one of serenity and an outpouring of love and peace.

I am very relaxed when I awake, choosing to put myself back into the dream, becoming:

'The Lucid Dreamer' travels between worlds.

Thinking of the book I am writing, my inner voice says:

'It's complete! You have written it in Jottings.' Hence the name of this chapter:

Mystical, Magical, Jottings.

To Educate. To Teach. To Learn. To Understand is to Know, is to Heal!

Once again, I find myself experiencing something and then seeking validation. I remember buying a book titled "The Lucid Dreamer" several years ago. I discovered it tucked away at the back of a cupboard.

IN LAK'ECH~THE TEMPLATE

I know I've walked this pathway before. The Divine Light and Presence are mine to hold. I stand transfixed in 'The Light.' Blissful tears roll silently down my face. 'The Light' integrates every cell of my body, transcends my very being, and transforms my thinking.

Meditation takes me into a spiralling vortex. Deep down, down, down, into Mother Earth 'Gaia.' Then up, up, up way out into the stratosphere. Dazzling Light explodes into my core, my being. Vibrating, pulsing. Vibrant colours - a vivid lilac hue and the deepest iridescent green - surround me, a density of colour I rarely experience. I luxuriate in integrating and accepting this gift. Flickering white light infiltrates the colours; I spiral off again. Download, spiral, pulse, and vibrate, moving into space as I swing from left to right, then right to left. My body is becoming the pendulum. Balanced. Pure 'Light of Love' surrounds and encompasses me. Tears of joy roll down my upturned face. My throat emits gasps of pleasure. Thought waves emanate to loved ones, and kindred spirits are within this circle. Then, like a pebble dropped into a still lake, ripples spread across the world to those in deprivation and hunger. Encircling them with Light, Love, Empathy, and Compassion. When I return to this time and place, I am at peace...

I learn a new word this weekend, accompanied by a special handshake. The word is 'IN LAK'ECH', a Mayan Word. A greeting, meaning:

I am Another You or I am Part of You. You are my Other Self. We are One. There is But One.

'The Template' validates where I am on my Quest. The facilitator said:

'Be aware of anything which may surface following the Ceremonies.'

I have worked through my issues with Reiki. I am surprised when matters arise within a day or two, validating the power of these ceremonial connections.

CHENREZIG INSTITUTE.'

February 2012

My Cousin Annie and I have booked a weekend seminar at 'Chenrezig Institute', a Tibetan Buddhist Study Centre & Meditation Retreat set amidst the magnificent Hinterland of the Sunshine Coast, Queensland, Australia.'

We begin our journey on the newly completed Ballina Bypass Expressway to Byron Bay. As soon as we leave, torrential rain slows our progress. It may be a hazardous journey to Chenrezig, as I remember seeing small creeks with low-lying bridges. The extreme weather conditions cause heavy traffic congestion around the Gateway Bridge in Brisbane. Finally arriving at 7.30 pm (6.30 pm Queensland time), it has taken us 4.5 hours, an hour longer than expected.

As we unload the car boot, the heavens let loose again. The umbrella jams as I try to put it up, so I scramble to put on my plastic poncho. A steep incline of steps carved into the mountain makes it challenging to manoeuvre ourselves, plus luggage. As the steps become steeper, I gasp for breath, the muscles in my legs screaming to stop. Halfway up, we pause, and a young man asks Annie if she needs help. Annie struggles with her heavy luggage, carrying a pillow and trying to hold up an umbrella, and she gratefully accepts his offer.

When we arrive at the office, I am panting, my heart pounding with the expended energy needed to reach this point. It is dark now, and I cannot read the notification on the office door showing which room is ours. Annie finds her torch. We climb more steps, then follow a steep pathway, directed by the young man helping Annie to number 8, at the far end of a block of huts, our accommodation for the weekend.

We drop our luggage onto the floor of the small two-bedroom room with relief, leaving small puddles where we stand. The rain has saturated my backpack, so I remove my belongings, hoping they are not too wet. I remember seeing the shower/toilet block the day I came here two weeks ago to check out the route and look at 'Chenrezig.' I prefer a 'dry run' if possible. It would not have been easy today without knowing the terrain and how to navigate our way here beforehand.

Desperate to use the bathroom, I need the torch to locate where I believe the toilet and shower room are. Outside, around the corner, there is a steep incline and a set of steps. Water is gushing along the pathway, making it slippery and dangerous.

Annie looks for a jug but only finds a hot water bottle. Dying for a cuppa, we brave the elements again and make our way downhill to the 'Big Love Café', luckily still open. There are tea-making facilities, open 24 hours a day. Filling up two mugs, we start the trek back up to the room again, holding the umbrella over the mugs so the water stays hot.

We are hungry, so sit on the beds to enjoy a vegetarian frittata and salad I have prepared, followed by banana and rosemary cake, a favourite recipe. I sit talking for a while, decide before going to bed to make my way outside, and go to the toilets again. The steep pathway is a torrent of water, turning it into a small creek. I met a lady, and as we chatted, she informed me that the class Annie and I are taking the next morning is being held in the community room at the bottom of those steps.

I say to Annie:

Do you want the bad news or the bad news?

Ugh! The thought of manipulating those steps again in the rain. The prospect causes us to giggle.

Exhausted, both of us find it difficult to sleep; the sound of the rain is deafening on the tin roof. Eventually, I doze off and dream of Tess, Annie's elder sister, who died of breast cancer; she is here with us. In the dream:

We are in a large white dormitory room. I lean over to kiss Tess as she lies in bed. The bed is wet, water is running down the walls, and parts of the timber ceiling beams are about to cave in.'

Annie wakes me at 2 am. She needs to go to the toilet, worried it will alarm me if I hear someone at the door. I use my 'Healing Journey' cassette tape to doze back to sleep...Awake early, a dream stays with me, not drifting off into the ether as dreams are apt to do, as I grasp to remember them...

I am here, in Chenrezig Rain Forest. There is a spider, the colour of a buttercup flower, large, round, and fat with fluffy, hairy legs. It runs into the palm of my hand, and I hold it gently. Another spider crawls into my hand, the same rounded body with bent-up fluffy legs, this one cobalt blue. I study them, marvelling at their colours.

A large group of people of all ages gather on the grass. I am looking up. In the sky is a collage of mosaic shapes, moving colours, swirling and twirling above my head, calling out:

'Look, look at the sky!'

I watched, fascinated, as the display finished, followed by another, swirling, exotic rainbow colour display interspersed with 'Sacred Geometry' symbols.

The images are flooding back as I type these words.

There is a giant hairy spider in the shower cubicle. Usually, I would choose another cubicle, but after last night's dream, I smile warily, keeping my eyes on her while I shower.

Breakfast is served at the Big Love café, featuring fruit, muesli, and toast. It is still early, and we sit and talk for a while. Volunteer staff arrive at 8:00 a.m. and turn on the espresso machine. The aroma of coffee was delicious as it wafted around us. Annie ordered a mug, and we relaxed for a while longer, admiring our surroundings and listening to the early morning calls of the birds.

Making our way down the steps, we pause at the bottom, searching for the Community Room, another 15 or more steps further down the hill from the car park.

The surrounding bushland is a luxurious, dense rainforest. Tibetan Prayer Flags dripping with raindrops are strung between the trees, creating a peaceful and serene atmosphere.

Due to the extreme weather, not all the booked participants have arrived—flood waters cut the road we used the night before to reach Chenrezig. The final number in class is 9. It amazes them that we have travelled 300 kilometres from Ballina to Chenrezig.

The Brochure reads...LIVING ETHICALLY ~

HOW TO CREATE INNER PEACE AND A HAPPIER WORLD.

'Living ethically and compassionately can bring us inner peace, which extends to our family. Friends, work colleagues, neighbours and communities. Understanding how we perceive those around us, and our experience, assists in developing contentment in our lives, bringing insight and the greater capacity to change our World.'

Lozang, the instructor/teacher, is an Australian Buddhist Nun.

She has been a student at Chenrezig Institute for 13 years. She is a University-trained Counsellor with a Master of International Studies in Peace and Conflict Resolution. Losang had taken her cloak two years before.

She is not as expected; she fits no preconceived ideas of piousness. She is open, honest, and forthright, and no punches are barred. I find her to be very refreshing and admire her.

During the two-day study, we participated in and listened to group discussions on the presented topics. We often separated into two groups to analyse a question and watched various YouTube clips and videos, listening to music with poignant and relevant words. At one stage, a rope is placed on the floor. We stand on one side. Lozang poses a series of questions to us, examining our conscience; we must answer 'yes,' 'no,' or 'don't know' (sitting on the fence), one foot on each side of the rope. Often, we cross the rope or stay put, deciding on our answers. It puts our lives, thoughts, actions, and morals under scrutiny.

Mindful thoughts, Conscious Actions, Kindness to Others. Recurring words throughout this course.

There are three daily breaks for morning tea, lunch, and afternoon tea. When facing a mountain climb, should you choose the steps or the path? The pathway proves to be an easier way up for me and is picturesque when we stop to admire the visual canopy of the surrounding bushland during the lulls in the torrential downpour. Towards the end, the path is challenging and steep, so I take a deep breath and go for it! The steps we use for the downward climb are sodden with deep puddles, forcing us to place each foot carefully.

Saturday Lunch at the Big Love Café is packed. It isn't easy to find a seat. Annie and I dawdled, browsing around the Dharma Shop before going into the Café. We overindulged at morning tea by sharing a delicious homemade Chocolate Mud Cake with a Berry topping, followed by a mug of chai tea for me, and Annie had a Cappuccino. The group squeezed into the lounge to make room. A vegetarian lunch of nuts, herbs, and Feta Loaf, accompanied by a Thai Lemongrass Salad, is delicious.

The day has been long. At 4:45 pm, we ascend the mountain to our room via the Gompa (Buddhist Meditation Hall), stopping to admire the Buddhist statues and plaques in the gardens.

Supper is quieter, as most students are day trippers from local areas such as Nambour and Caloundra. We are offered a large bowl of pea and vegetable soup. Pea soup has never been a favourite of mine, but this is delicious. We sit, chat, and listen to the serenade of frogs and crickets.

Saturday night, I slept like a log. Annie was in and out before I awoke from my dreamless, deep sleep.

After breakfast, we arrived at the Community Hall, realising we were too early. We walk to the 'Garden of Enlightenment', stopping to take photos. We arrived at class ten minutes late and apologise for keeping the group waiting.

Lozang guides us through a 5-minute 'breath awareness meditation.'

I spiral into the vortex, a luminous deep green, a vivid violet haze filling my soul, my being, swaying gently as I spiral. Reluctant to leave this limitless space to return to the present, grounding myself in the room.

The day before had been enjoyable from my perspective. Lozang asks:

'Whenever I strike the bell, stop whatever you are doing and go into a one-minute, breath awareness meditation.'

Although meditation is a part of my life, entering it without first contemplating is a unique and refreshing experience for me.

Lozang plays a track from the internet, specifically from YouTube, titled 'Civil War' by Guns N' Roses. Giving an insight into why she does not fit my pre-conceived idea of the mould of a Buddhist Nun. Instructing us to listen carefully to words and video highlighting:

'Mans' Inhumanity to Man' The track delivers a powerful message...

'I don't need your Civil War, whilst the rich it feeds, it only buries the poor.'

By the end of the YouTube video clip, I am emotionally drained and in tears.

On Sunday, the weather cleared, with a blue sky and sunshine, and the flood threat was gone. We are relieved, as Annie must return to work in Coffs Harbour early Monday morning.

Once again, lunch is delicious: vegetarian curry with boiled rice and a vegetable samosa.

The final exercise is titled 'The Tent.'

We split into two groups. The Question posed:

There has been a disaster; you have no home, shelter, or possessions, just a tent.

How Big is your Tent? Who will you invite into Your Tent?

The following are my thoughts and feelings:

I see the analogy of 'The Tent' as the apotheosis of the entire course of teachings.

Coming at the end of the session is no coincidence.

The question posed is to 'test the mind.'

How do we now perceive those around us?

Has our way of thinking changed?

Have we truly grasped the meanings of the words?

Have the lessons taught affected our hearts?

i.e. Respect for All Human Beings.

Kind Open Hearts to People.

Mindful Consciousness in multiple conditions.

'The Tent' enables us to embody these aspects of respect, kindness, and mindful tolerance towards our fellow human beings in times of adversity.

It offers us the freedom to let go of materialistic clinging that holds us back on our path. This realisation brings a significant levelling of humanity, presenting an opportunity to become caring, empathic, and compassionate in service to our fellow human beings.

There are no exclusions in life; everyone who enters our lives is there to teach us something we need to know, whether we choose to learn that lesson or not.

There is no 'control' over life and death; we travel our path and die. Trying to control these aspects of our lives feeds the desire for power and ego. Excluding those you find undesirable won't bring contentment. The keys to inner peace, acceptance, and contentment are:

'Embrace life and everyone you encounter on your journey, warts and all!'

Trust in the Universe, Your Highest Self, Your God, however you perceive these words. Respect and accept the differences in beliefs that abound around the World.

Don't be complacent. Please don't think that it can't happen to you! The Earth is fragile; we are fragile! Put yourself in other people's shoes; for example, the refugees of the world feel their pain. What's it like to lose everything you own? Even worse, to lose your loved ones—your sons, your daughters, your parents, your grandchildren, your partner—because of war, floods, or earthquakes.

Please: Think From Your Heart. Be Compassionate. Embrace with Love.

Lozang said:

'This is happening in the world right now. Millions of people are homeless and starving. Do your research; don't just listen to the media reporting fear and negativity. Talk to a refugee, speak with an Indigenous person, and form your own opinions.'

PEACE will be achieved when we, as a Human Race, realise...

ACCEPTANCE and RESPECT for each other, regardless of our differences.

We are Human Beings, living on this tiny planet we call Earth, orbiting around the Sun, our 'Life Giver.' The Mayan Word 'In Lak'ech' I learnt recently is appropriate.

I am Another Yourself, I am Part of You. We are One. There is but One.

Conscious apt words, when applied to the way we live.

Summary of my impressions of this weekend:

Thought Provoking. Challenging.

The course helps me assess my current spiritual state. I received an email containing a gut-wrenching YouTube video that brought tears to my eyes. I dubbed it .... Theme Song for Planet Earth.

'Tell Me Why' Declan Galbraith

GOB SMACKED!

Baz and I have been staying with Naomi, Andrew, and Aleisha. Naomi has been in Royal North Shore Hospital having a tumour removed from her left thyroid. This morning, after a long wait, she received the pathology results. The tumour was benign.

After ringing David to let him know, I entered the caravan and had an intense third-eye connection. The pressure stayed, similar to the intense connection to Spirit I received at Naomi's house, in their hallway, on the anniversary of my mother's death. Greeting Spirit. I meditated, calling forth my guides, surrendering to the Universe, channelling back through the third-eye portal, in gratitude for the positive results.

We discussed Naomi's rapidly growing throat tumour tonight, and I called my friend Alison. I told Alison I felt calm.

She replied: "You gobsmack me. You are so whole, so radiant, so happy."

What could I reply to such words? I was humbled, replying:

"Thank you."

PERUVIAN SHAMANISM

It is Good Friday. Today, I attended a workshop at the Starlight Wellness Festival in Bangalow, entitled "Peruvian Shamanism." I realised when I saw the lecturer that I had previously participated in this same workshop and enjoyed it. We stand...

Facing: SOUTH-SNAKE—TRANSFORMATIONS A snake has a bodily connection with the Earth and then lets go, symbolised by skin shedding. You are not your body. It is just matter.

Facing: WEST- JAWA Letting go of the EGO.

Facing: NORTH-HUMMINGBIRD Appreciating the bounty of this Earth, taking the nectar.

Facing: EAST-EAGLE SOARING New Life New Beginning.

CENTRE: Connecting with all. In and out, as above, so below, the God connection. Healer within, manifesting, no negativity, connecting with:

Earth, Water, Fire, Air, Light. Balanced Chakras.

To fully access balance, connect to the heart, embracing both the masculine and feminine aspects of oneself. Accepting ourselves as Earth Keepers,

Committing to Sun Consciousness. Acceptance of Awareness into our DNA.

Accepting ourselves as 'I am the Creator!' Cosmic Mind, Cosmic Consciousness.

Connection to the sky. Unlimited Power. Connection to the Heart Mystery,

LOVE. That says it all. I resonate so WHOLLY with these words.

LOVE SYMBOL

I attended the Sacred Ceremony at the Mongolian Yurt, Temple Byron, for six days. Byron Bay. NSW. I repeat the first three ceremonies, followed by the next six. During the first day of meditation, I spiral and sway, moving into Spirit, the familiar pressure on my third eye palpable. By early Wednesday morning, before getting out of bed, I try to explain the first ceremony of gazing into the mirror to Baz. I have completed the 1st Ceremony three times now. I choke up, the words locked inside, my body trembling. I need to inhale deeply, to come back into equilibrium as I describe looking into the mirror, forgiving my father for abandoning me. I forgave him many years ago; the anger and entrenched hurt had long since dissipated with the help of the healing powers of Reiki.

The Temple gardens are magical. This morning, I arrived early to take photographs, then place my meditation stool and purple cushion in the same place to the right of the central column in the Yurt.

In the mornings, a lecture is followed by a description of ancient sacred geometry. At one stage, whilst meditating, I believe the overhead light had been switched on. I opened my eyes and, realising it hadn't, saw that the sacred geometry was spiralling in the candlelit room. I had been transported into 'The Light,' once again.

The symbols described are being transcribed onto paper. I mentally imagine them. At one stage, the speaker, holding up the sheet, asks:

"What do you see?"

I raise my hand, saying:

"I see Love." The lecturer replies:

"It doesn't say Love," I say.

"That is what I see!"

The word "LOVE," a powerful and universal concept, appears on the paper when the symbol is completed. The presenter says...

"Your life must be focused on Love to have been able to see that!"

Yes, my life is focused on Love, I'm Blessed.

On the fourth morning, a sun-filled blue sky greets me. Mary-Jane is there with her guitar. She has been invited to attend each day to sing before the sessions start, as her voice is glorious. As I arrive, she calls out to me.

"Just look at you!" she says.

I've been wearing purple daily, my favourite spiritual colour. This hue resonates with my inner journey and personal growth.

We hug, she inquires:

"How are you?"

I reply from my heart as I am bubbling with joy:

"I love every cell of my body!"

She looks into my eyes, then starts to cry. Within minutes, she is singing those words,

'I love every cell of my body', incorporating them into her song.

When I approached her later, she thanked me. Her songs are usually melancholy, reflecting her thoughts and feelings about herself. Now I've shown her how to love herself. We hug, she cries, through her tears, saying:

"Thank you, you are a great healer!

Before entering the Yurt, I stopped to talk with a Portuguese man, telling him I lived in Portugal in 1978/9. He says:

"That was the year I was born."

During the break, Mary Jane cried again, so I hugged her. Someone has commented on how much she has changed from the first day. She tells me they are tears of joy and says, smiling into my eyes:

"This is your fault!"

Throughout the week, I meditate easily, with noise and chatter not interfering with my ability to enter a calm, gently spiralling, and balancing space. By day five, the presenter refers to the negative 'stuff' that people experience, the need to talk, and the desire to offload. For example, someone has lost their business and partner in the last few days. They invite people to share experiences. There is silence. My voice comes from within, describing the intense bliss and joy I experience meditating, moving into 'The Light.'

My voice breaks with emotion as I relive the experience.

The lecturer says:

"Well, that will allow you to integrate."

Later, the young Portuguese man sitting behind me tells me how my little speech resonated with the way he was feeling, saying:

"You're an inspiration to everyone!"

WOW! What a great week I'm having, thank you. I stayed back after the session to chat for a while. As I leave, I see the guy who has been playing the Didgeridoo. I compliment him, saying how much I enjoy listening to him. We hug and chat. I learn his car has broken down, and he needs a lift to Bangalow, so I offered to drive him. His name is Ollie. It's getting late; I guess Baz will wonder where I am. Try to ring him, but there's no answer. Stop on the highway 10 minutes later and try again. He answers, saying in a very peeved voice:

"Do you know what the time is?!"

I suppose I'll get the silent treatment when I get home, which dampens my spirits.

Sunday morning, arriving early again, I do Tai Chi, enjoying the tranquillity of the gardens at Temple Byron before everyone arrives. I talk with a young Frenchman sitting at the table. He says he is a Spiritual Paintings Artist, proudly showing images of artistry from his iPhone. Then he looks at me:

"People are drawn to you and your vibration; you need not say very much, they see your Light."

I thank him, and I am grateful for his words. During the last Ceremony, the facilitator says:

"Integrate, totally integrate!"

I melt, I sob, I integrate.

I am totally at one. Thank you.

THE SUMMARY

This Spiritual pathway I have navigated for twelve years has carried me to a blissful, emotional state. These last six days have been chaotic for some and peaceful for others. I witness it all. This is 'Life.'

I recall the words that Mary Jane, the singer, the Frenchman, and the young Portuguese man spoke. How grateful I am to the Universe.

My villa is a tranquil space. As I talk to Baz, tears flow; peace is palpable, except for his racking cough, which permeates like a shock wave.

I sit at the breakfast table reflecting, trying to paint a picture for my husband and partner of 50 years. It is a picture he cannot visualise; his journey has not carried him along this pathway.

'Joy' overflows as I remember the words spoken on the second day:

"You are already there, we are all already there."

My inner voice replied, saying:

"I know, I know." It is the wisdom of the 'knowing.'

I cannot continue to discuss this with Baz; my throat constricts as the tears flow, and there are no words to describe

bliss, except *'bliss.'*

peace except *'peace.'*

REFLECTIONS

Whilst in the shower this morning, another piece of the puzzle fell into place. I realised the insights I gained from Colin's death. Col took 'Methotrexate,' a cancer-fighting drug, which seems to have positive side effects, alleviating the debilitating condition of chronic psoriasis. Psoriasis is an autoimmune disease that causes rapid growth of abnormal, overabundant skin cells. Both Col and I inherited the gene from our father. I reached this conclusion, despite not knowing my father, as none of my cousins on my mother's side of the family suffer from psoriasis. This disease caused Col immense distress. When he took Methotrexate, the condition improved. His medical practitioner advised him to undergo regular blood tests. At one stage, they informed him that Methotrexate was adversely affecting his liver. When he stopped, the psoriasis ran rampant. Several years later, he died of liver and kidney failure.

I had flown to Victoria for a work conference and hadn't seen Col for a while. He came to Tullamarine Airport so we could spend time together. I thought about how gorgeous he looked—so tall and tanned. Strangely, he didn't like the heat. He took after Mama; she never exposed her English complexion to the extreme Australian conditions, unlike me, a 'Sun Goddess.' I realised years later that his tanned skin was likely the result of the drug on his liver, which caused high levels of bilirubin to circulate in his bloodstream and throughout his body, leading to the tanned or yellow hue of his skin. In my heart, I often wondered. It was I who mentioned Methotrexate. I remember sitting in the Rumpus Room at my home in Adelaide, South Australia, reading an article titled 'Psoriasis and Methotrexate' to him over the phone. Had I not told him, would he have ever taken it? I have this searching medical mind; the knowledge comes naturally to me. I console myself that the doctors had told Col it was affecting his liver, and he chose to continue taking the drug, not realising the complete and utter consequences.

In his early twenties, he contracted Viral Hepatitis during an epidemic in Sydney in late 1959. Did this episode damage his liver? Maybe it had a contributing effect. I read that the liver is one of the few organs in the body that rejuvenates itself, so I doubt this hypothesis. As I edit this book, I've been reading about Methotrexate, having picked up a second-hand book in Hervey Bay, Queensland, when I was there, entitled:

'The Emperor of All Maladies.' A Biography of Cancer.

Winner of the Highest Award for Non-Fiction,

The Pulitzer Prize - Author Siddhartha Mukherjee.

I found it to be a fascinating book detailing the history of cancer.

FOLLOW YOUR HEART

E ntering the dining room this evening, a card from Spirit Oracle fell out of the rack holder and onto the floor. I take this as a sign to read the cards, as I shuffle several of the cards stay together, after prising them apart, I'm told:

Enjoy the Journey of life. Be not afraid of its mysteries.
Take a chance and follow your heart, for an angel guides you.
This confirms if you have been wavering about proceeding with something dear to you. Just do it!'

I have been wavering about going on holiday to the UK next year. It is my 70th year, and I want to complete 'The Circle' by returning to where my life began. This message provides validation, my confirmation. I will go! Second card reads:

'*Stand up for what you believe in, regardless of the consequences.*
Speak your truth regardless of what others may think
It's time to stand in your Power.
Shine for all the World to see.' WOW!! How true is this of me?

Quotes from 'Spirit Oracle' Cards Copyright 2005 Toni Carmine Salerno

RESPECT, COMPASSION, CARING, LOVING

When I read, I write. Reading inspires me to write, and both are my primary sources of enjoyment. Recently, I bought several books from the second-hand book sale at the Ballina library.

'**1963–The Way We Were**' attracted my attention.

Baz and I were married in April 1963, and JFK (John F. Kennedy) was assassinated in November. One never forgets where they were and what they were doing when they hear news of this magnitude; the memory imprints itself into the psyche.

A second book titled '**Mandela**'. This morning, after reading 'Mandela', I wrote.

"In conflict, no side is blameless; both sides are guilty of perpetrating wrong. We need to understand from Compassion.

Every human on this planet deserves respect. If we respected others' differences, starting from a pure place, a pure perspective, the necessity for racial, religious, and cultural war would cease to exist.

It is greed, materialism, the need for more and better, the need for power and control that perpetrate the continual cycle of war and destruction, hunger and suffering bestowed upon so many millions of humans throughout this place we call home. Our Earth." Keywords to World Peace...

Respect, Compassion, Caring, Loving.

Profoundly simple! At the same time, it is so challenging to achieve.

HAND FASTING CEREMONY

D*ecember 29, 2012*
Dave and Kez have been together for six years and have decided to 'tie the knot.' The Ceremony takes place on the beach at Kingston Park Coastal Reserve in Adelaide, South Australia. They chose a wonderful way to honour their love by holding a...

The "Hand Fasting Ceremony and Rituals" were initially performed by the Greeks and Romans before traditional wedding ceremonies, and later by the Scots, Irish, and Ancient Celts.

The connection between hands and heart symbolises the union of two lives joined in Spirit, Love, and Trust. Witness is the Eternal Spirit, Great Life Source, The Higher Power. The bringing together of two hearts in Love.'

The children serving as ceremonial attendees are Jorgia and Lachlan for David, and Tayla and Casey for Kerry. Each family carries their favourite colour ribbon and balloon for the hand-tying ceremony, symbolising the coming together of the two families into one.

Baz and I have driven from Ballina in Northern NSW with the caravan in tow, while Naomi, Andrew, and Aleisha have flown in from Sydney for the event. It's a typically hot, sunny Adelaide day, and gentle waves lap at the edge of the scorching sand. Family and friends gather. As the Marriage Celebrant reads the chosen words, Jorgia steps forward first and ties an orange ribbon around Dave and Kez's hands, followed by Tayla, who opts for aqua, and then Lachie, selecting a vibrant green. Casey finishes tying with a purple ribbon. Celebrations follow at the Blue Swimmer Room, Seacliff Beach Hotel, and then continue into the night at Dave and Kez's home, perched on a hill overlooking Adelaide's city lights and the Southern Ocean.

INSIGHT CLARITY ACCEPTANCE

January 22, 2013, 4:40 am
  I receive an insight...
  There's a small window of opportunity, a time frame when we face adversity, sorrow, grief, and suffering. It's our choice where we go from here and how we handle our lives. We either embrace or reject the suffering. If we reject it, push it away, and cut it from our thoughts and lives, we may choose the path of depression. We might turn instead to alcohol, dependent drugs, or whatever we grasp to ease the pain of our existence. We lose the value of 'self.'

  Instead, we may embrace the suffering, breathe it into our lives, and accept the circumstances. Sitting, reflecting, listening to the silence, and meditating, we find ourselves on a pathway of discovery. This choice helps release the chaos of the mind, 'monkey chatter,' and lifts us beyond our daily trials and pain, allowing us to know and love ourselves, our higher selves. It grants us the wisdom of insight and clarity to develop inner peace, which then radiates to those around us. We become compassionate, empathising with the suffering and pain of our fellow human beings.

  We are One. One Race. The Human Race. One in Compassion.

  To embrace suffering is to step onto the path leading to spirituality, inner peace, wisdom, happiness, and love. We can serve humanity from this enlightened state to encompass, surround, and embrace friends, loved ones, and the greater community. Compassion flows from the heart and the whole being. The compassionate soul can empathise, for we are all one in suffering and joy on this little planet we call Earth in a vast cosmos. I jotted down the following words, which came from my heart, although I may have read them somewhere.

Transcendence comes through acceptance. When you deny the existence of something, you remain at the same energy level as the problem. However, when you accept and open yourself to healing, you free yourself from that energy and transcend.

The dictionary defines transcendence as:

"To be or go beyond the range of limits of normal or physical human experience, existing apart from or not subject to the limitations of the material universe."

Transcendental Meditation:

A technique for detaching oneself from anxiety and promoting harmony and self-realisation through meditation and the repetition of a mantra.

"A 19th-century idealistic philosophical and social movement that taught divinity pervades all nature and humanity."

I believe this movement is 'The Theosophical Society', which resonates with me. Four decades ago, my business partner at the time, recognising traits in me I was completely unaware of, recommended that I buy a book titled 'The Voice of the Silence' by H.P. Blavatsky. Although I searched several bookshops, I was unable to find it. The title and name of the author, however, stayed with me. Many years later, I found it in a metaphysical new age bookshop in Adelaide. While reading the text, I struggled to grasp the words and their meanings. Eventually, in my fifties, the book 'jumps' out at me from my cabinet. I reread the words. Now the words come to life; they resonate within my being, and I marvel at their teachings. I've learned that spiritual knowledge finds you when you're ready to receive it.

Madam Helena Petrovna Blavatsky, author of "The Voice of the Silence," the book I took so long to find and understand, was one of the founding members of the Theosophical Society in 1875. The book is based on her teachings and principles.

"*Since all souls are divine, all souls are equal. There are young souls and old souls, but all are brothers. Despite differences in birth, capacity, environment, race, creed, sex, caste or colour, or goodness or wickedness, all men form an indivisible brotherhood. All of us, high or low, ignorant or wise, make a chain, and the stronger grow by helping the weaker. Brotherhood is the law of growth for all men, but this Brotherhood extends to all animals, birds, fish, even the plants, mountains, and seas. We grow by our unity with all things. The Divine nature which is latent in them as in us, helps our inherent Divinity to step forth in its beauty.*"

"*This understanding is the heritage of every soul. But he will possess it only when he learns to be a brother to all that lives, for Loving action is the Divine Wisdom at work and whosoever acts lovingly will inevitably come to this Wisdom.*"

Quote from 'The Theosophical Society' pamphlet 'Vital Questions Answered.' C. Jinarajadsa

'MOVING DIMENSIONS.'

April 2013

Baz and I have just returned from a 23-day cruise aboard the Cunard Queen Victoria to celebrate our 50th wedding anniversary. We had a fabulous trip, visiting, among other places, Bali, Manila, Shanghai, and Hong Kong. I found China fascinating, touring ancient monasteries and witnessing Buddhist ceremonies.

We followed the cruise with a family reunion at our home, where over 50 relatives from across Australia gathered. A 'special occasion'. The following weekend, we invited friends to join us on the Richmond Princess, a small boat in Ballina, for a tour of the Richmond River.

As part of our celebrations, Baz suggests I include a photograph in the Sunday Telegraph and the local newspaper, The Advocate—photos of us from our wedding 50 years ago, alongside present-day images. I agree; I think the articles will be fantastic for my scrapbook.

Last night, I attended the 'Space' meditation at Ballina. The speakers' topic was "Transcendence Healing." I realised during the talk that I've reached a point where I'm moving dimensions. This concept of 'moving dimensions' refers to a shift in my spiritual understanding and experiences. Physically, I moved dimension by travelling overseas, and when I meditate, I also shift dimension by moving into The Light. I am becoming my Ethereal Body, vibrating within that body. Now, with greater clarity of speech and a deeper understanding, I can explain what I believe is happening. This sense of accomplishment and growth in my spiritual experiences inspires and motivates me to share them with you.

Vibrating energy moves me into the 'Golden Mean Ratio,' becoming my 'Ethereal Body' or my 'Light Body.' Over the years, the vibrations have changed. They were initially irregular, and I didn't know what was occurring.

Now I'm aware. The movements are structured and follow a pattern as the meditation progresses. My heart pounds, first spiralling, then swinging back and forth like a pendulum, and then circling. My chin tilts upwards, and 'Light' bursts into my brain. My head vibrates, pulsing 'The Light.' I'm aware of these movements, yet feel removed.

I thanked the presenter last night for clarifying and supplying descriptive words to convey my experiences over the past few years. I am: 'moving dimensions.'

TEMPLE BYRON'S HEALING TEAM'

At the Starlight Festival in Bangalow, whilst talking to Rama, a healer at Temple Byron, he advises me:

"Temple Byron is looking for Healers."

1 May, 2013

I am invited to join 'The Divine University Healing Team' in a high-frequency healing space, where I will connect with Enlightened Masters and Archangels. Voluntary public service every Wednesday night at Temple Byron, Byron Bay, NSW. Giving of myself, opening and igniting chakras, activating and expanding to connect with the 'Universal Family of Light,' through this sacred portal.

I attended the Lotus Temple in Byron Bay, NSW, for several years as a participant, lying on the floor, receiving; I will now be giving. My sacred connection to hearts and the Universe manifests itself once again. After singing the opening Mantra to the participants, I walk over to a lady on the far side of the room. She has wrapped herself in a pink blanket adorned with hearts. My first healing connection once again brings me hearts.

I give her Reiki and notice a tear in her eye. I move on to another person, placing my hands on three people before the final mantra concludes the meditation.

Afterwards, I joined other team members for a bite to eat at a local café for a 'get-to-know-you chat.' This sense of community and shared purpose is a significant part of my healing journey.

8th May. Tonight, while working and giving Reiki to one of the other healers, she tells me she had an incredible healing, saying:

"It was you, wasn't it!" I nod replying

"Yes, just my physical me, I am the portal."

As a healer at Temple Byron for the past seven weeks, the hugs and thanks I receive from people after each session fill me with a deep sense of fulfilment. Last night, a lady asked:

"Is this your job, as a Healer?"

"No, it's just who I am," I tell her. "I'm retired."

"You are a great Healer."

As we chatted, I shared with her how I came to work for the Divine University, feeling a strong connection with the Divine.

"I remember you from the Lotus Temple, they are fortunate to have you here!"

On the way home, I give thanks and gratitude for the experiences and learnings that have brought me to this point in my spiritual journey.

Eileen has emailed me four YouTube videos. Validating learnings and experiences over the last few years. Entitled, "Inner Worlds, Outer Worlds." I learn,

"One who awakens the Kundalini in their lifetime is the living manifestation of the Divine."

I know precisely when my Kundalini awakened: June 14, 2001. It was a dynamic occurrence.

After a 'strange' dream, I awoke with the words 'Kundalini, Kundalini, Kundalini' going around and around in my head. To my knowledge, I had never heard the word. Discussing the whole episode later with my Master Reiki Teacher, he told me:

"Your Kundalini has Awakened."

A significant milestone on my spiritual pathway.

"To balance the inner and the outer, Aristotle referred to:
The Golden Mean."

'The Golden Mean Ratio' is a concept that symbolises balance and harmony. I am that Bridge. I have achieved a serene balance between my inner and outer, embodying the principles of the Golden Mean Ratio in my spiritual journey. This balance brings a profound sense of peace and tranquillity to my life.

'The Golden Mean Ratio', total joy, and inner bliss.

I sit in 'The Light', and it is magnificent...I am Blessed.

'THE VOICE.'

M*ay 18, 2013*
    I am staying with my close friend Lynne in Adelaide, South Australia. My grandson, Lachlan, is performing at the 'Adelaide Festival Centre.' He auditioned and was chosen to play a part in the stage production of Chitty Chitty Bang Bang at the Festival Centre as one of the lost children, a role he had been preparing for with great dedication and enthusiasm.

I sit next to Dave in the theatre. He is so proud of his son. At one point, glancing over at him, I see tears in his eyes. These are the momentous moments of our lives, when being a parent and grandparent is rightfully rewarded.

I stayed in Adelaide with Lynne for a week, enjoying the chance to reconnect with old friends and go out for lunch, a movie, and coffee. While sleeping in her spare bedroom, I had a dream.

Answering the telephone, I hear his voice calling my name.

"Brenda, Brenda."

It's the voice of someone long lost in my life, returning in a dream state. The voice feels so real and close that I sense he's in the bedroom. I wake up confused, and the dream unsettles me.

Returning home to NSW, I discover that my ex has seen the 50th Wedding Anniversary photograph and contacted me by email through the Sunday Telegraph newspaper. I haven't thought of my first love for many long years. We met when I was just 15 years old.

Stepping onto this spiritual pathway, in my mind, I think of myself as:

'The Universal Dancer Dancing to the Beat of the Universe.'

Incredibly, his email address incorporates the word 'Universaldancers.' I am blown away, and my intuition tells me the Universe has shown its hand. We started emailing each other and discovered that we share many similarities. Both of us are conscious of our spiritual connection to the Universe. Metaphysically 'Souls in Synch.' He is a Poet; I am a Writer. We share a love for the same music and are passionate about the rock and roll beat of our era. My thoughts are chaotic; memories of my teenage years with him flood my consciousness, accompanied by constant mental chatter, and my sleep is disturbed. I experience the full spectrum of emotions towards him: love, heartache, anger, fear, hurt, and frustration. How could this be! It is unbelievable! In my mind, he becomes my Svengali. My peaceful bliss was shattered, and my life was turned upside down. Why is this happening now? Did the Gods see me sitting peacefully in my blissful life? They heard me boast and decided to teach me a lesson. Weeks before, they had guided me to the sanctity of Temple Byron, taking on the role of a Healer and opening myself up. It is from this sanctioned temple that I needed to meet this challenge.

Sally, a recently gained psychic friend, a trained counsellor and psychologist, says:

"Something has not been forgiven or healed in your life. I feel it was when you were a teenager."

The penny drops! She is correct—the proverbial layers of the onion. I had not thought about those painful years and had buried the memories of the heartbreak deep within. Sally explains:

"We think we are done, then another layer emerges!"

How right she is!

THE YURT ~ ONENESS BLESSING

A fter returning from Adelaide, Eileen and I went to Temple Byron Yurt. This exquisite Mongolian Yurt is set on 3 acres of tropical paradise, surrounded by lush gardens and water features. The gardens are abundant with stunning crystals that catch the eye whichever way you look. Walking through the gardens creates a sense of peaceful tranquillity.

My experience of receiving the 'Oneness Deeksha Blessing' six or seven years ago in Adelaide was unique and holds a special place in my memory. The Yurt was filled with 20 people, and I sat in the inner circle on my meditation stool, dressed in my usual purple attire. With three drops of oil on my inner left hand, wrist, and forehead, the anointment process was a profoundly spiritual moment. As the facilitator invoked Quan Yin, I felt a profound connection to the divine.

As the evening progresses, I'm carried into a deep meditation. I feel I am hardly breathing, a long way away. I am still present and conscious of spoken words, but I do not wish to participate. I am just in a mesmerising space.

The presenter discusses Quan Yin, explaining that he has visited Thailand, where he attended an extensive open parkland featuring life-size statues of Quan Yin. He feels something is missing on the statues 'breasts.' Learns that Quan Yin was male and had surrendered himself. Thus, he opened up to the feminine side of his nature, becoming compassionate, nurturing, and caring, and incorporating both aspects of his being. When being asked to offer feedback, I say:

"I work with her daily, calling forth Quan Yin, Goddess of Compassion. I will invoke her as the God and Goddess of Compassion."

Then, explain how I received the Oneness Blessing six or seven years earlier in Adelaide and how I have now surrendered my life to the Universe. I meditate to 'The Light,' experiencing peace and bliss....

He replies, 'Hallelujah!!'

A second meditation follows, in which the seven facilitators place their hands on my head.

Sitting on my stool, I find myself in a quiet space, meditating, spiralling, swinging, balancing. The first person places their hands on the top of my head. I become still, and darkness envelops me. One by one, after each connection, I revert to a balanced meditative state.

During the fourth blessing, my head lifted, my neck extended, and my senses exploded. 'LIGHT' engulfed me. I gasped with pleasure, sheer bliss, sobbed, tears streaming down my upturned face. My body took over my head, physically pulsing 'The Light.' I was euphoric. Conscious that someone else had touched my head again, and moved on.

Then someone breaks the spell by tripping over my legs. By the time the seventh and final facilitator arrives, I've resumed my balanced meditative state.

'Open your eyes, keep them soft, unfocused, conscious of all surroundings.'

I'm not used to meditating with my eyes open. It's an enlightening experience. I become aware of my heart beating and expanding. I gaze into the facilitator's eyes before lying down to reflect on the evening...

I am at Peace...

SIMPLE ABUNDANCE

As I eat breakfast this morning, I glance through the Jasmine archway into my little walled garden. Abundant roses are blooming, and yet it is the middle of winter in beautiful Ballina, Northern NSW, Australia. Locally, Ballina is referred to as 'Paradise.' The Poinsettia tree is ablaze with red flowers, while the white Sasanqua Camellias and deep pink Azaleas complete the idyllic scene before my eyes.

I read a passage from "Simple Abundance-A Day Book of Comfort and Joy."

The author discusses the need for pruning, ideally voluntarily. I interpret this to mean pruning not just from our gardens, but also from our thoughts and lives, discerning what is real, meaningful, and essential for our happiness, regardless of the pain one may encounter.

These words resonate with me this morning. My happiness is my caring, loving husband, my little villa and walled garden, the peaceful place I spiritually reside. These are my greatest gifts. I've been on a roller coaster ride for the last few months following the email from my first love, and my ego was boosted. It is an illusion.

THE MEDIUM

The energy in Temple Byron tonight is palpable. The pure celestial tones of crystal bowls emit powerful sound waves, promoting deep relaxation and out-of-body experiences. The opening mantra sung by us, the Healers, carrying the participants, prostrating on the temple floor, into another space, transcending them. My thoughts flash back to 'The Lotus Temple,' and my sadness when it closed. Now, so full of abundance, Temple Byron has more than filled the void.

There are regulars, and we share hugs after each session, along with newcomers from around the globe. Byron Bay, NSW, is a popular spot for overseas travellers. Word of mouth has spread about a "Sound & Healing Night," a donation-only event that draws visitors to the Temple door. Seeking peace from a troubled world, many experience the sheer joy, bliss, and happiness within the Temple's walls and tranquil gardens. Two regulars, Val and Eve, often bless us with their presence. Val is a Medium. She approaches me after the healing, we hug, thank me, and then excitedly says:

I saw you in your last lifetime; you were a nurse in the previous World War, wearing a nurse's cap with a red cross. You didn't like the noise of the bombs and quickly returned to this lifetime.

I have always had an affinity for medicine and a profound comprehension; these words are comforting. I had a dream of a previous lifetime in Portsmouth, UK, where I witnessed the countryside, houses, and the surrounding area. My inner knowing, as Val describes her vision, is that I died in Portsmouth during World War II. Portsmouth, being a military stronghold, was heavily bombed by the Germans. Val chatted on. I also saw you as a man in another lifetime, looking through a microscope. This information aligns with the medical knowledge that comes second nature to me—Val's validation.

ONENESS CONFERENCE

September 14 and 15, 2013

I spent the weekend at the 'Oneness Conference' on the Gold Coast, Queensland. Over the past 18 months, I've reconnected with the Oneness Group in Bangalow, Byron, and Ballina and decided to attend this conference. I dropped off all my gear, including my yoga mat, purple pillow, books, meditation stool, and rug, and went to the bathroom. When I came out, a lady said:

I love all your purple!

She introduces herself as Lyn and also introduces her daughter-in-law, Beverley. As we chatted, I discovered that she has written and published several books. Lyn and I have an instant connection; we're alike, both being writers.

The weekend is filled with meditation. Saturday is spent with Pasquo and Lisa, as Pasquo demonstrates some astronomy and the impact of the changeover from Pisces to Aquarius on the world. We are transitioning from a self-centred, materialistic energy to the sharing and compassionate energy of Aquarius. This process takes a few hundred years to achieve, and we are now in the midst of it, hence the widespread unrest in the world. 'The Oneness Philosophy' is the coming together of all religions and all people and becoming 'As One.'

Profound trance meditations move me into 'The Light' five times in just a few hours. During one meditation, Lisa carried a sash, paused in front of each person, and placed it over the back of their necks. As she neared, I experienced an intense, palpable energy. Lisa positioned the sash on my body, my head lifted, my neck extended, and I shuddered. I spiralled into a full energy release, up into brilliant, illuminating 'Light '-OMG!

Afternoon activities include energy movement, dancing, belly breathing meditation, focusing on each chakra, and circulating breath around the body. One surprising distraction for me is that a few people laugh raucously during deep meditation. While I am brought to silent tears of bliss, I find it somewhat disquieting.

The session goes overtime by an hour. I ring Baz before leaving; he watches footy on TV and isn't too concerned. I leave the resort at 6 pm and arrive home at 7.15 pm. Good timing, an hour and a quarter. However, I find the last 20 km tiring. After a luxurious spa, I go to bed at 9.30 pm and sleep deeply.

Sunday morning, deciding to leave later. On arrival, I meet Lyn and she says:

"I have a present for you."

She hands me an autographed copy of the book she has written. It's a surprise to start the day.

I find myself seated between two of the laughers, thinking to myself, how ironic! At first, it crossed my mind to move away, deciding:

'No, this is where I am to overcome this irritation. It is a challenge.'

There is a short intro meditation with Lisa and Pasquo, followed by a group meditation with Rahasya and Nura, whom I met in Temple Byron. I again experience 'eye contact' meditation, and Nura's serenity brings me to tears. She talks of being at one with our Divinity. I connect and resonate with her words.

There are six sessions: three deep-trance meditations and three eye-contact meditations. I am in my element. Connected to illuminating, iridescent 'Divine Light'.

I visualised a deep purple mountain with a green aura at one stage. The mountain peak is a white, pulsating circle of glowing light, radiating out and pulsing back, a magical sight. We move around and change positions after each session. In the last session, I was towards the back, in the middle, sitting next to Lyn and Beverley. I am glad this position gives me a broader perspective on the other participants. I see a few others spiral as I do, one young woman to my right, lifting her head up and backwards, extending her neck in the same gesture I do when I am one with 'The Light'. Lisa moved and vibrated her head and body. She is obviously in a state of extreme bliss, as I am. I hug her afterwards. She says:

"It is the Kundalini energy moving through the body; nothing you can do about it."

Deep, powerful music plays after each meditation, and I vibrate, moving every cell of my body. I am grateful for the deep connection and the hands-on experience. I usually give Reiki, and it's lovely to receive it.

I drive away at 6 pm, switch on the radio, and wow! Incredible how things occur.

A programme describes a play at the Sydney Opera House: *The Life of Swami Vivekananda*. During his lifetime, his goal was to unite the world's religions. This weekend has highlighted these beliefs in a truly amazing way. I arrive home at 7:15 p.m., somewhat tired from the weekend activities and the long drives. Baz makes baked beans and cheese on muffins for me and a cup of tea. Yum!

The words I write following this weekend are:

We know when we awaken because our lives change profoundly, we become our truth, and come to know our divinity.

Buddha was asked...

"What have you gained from meditation?"

"Nothing."

However, Buddha said:

"Let me tell you what I have lost.

Anger, Anxiety, Depression, Insecurity, Fear of Old Age and Death"

Marvellous!!!

CHIRON THE HEALER

*N**ew Year 2014*
I heard these words in a song today:
"Some things that are buried will rise again."
I say to my ex: "No more emails!" He replies: "Look deeper."
I Google 'Chiron', his chosen channelled spiritual name. My problems are exacerbated tenfold, and my turmoil is heightened.

Chiron is the Planet of Healing, discovered in 1977 and named after the centaur in Greek mythology. Chiron is symbolised as "the wounded healer." He represents our deepest spiritual wounds and our efforts to heal them.

Derivatives of the name Chiron are:

CHIRAL–The polarisation of 'Light,' from one hand to another.

CHIROS–Timeless time–the eternal moment reached when I meditate.

CHIROTHESIA–Hand Energy–the warmth in my hands when giving Reiki.

CHIROTONY–Blessing without Hands.

CHIRURGERY–Ancient name for surgery.

CHIROPRACTIC–Healing of joints/bones by manipulation.

CHIROMANCY–The Magical Divination form of Chiron is Tarot and Palmistry.

Chiron embodies all that is cherished in my life.

How can this be? Is he a Twin Flame or a Spiritual Partner? I'm caught in a dilemma where every decision will have undesirable consequences. So many lives are involved, and there will be so much hurt if I walk this pathway. I need help. Time and again, during the turmoil, I throw it up to the Universe, putting my trust in its hands and surrendering my chaotic thoughts.

As is my practice, I visit the Starlight Wellbeing Festival in Bangalow and attend a 'Shamanic Ceremony' workshop. The card that arises for me is 'Chiron the Centaur.'

Shocked, I hold it, feeling numb, staring at it. I'm also given a book: **'Transference Healing Animal Magic.' Author Alexis Cartwright. Words stand out to me: I have paraphrased -**

If you have chosen this card today ...

... "You are given an excellent opportunity to become conscious of wounding that has been lying dormant within the DNA/etheric body and unconscious mind......

... possibly an unresolved old relationship.

I learn from Alexis:

Chiron brings core wounding into consciousness and supports its healing, helping you reconnect to your Higher Self. Chiron symbolises the 'rainbow bridge' of reconnection to Spirit, which allows you to receive the 'gift of healing' to enhance your self-healing abilities and the key to enable you to support others in their quest for healing.

Synopsis: Chiron has returned to my life as a gift to help me awaken to a higher level of consciousness. I want to acknowledge the Healer within me, work with this energy, and support my ascension by using my Reiki Master's knowledge to teach, guide, and share this wisdom.

I ride a roller coaster. It helps me offload my turmoil to Rama, a colleague from Temple Byron who is a trained counsellor. Rama advises me concerning Chiron.

"Research your Soul Family."

The feelings settle. As is often the case with 'Reiki,' written words arrive in my hands while reading a book by a favoured author entitled,

"The Wisdom of James Allen."

The book provides me with insight, clarity, and answers. Addressing my journal, it takes me back to March 8, 2011, reminding me that I had attended a workshop at the Lotus Temple in Byron Bay when Qala carried me into a deep trance meditation. This spinning vortex expanded and opened my Heart Chakra. Her words:

"... Everything is balanced. Karma is clear except for one aspect that is deeply buried. Quan Yin will help you with it. It has to do with your base chakra, your feminine, your sexuality."

Now I understand what she was referring to: my broken teenage heart, the buried hurt from that time. Writing this chapter of my life has been cathartic, as I see the puzzle pieces fall into place and realise the role each piece plays in completing the whole. My greatest challenge and most profound healing are happening now. I wonder about the outcome. One minute, one step at a time, one day at a time. This week marks a distinctive shift, an opening of the heart, as I still work through the hurt, pain, and anger. I gently accept what is right. Now.

In my life, two 'Capricorn' men walked away from me. First, my father was born on January 7th, and then my first love, Chiron, was born on January 6th (of course, I didn't know him as Chiron then). There's a sense of sadness in the missed opportunities of both relationships. Capricorn and Virgo (my sign) are an ideal astrological combination. I worked through the abandonment issues with my father using Reiki healing. I had forgotten the hurt and heartbreak of my first love and buried it deep within my psyche. I know life is a cycle, replaying events until the lesson is learnt. I hadn't learnt this lesson!

Many years have passed. Reiki has taught me that when I confront the hurt and the pain, I must cleanse and purify, and only then can I move through it. Bringing it to 'The Light.' Reiki and meditation have led me to a life of serenity and peace.

Now, the realisation is that the issues with Chiron must be resolved and worked through. He emailed me a YouTube song, apologising for the hurt he caused.

'I Apologise', Billy Eckstine. As I listen to the words, forgiveness ensues.

Paraphrased from www.cafeastrology.com

(Excerpts taken from Internet 'Healing the Ancient Wound–the Journey of Chiron,' Copyright © 2004 Dwight Stevers. BA

Copyright © Alexis Cartright. Published by Tranference Healing ® Pty.Ltd. All rights reserved. Reprinted by permission

MUTUAL GIFTS

Yesterday at the Starlight Festival, I was sitting in the workshop room when Rama arrived for his 'Wholly Men' presentation (usually reserved for men). I asked Rama for permission to stay. It wasn't unusual; it reminded me of my career days in the 80s when I worked in the food industry in Adelaide, South Australia, a male-dominated field. I attended 'FIDO' (Food Industry Discussion Organisation) and sat in a conference room with 25 men, being the only female. I learned why I'm drawn to stay...

While sitting at breakfast the next day, I told my husband about a man I met at the workshop named David. After returning from his father's funeral, he and his wife were on their honeymoon. They are 'bikers.' A car hit her, killing her, while the driver was asleep at the wheel. David told me:

'Her dying had led him to his spiritual path.'

I shared with him details of my brother's death 20 years ago, saying

"She has given you a 'gift', your gift of spirituality, the greatest gift of all."

THE MESSAGE

Tonight, at Temple Byron, after the 'Healing Session', Val the Clairvoyant says:

"I have a message for you."

Putting her hand to her forehead, she thinks for two seconds:

"They (Spirit Guides) told me to tell you, not to worry about money, it's being fixed, something is happening."

I am worrying about money. Baz and I returned from a trip to Sydney for his sister-in-law's funeral. On the return trip, a Police Patrol stopped us at Port Macquarie. The officer informed me the car was unregistered.

No! I explained that I had registered it online. The officer accepted my explanation and instructed me to contact the RTA upon my return home. However, he still had to issue me a traffic infringement fine of over $600.00.

North of Coffs Harbour, we were pulled over again. The officer said we couldn't continue our journey in an unregistered vehicle, insisting we pull off the road and issue another fine, bringing our total to $ 1,224.00. Stressed beyond belief, I cried; Baz contacted his mechanic in Ballina. Within half an hour, the mechanic rang back saying:

'All fixed.'

When I returned home, I rang GIO Insurance to find out what had happened. They told me the systems had gone down, and there was no record of my request to complete the registration, so it was my fault.

Next, I rang the Police Helpline. I needed the second infringement notice number, and I planned to appeal the decision. They put me through to Coffs Harbour Police Station. Talking to an officer, he could not find any record of the offence, and transferred me directly to the officer involved.

Speaking with the officer who had booked us was a revelation! He said he had phoned me (20 seconds ago) on the home line listed with the RTA, and had been informed I had not lived there for three years. We were both ringing each other at the same time! He sounded confused and said he thought I was calling back from a missed call, realising that was not so.

'That's OK, it's the Universe looking after me.'

Telling him I intended to claim leniency due to extenuating circumstances, he said:

"I had decided not to go ahead, so I was ringing you."

I replied: "If you were with me now, I would hug you!"

He said they (meaning the police) were not out to 'get people' and that he was writing a 'caution' saying:

'After he left the scene, he realised we had registered the car on the spot over the phone.' He advised me of a website where I could find registration information. I thanked him, replying:

"Good advice. I should have followed it up, instead of assuming they had completed it online."

Once again, I was emotional; it was pure affirmation. I was loved and looked after by the universe—validation from Val the Clairvoyant and her Spirit Guides.

Writing a letter to the Police Department, detailing the sequence of events, I received an answer...

Result: 'Fines Waived!' At the time, there was confusion surrounding vehicle registrations due to the abolition of 'Registration Car Stickers.'

SPIRIT ORACLE CARDS

T hree cards are on the dining room floor, having fallen from the small stand of the bookcase. I read them in the sequence in which I pick them up.

ELECTRA: *Electricity! Thunderbolt! Activation!*

You are subconsciously connecting with the incredible power that lies in the energy of the stars—intergalactic transmission from a place beyond time.

A message is coming. Be open-minded.

PATIENCE: *You are entering a time of great love and peace.*

Be patient and allow the current storm to clear.

Resurrection, no more wounds.

Only love is predicted for the future.

RESPONSIBILITY: *Do what feels right for you above all else.*

It is impossible to please all parties in the present situation.

You have responsibility only for your own life and actions.

Others must take responsibility for themselves.

How relevant these cards are in my life right now!

SYMBOLIC RETURN.

M*arch, April, May 2014*
I leave my home in Ballina, NSW, Australia, on 22nd March to travel to the Orkney Islands, Scapa Flow, Scotland. I will meet my two cousins, Annie and Bec, at Sydney Airport. We are travelling together to Glasgow via Dubai on Emirates Airlines.

We thoroughly enjoy Dubai's culture, food, and the exotic aromas of souk markets—the Yin and the Yang, the light and the dark, exotic mystery abiding. When we visit the Jumeirah coastal residential area, we hear the 'call to prayer' over loudspeakers around town. I find it evocative and calming.

We spent several weeks in Scotland with Annie's son, Mike, Vic, and Maddie. Mike is working for the Commonwealth Games in Glasgow. We toured the magnificent Scottish Highlands, visiting historic castles, estates, and a whisky distillery. Celebrations were held for an extended family gathering in a picturesque B&B for Mike's 40th birthday. The next part of our journey took us by train from Glasgow to London, where we could enjoy the tourist attractions. Annie, Bec, Mike, Vic, and Maddie have booked a visit to Paris. I hired a car in London, as my heart calls me elsewhere.

I visit my mother's long-lost family in Cornwall, who welcome me with open arms. They hang a banner from the ceiling of the local church hall that says, 'Welcome Binkie' (my nickname), to celebrate a large family reunion. I spent several days with my 88-year-old cousin, who reminds me of Mama at the same age, even though they never met. After visiting my Cornish family, I head north towards Scotland.

North of mainland Scotland, where the Atlantic Ocean and North Sea converge, lie the islands of Orkney. These islands were the ancient home of the

Viking Norse Warriors, Celtic Nobles, Shamans, and soothsayers. At the heart of the Orkney Islands lies Scapa Flow, a vast expanse of calm water that serves as a haven for seafarers. Here, in this ancient place steeped in a spiritual heritage, seventy years ago, the first stirrings of my life began.

This journey is a Spiritual Pilgrimage for me in my 70th year. It's fitting that towards the latter part of my life, I visit the beginnings of my life. There is a call to make this journey, opening the doorway to my soul, completing my life circle.

I found these touching words in a brochure whilst visiting Scotland, so apt in describing the Orkneys!

'An ancient magic hovers above the Orkney Islands, endowing the islands with an allure that lodges firmly in the soul.

It's in the misty seas, where seals, whales, and porpoises patrol lonely coastlines,

It's in the air where squadrons of seabirds wheel above the huge nesting colonies.

It's on the land, where standing stones catch late summer sunsets and strains of folk music dispense in the air before the wind gusts shut the pub door.'

This pathway allows me to weave another section into the tapestry that is my life.

Quoted from 'Lonely Planet Publications Pty Ltd.'

EMOTIONAL ENDINGS

F*riday, 13 June 2014*
Referred to by some as 'Black Friday,' I am at my computer when it crashes. It switches off, then reboots. The words that appear on the screen after rebooting are these:

"A mind stretched to new dimensions never returns to its previous state."

Wow! That's an immediate message from the Universe if ever there was one! I needed that message, and tears brimmed from my eyes, threatening to spill...

I enjoy using my computer to answer emails, write, create short stories and memoirs, work on this book, and keep a spiritual journal. Now, as I try to step back from this crazy turmoil by not responding to emails from Chiron, I find myself facing two angry men. I never lie; it's not part of my psyche. Baz has accused me of being dishonest with him. Is silence, not divulging, considered lying? Deep within my core, I know it compromises my truth, which does not sit well with me. Happiness does not arise from hurting others. Our relationship with each other is not the issue. Hurting Baz was never part of this equation. I remind myself that this is all part of the healing process, the pain of a first love's heartbreak. Bringing the hurt into the light sets me free. It's not just about me; life isn't like that. So many lives are intertwined, and I could hurt many people. Baz loves me; he tells me so every morning, waking up to greet me with 'I love you,' and he shows affection. I love him; he is a good and gentle man, and it's inconceivable to hurt him. I've done so without intention. We've been together for so long; our lives and spirits are intertwined. His fear of loss and separation manifests as anger. I have asked him to trust me. This has left me drained; a void has entered my life. This morning, I find myself in a melancholy, emotional mood. Desist from using the word depressed. I had a fall—the second one—this time injuring my left wrist and crashing onto the tiles on my left hip. Now I'm sitting in the Summer Room, rather than at the laptop in my office, eager not to upset Baz.

The ninth of the ninth—9th day of September and the 9th month—Full Moon in Pisces, meaning... 'Emotional Endings.' ~ So apt in my life.

Ballina Scenic Lookout features long, curving, pristine sandy beaches that flank a steep incline leading to the viewing platform. It's a magical night with a clear sky. I arrive before the moon rises. Dozens of other people stand around me, silent, marvelling at this spectrum. I remain still, contemplating nature as the full moon rises above the horizon, illuminating the dark, rippling waters and creating steps to a blackened sky. For a long time, I've wanted to visit Broome in Western Australia to witness the famous 'Stairway to the Moon.' Now, I don't feel the need; I'm seeing my own 'Stairway to the Moon' right here in my hometown of Ballina, NSW.

Nature has its unique way of cleansing our emotional turmoil.

Having Googled, it appears this quote was adapted and paraphrased from a quote by US Author & Physician Oliver Wendell Holmes (1809-1894)

THOUGHTS IN CONFLICT

S unday, 26 September, 5:30 am
A young magpie wakes me, calling from my walled garden. It's a gorgeous spring dawn with blue skies and a hint of a playful breeze. As I sit in the morning sunshine, feeding him strips of meat, he rewards me by singing a sweet song. I do not allow my thoughts to dwell on the fact that the strips of raw beef I am feeding this bird were once a soft-eyed, gentle cow not long ago. I shudder, finding it difficult to put these words to paper. Additionally, a minor concern on my mind is the baby doves, newly hatched just two days ago, in the Star Jasmine archway. It is not safe for them with a magpie calling to see me.

The Summer Room is serene, with the morning sun's rays filtering through, filling every nook and cranny. Baz and I enjoy our Sunday breakfast together. I listen to the haunting refrains of "Deja Blues" by Steven Halpern, one of my favourite CDs, while watching tiny ants scurry about, so busy in pursuit of life, oblivious to my presence towering above them. A simile passes through my consciousness. Is this how humans, on this tiny planet we call Earth, are seen by a Higher Force, a Higher Being? Are we scurrying around in the unconscious pursuit of our lives, vulnerable every second?

Life could end with a foot stamp, a colossal earthquake, or the Earth tilting on its axis, sending every living ant, every living being, and every living human into oblivion and the unknown forever.

The Human Spirit: "Oppression leads to Radicalism. The 'oppressed' spirit will 'break through' in the form of radical ideology to grasp at hope for survival."

Life is filled with unique beauty, devastation, and horror. Although my thoughts this morning were conflicted, my spirit felt no longer oppressed.

I've let her go!

CHRISTA ~ THE EMBODIMENT

Yesterday, I enjoyed sitting at my computer. I haven't done much since the upset with Baz over the emails. It's a part of my life I've been missing; this loss was bringing me down, making me unhappy, and even sick. So, I stood in my power, emailing out and reconnecting. Last night at the Temple, three people commented on how I was 'Glowing'. I felt the shift; it was palpable. By taking that step and doing what I enjoy instead of feeling oppressed, the load had lifted!

After the healing session, seven of us went to the 'Red, Hot & Green' Café in Byron. We shared stories. I told them how, after channelling the name 'Christa', I had been using it as a pseudonym in my writing for several years, saying:

"I would like to be known as Christa at the Temple from now on," Kaliana says:

"Now you have taken on the name of Christa, perhaps your book will be published."

Kaliana prayed to the Universe, asking for the right people to come my way. One of the other healers asked if I thought my book would help others who have also lost a loved one.

"Maybe," I reply. As we leave the café in the centre of the square, we share a group hug, forming a circle. Kaliana sings:

"Happy Birthday to You, Happy Birthday to You, Happy Birthday Dear Christa." Everybody joins in "Happy Birthday, Happy Birthday to You, Christa."

Christa is acknowledged as a true embodiment of self on October 16, 2014.

THE JOB

My spiritual journey has reached a point where Spirit is calling me to take on a teaching role. It is early 2015. Who would have thought that when Col died, this would be my future?

I was invited to fill a lecture vacancy when a Reiki master was unable to attend the Body, Mind, and Spirit Festival. I gave lectures and guided meditations, stayed busy, and enjoyed it. Afterwards, several people asked, 'Do you teach Reiki?' Although I received my Usui Reiki Master's degree in 2002 and my Karuna Reiki Master's degree in 2003, I hadn't given much thought to teaching. 2015 was the year when I was asked to 'Step Up' by the Universe. My first Reiki student attended the lecture; she was keen and receptive. Samantha is young, in her early twenties. I offer Reiki Level 1 tutoring for free; it feels 'right' with the Universe. Her 'thank you' came with a contribution of a pretty 'Reiki hand' suspended on a chain, which dangles from the rear vision mirror in my car. I am reminded of Qala's words:

'You have a job to do; you don't know what it is yet. You have been preparing for it for about seven years.'.....

I am no longer unaware of the job. I revel in serving at Temple Byron, teaching Reiki, and sharing the knowledge gifted by the Masters and the Universe. Chiron returned to my life to awaken me to a higher level of consciousness, acknowledging the 'Healer Teacher' and enabling me to work with this energy, passing on the divine 'gift' and lifting me to a higher level of existence. The words: 'Healer Heal Thyself' enter my consciousness. I had been holding back until the hurt of a broken heart surfaced to the 'Light', and my healing had fully taken place. Now, I access and use Reiki. Meditating. Merging. Stepping into Self-Mastery to become One with my Highest Divine Self, in 'Light', 'Love', and 'Compassion.' With Universal guidance, I can step up to the job. I am in deep gratitude.

INTEGRITY

S*ummer/Autumn Equinox New Moon*
Solar Eclipse, 20 March 2015

There is a gathering at the 'Healing Heart Gateway' in Uralba, a ten-minute drive from my home in Ballina. Usually coming together for 'Full Moon' meditations once a month, this is the first 'New Moon' gathering. The first meditation relates to 'Equinox New Beginnings.' ~

Let go of everything that is not serving me in my life. Acceptance comes from moving on and letting go. I surrender: 'whatever will be!'

I draw a Tarot card, the **Nine of Wands**.

Meaning: You will face the challenges ahead by leveraging your reputation, experience, and courage, which will give you a sense of purpose.

Keywords: Spiritual depth, preparedness, accomplishment.

Gifts: Integrity

Advice: You have strength in reserve. Use it!

How true is this? Memories take me back to January 1994.

Reminiscing:

I am standing in the Church listening to the Eulogy for my dearest brother Colin, my heart weeping, my body shaking, I cannot see through my tears. My voice soars to 'The Lord is My Shepherd.' I hear my Mother sigh with relief as she joins in the hymn. Mama has always had a sweet singing voice. We enjoyed many happy times, curled up in bed together when I was a little girl, singing and reading the Sunday paper and comics.

The congregation stands to begin the walk to receive Communion. Mama pushes me forward, but Baz remains; he is a member of the Church of England, and neither of us has attended church for many years. I have not sat in a confessional box since 1963, when, taking the pill, the Church told me I was sinning! OMG! It's time to step away. I know Mama; she is worried about appearances! What will people think? I feel like a fraud going to receive Communion.

Now, as I write these words, it is...March 2015.

I recall last Easter 2014, when I was in Cornwall, UK, visiting a long-lost family member. I had never met relatives on my mother's side of the family.

My newly gained cousin, a grand old lady of 88, reminds me so much of Mama at the same age; they have the same mannerisms. She invited me to attend Church with her on Palm Sunday.

I sat in the family pew of the Church called Saint Petroc Minor, St Issey, Cornwall. It is the 'High Church of England' and has been the Family Church for centuries. My cousin told me to look at the Baptismal Font, which dates back to the 14th century. It is 'special'; the whole of this little church is rather 'extraordinary'. I was given a palm and moved to the carved wooden altar to receive Holy Communion.

I realise that I am now at peace with my GOD within. I am accepting and willing, knowing my true purpose: *to serve.*

CONTRASTS & DIFFERENCES

I am waiting for Baz to join me for dinner at the table. I had a friend over earlier, and we enjoyed a day of giving, including Reiki, a hot tub, a spa, and a tarot reading. The Tarot cards are still on the table. Leaning over, I draw a card from the pack.

'Two of Cups.' Depicts two lovers, hands toasting each other with champagne flutes, their faces reflected in the glasses. I'm not sure where this is leading. I put the card aside to eat my meal.

Then I do something I would not normally do: hand the tarot pack to Baz, inviting him to take one. He shuffles, dropping two cards, then decides to go with the one face up on the floor. It is a Major Arcana, 'The Lovers', depicting two lovers not touching. They are separate entities that, when together, create a whole. Traditionally, this card is about being at a moral or ethical crossroads:

'The Lovers'

Keywords: Divine union, balance, completion.

Meanings: The Lovers represent relationship, intimate communication, and choice.

Gifts: Intimacy, union, connection.

Advice: Enjoy the contrasts and differences.

As I read the advice, tears spring to my eyes. I read it as the Universe resolving my fears and worries; Baz and I are not doing things together much anymore. We seem to be on different paths. NOW I read my card:

'Two of Cups'

This is a card of recognition and romance. The two lovers from the Major Arcana connect once more. Now, I realise the deep connection between the cards, one drawn by Baz and the other by me!

Two polarities. Light & Darkness. Male & Female. As Above, So Below.

"Lovers are crossing and mirroring each other.

An intriguing feature of the Two of Cups is the pair of faces reflected in the cups, a metaphor of how the depth of our love reflects in the quality of our relationship."

In addition, it says:

"The success of our relationship depends in great part on how we see ourselves reflected in the eyes of our loved ones."

Keywords: *Good rapport one-on-one, kindred spirits, warm friendship, attachment.*

Gifts: *Emotional connection.*

Advise: *Enjoy the rewards of a loving partnership.*

WOW!! Some chance reading that was. The Universe is giving me the answers and insights. Thank you. Once again, I am grateful.

Quotes from: 'Gateway to the Divine Tarot' Copyright © 2009 ~ Ciro Marchetti Llewellyn Publications

IT IS AS IT IS AS IT WAS MEANT TO BE

After immersing myself in the Easter ' Starlight ' Wellbeing Festival for the past four days, I find myself in the summer room, savouring a cup of chai tea. The words from the book I'm reading, a reflection of the Tao Te Ching, Lao-Tzu's wisdom, profoundly resonate with me...

"The Book of Wisdom" was written approximately 2500 years ago.

To fulfil one's destiny is to be constant. To know the constant is called insight.

"To know the way, understand the Great within yourself."

"You need not fear the darkness when the Light is shining everywhere."

Six months ago, I could not envisage myself lecturing and teaching. Yet here I am, having been invited to be a 'workshop presenter' at the Starlight Festival. Over the last four days, I spent an incredible time giving six lectures, including two guided meditations. My life journey has led me to this point, teaching me the needed skills. Every job I experienced in my career relates to where I am now. Strangely, I had walked the pathway for 70 years before coming to this understanding.

NO VOID

M*ay 11, 2015*
I have not needed to visit a clairvoyant for a reading for many years, as the Universe has provided all the clarification I wanted. The chaos my thoughts of Chiron have engendered, I have now decided that additional advice is warranted.

I met Ava, a Clairvoyant, at Murwillumbah, NSW. One of my Reiki students referred her to me. My home address and her business address have the exact numbers: 1/9. The numerology meaning is the beginning and the end. My intuition told me she was the 'right' Clairvoyant to visit. Ava asks me a question. I say..."Is Chiron my Spiritual Partner?"

Ava sits still, looking at the floor, silent, pondering. She lifts her eyes, replying...

"I see darkness around him. No, he is not your Spiritual Partner. This is a drama in your life, one of your own making!" She touches her solar plexus, coughing: "It is painful, and you need to address something.

We chatted for over an hour; her words validated and clarified my thoughts. It was necessary to hear them from someone else. I felt there was a 'void,' no one to fill the role of Spiritual Partner. After visiting Ava, I realised there is 'no void,' and there has never been one. When I stepped into my power as a Reiki Master, I was all I needed to be. Self Mastery. Baz is part of that scenario. I created the illusion, thinking I needed a 'Spiritual Partner'. I am given these words...

"A world without boundaries is opening to you. Anything is possible, remove any doubts or fears, knowing the only limits are the ones you create yourself. Higher mind reconciliation, loving vibrations, mutual exchange of love. Past wounds can now be energetically healed, all negative attachments reconciled and released."

THE UNWELCOME VISITOR

The decision to attend the Camel Races in Tara, outback Queensland, Australia, was a compromise made in default. A Yoga Retreat had booked me to present a Reiki Lecture, but due to insufficient attendees, they cancelled it. Hence the fateful decision.

We left our home in Ballina, driving to Casino, NSW, through Stanthorpe and Warwick in Queensland, and arrived mid-afternoon at Clifton. We parked 'Little Molly', our imported UK Caravan, on the Showground overnight. Tonight, it would be a Full Moon, a 'Blue Moon.' The Australian landscape, with its vibrant sunsets and iridescent moonrises, consistently inspires awe.

I watched mesmerised in wonder as the golden yellow rays of the sun sank deep into the western horizon. Simultaneously, in the east, the iridescent silvery glow of the enormous full moon rose into a cloudless indigo blue of the evening sky. As a voluntary salute to the vision I witnessed, I lifted my arms in surrender and shouted out loud from my heart.

"I love this place!"

Elated, I felt inspired to practice Tai Chi, meditating and losing myself in the energies. Afterwards, filled with sheer gratitude, I stood still, marvelling at the vast expanse of the Australian sky.

Friday dawned.

On the outskirts of Toowoomba, Queensland, we paused, unsure of the way to Dalby and Tara. Whilst setting the Satellite navigation, an inquisitive Police Officer approached our car, and smiling, he said:

"Have you stopped to give a voluntary breath test?"

Baz obliged. After the police officer assisted us with directions, we were on our way.

SPIRALLING TO THE LIGHT

The road to Tara was long and narrow. We travelled at 80-85 kph, feeling comfortable at that speed, annoying a 'truckie' as he roared past us at the first opportunity. Prickly Pear trees, soon to burst into a blaze of spring flowers, lined the bushland road, kilometre after kilometre. In my mind's eye, I envisioned a blaze of colour, saying out loud, 'It will look spectacular here in two weeks.'

Tara is a typical Australian township, larger than I had envisaged. The population of around 2,000 residents was inundated with another 10,000 tourists for the biannual Camel Race event. Camel effigies guided us towards the showground. As we entered through the gates, my heart sank to see row upon row of caravans and motorhomes sandwiched into a dusty expanse. With the willing help of several experts, Baz manoeuvred Little Molly into a tiny space, so narrow that we couldn't put out the awning. Once we settled in, we walked a long way through the dust to the entrance gate, only to be refused entry because we weren't wearing the required wristbands that had been provided. Baz growled:

"I'm not coming back!!"

A shuttle bus was parked nearby. The obliging driver took us to our caravan and waited while we collected the wrist straps, then returned us to the entrance gate.

As dusk fell, the night sky illuminated with fireworks, a cherished pastime of mine, and I took a deep breath, the sharp scent of gunpowder bringing back memories of my childhood days.

Saturday dawned, and the showground was buzzing with excitement. Market and aromatic food stalls were plentiful. Baz placed a bet on the first Camel Race, the name appealing to him, 'Rock a Tock' reminding him of a rock & roll band in Ballina. He won, pocketing $20.00 and recouping his original $5.00. I bought raffle tickets for prizes I didn't want. We watched belly dancers sway to enticing music and then found a seat to listen to the performing artists on stage. Happy hour, food, wine, and chatter followed.

Sunday dawned.

My friend Jeannie and I drove into Tara town, wandering in and out of little shops, soaking up the town's vibe. Val, my clairvoyant friend who attended Temple Byron, advised me to buy a Citrine (yellow quartz crystals). Her advice...

'Place one into the furthest left-hand corner of your home from the front entry.' This action, she explained, provides:

'*communication, clarity and vitality.*'

I found the perfect piece at a Crystal New Age shop. Val also suggested putting three gold coins under the mat at your entrance for abundance.

Baz and Graham had taken the bus into town, and we sat together outside the local bakery, enjoying coffee and cake in the winter sunshine. The weather was lovely, not as cold as expected. Later in the afternoon, we discussed the route home. Baz and I preferred to stay out one more night 'free camping' on the way back. We had no idea of the fateful events to come.

As is the norm, Little Molly attracts plenty of favourable recognition. Wherever we stay, Molly fascinates people with the fact that such a small, compact caravan has so many features: an en-suite with a vanity, shower, and toilet; a built-in wine bar; hanging space wardrobe; large storage areas; an added fold-away table; an oven; a fridge; a microwave; and more. Many people received the guided tour. Baz and I decided, after selling the Winnebago, to stop travelling. When we saw Little Molly in a paddock on the way to Lismore, we fell in love with her and placed a deposit on the spot.

We sat at Happy Hour reading a variation of the traditional Tarot cards. **'Animal Magic Transference Healing Cards'**

I purchased them just a week ago when I attended the Moon Meditation group. This gathering helped me familiarise myself with the cards. I may never have embarked on this journey had I been better at reading the cards a few days prior to the trip. Only in hindsight do the cards become crystal clear.

Monday, 3 August 2015

I stood at the sink after breakfast in Little Molly while Baz packed up outside. I thought to myself, why? Why do we leave Ballina? Paradise, beaches, and green rolling hills are places where people from all over Australia and the world visit, only to end up in a dust bowl for the weekend. I expressed these concerns to Baz as we drove out of the showground gates.

I didn't enjoy the weekend since Baz's snoring had been chronic. Getting a good night's sleep was impossible in such a small space.

At 9:10 a.m., I reached for the Sat Nav and pressed the home button. Instantly, a horrendous noise erupted in my eardrums; the whole car shook and shuddered. My racing mind thought... "We've been hit by a truck!"

"OMG! What was that?"

"It's a Roo!!"

Moments before, Baz had spotted the large kangaroo as it hopped across the road, heading directly towards the car. After getting out of the car, we examined the damage. Shocked, Baz said...

"Look at the caravan!"

There was a gaping hole where the large front picture window had been. As I walked to the caravan and peered through the hole, I immediately realised that the big grey roo was inside, sprawled on the kitchen floor – an unwelcome visitor.

I flagged down a car and told him what had happened. Soon, other people surrounded us—travellers, hugging us in shocked disbelief! The young man stepped into the caravan and cleaned up the blood and bits of shattered debris. Meanwhile, our close friends, passing by the scene, stopped.

Jeanie says:

"What happened?"

"A Roo hit us! It's in the caravan."

The helpful young man says:

"Would you like me to take the Roo out?"

I'm relieved; I don't want Baz to have that job. Half afraid it might still be alive. He dragged the dead kangaroo out of the door by its tail, bouncing it over the steps to the ground. My heart reached out when I saw it lying there.

'Oh! poor thing.'

I dropped to my knees and placed my Reiki hands on the warm, soft, furry body, gazing at the badly battered and bloodied face.

Someone said, 'Take photos for insurance.'

Baz was at the front of the caravan with a group of people, pondering their next move, when someone else spoke up:

'No! You can't tow the caravan, it's too dangerous.'

My mobile phone, which had been out of range all weekend, couldn't even get an SOS. Jean and Graham stayed with us for three hours; luckily, Jeanie's phone worked. We spent the next hour and a half on the phone with GIO Insurance, detailing the accident while they completed the paperwork. During the drama, I realised there was substantial damage to the car as well. Confused by the amount of glass on the back tray and inside the vehicle, a woman pointed out, saying:

'The Roo smashed the back driver's side door and window, before catapulting into the front of the caravan.

The Kangaroo had missed Baz's head by centimetres.

Baz and Graham taped the smashed window with a tarp and duct tape.

Jeannie said:

"Look at you. You are not crying. You are so calm."

Gratefully, I replied:

"It's just a car and caravan, and we are alive! It could have been so much worse."

I was focused, getting on with transferring my personal items from the caravan to the car.

The GIO advised us against driving the car, as it was not roadworthy without the driver's mirror and tail lights. Baz insisted, convinced that we would be fine. We limped back to Toowoomba, leaving Little Molly on a farmer's property beside the accident scene. A tow truck would collect it later in the day.

In Toowoomba, we bought a small cosmetic mirror from Chemist Warehouse to replace the damaged driver's mirror and make driving easier. Feeling mentally fatigued, we checked into a motel.

I texted both our kids, Naomi and David, to tell them about the horrendous accident, and Dave rang back saying:

You had to know I'd ring immediately after sending a text like that!

I described the accident to him, still holding back tears.

When Nomi calls, her comment is, "Oh my God!"

We're having dinner at the Motel restaurant and don't want to drive the damaged car at night.

I couldn't sleep, seeing the dead kangaroo's bloodied and battered face when I closed my eyes. Instead, I sat up in bed all night. I watched television, but I wasn't concentrating or absorbing anything. My mind is numb. Baz is snoring beside me.

Tuesday dawned.

When we arrived at the crash repairer, he told us in no uncertain terms: "It is a write-off!"

We took out more personal items from the van. Then we walked away, not looking back. Holding onto each other, we paused to hug, both in tears.

Toowoomba, Queensland, is situated at the top of the 'Great Dividing Range.' As Baz drove down the steep mountain road with a 10% gradient, the steering wheel vibrated, and we realised the car might have sustained mechanical damage. The insurance company offered us a hire car as part of the insurance policy, but Baz declined, wanting to get home quickly. Exhausted from the trauma and lack of sleep, I said:

"Now you will kill us in the car just because you didn't want to take any advice!"

Ballina was a long drive home.

Wednesday dawned.

I rang my dearest cousin Annie to relate the accident, tears flowing when describing how I placed my hands onto the soft, warm body of the dead Roo.

The following week was exhausting. I had to repeat the story to shock and concern friends and family. Sleep evaded me, and I ran on adrenaline. Reiki and meditation are becoming my saviours. My healing hands are soothing and comforting.

I phoned Peter, the local UK Caravan Importer from whom we bought Molly, and a UK Bailey caravan agent in Gympie, Queensland, sending them graphic photos of the accident scene via email. Each doubts whether the parts are available and whether the damage is too extensive. In denial, we refused to accept the obvious.

On Tuesday, we shopped at Aldi, stocking up on food for the fridge and pantry. The car would be away for repair. I sat with my feet flat on the floor, waiting while Baz returned the trolley. The motor wasn't running, but distinct vibrations were coming through the floor. It was strange; they were travelling through my boots, into the soles of my feet, and up my legs. When Baz returned, I asked him if he could feel it.

He said: "No."

"Strange you can't feel it, it's so strong!"
Insight: Einstein showed us...
"We are made of atoms, energy, vibration."

Part of who I am is that I pick up energy vibrations. I search for reasons in my mind. The car was shuddering! Perhaps it was delayed shock waves resonating through my body. I know life is an illusion—atoms and particles vibrating into existence. However, I found it challenging to grasp this concept.

Friends came to our rescue, and we borrowed a small car while ours was being repaired. Exactly one month later, GIO Insurance advised that Little Molly had been declared a write-off. The money will be transferred into our bank account. We returned to Toowoomba with heavy hearts to collect more items that weren't damaged in the accident. It was worse to see our dear little caravan so battered, exposed to the elements, dirty and untidy, sitting in a paddock with other bashed and damaged vehicles.

THE POWER OF THE UNIVERSE

The Universe's display of power was awe-inspiring. It demonstrated how easily Barry could have been taken from us; he could have been killed so effortlessly. The kangaroo missed his head by centimetres, allowing us to continue our lives together.

While recounting the scene to my cousin Annie, the emotional weight of the kangaroo's death hit me hard. The memory of its body beneath my hands and the bloody, battered face broke me. I couldn't help but cry, my voice catching as I shared this with her.

The first reading of the Tarot Cards I purchased before heading off to Tara on July 30, 2015, foretold the event.

First card drawn... THUNDERBIRD Lightning Spirit, Guardian Spirit. The Thunderbird acts as a servant to the Great Spirit, the Universe. It serves as a conduit to forces that defy understanding. Divine messenger.

Second Card: THE BUFFALO Key Word: Sacrifice. The Roo represented the sacrifice, allowing us to live in the moment truly.

Third Card: GARGOYLE Key word: Guardian Protector. Divine Protection.

The Message: In an instant, our life as we know it could have shattered. Instead, we walked away unharmed, under divine protection.

'Transference Healing Animal Magic' *Earth, Mythical and Elemental Animal Magic Ascension Cards* Copyright © owned, published and distributed in Australia by Transference Healing® Pty. Ltd., www.transferencehealing.com.[1]

---

1.   http://www.transferencehealing.com/

SENTINELS ~ STANDING STONES

September 22, 2015 ~ Equinox Celebration

S I travel to Tyagarah, a private property north of Byron Bay, NSW, for the Equinox Celebration, a sacred ceremony around a circle of 'Standing Stones.'

Twenty-two is the Master Number in Numerology, representing balance. Coincidentally, 22 people attended the ceremony: 11 women and 11 men, symbolising the balance of masculine and feminine energies. The theme of the Equinox is complete balance.

An ancient mango tree, *along with natural running spring water, Yin, is* on the property. Yin and Yang. Male and Female. Light and Dark. As Above, so Below.

WOW! NOTHING is by CHANCE!

As I ascend a stone stairway, I enter through a Portal Archway. The standing stones resemble sentinels guarding this sacred earth, adorned and draped with silk ribbons in the colours of the rainbow. An aura of mysticism envelops the scene. As the full moon rises in the darkened sky, we sing and dance around the standing stones. The words to the song...

'When I See Thee, I See Me, (for we are One). When I look into your Eyes, I see Love.'

My inner voice replies... *'Yes! Light & Love.'*

We share food in the evening and gather around a campfire, accompanied by the sounds of guitar, drums, singing, and chanting. It's magical!

DETACHMENT

In the process of living, learning to detach is a crucial aspect of life. Letting go externally deepens our inner connection to the soul. One cannot 'detach' until one has experienced pain, loss, grief, and love. When these emotions become part of who we are, we can release them and detach without fear of consequences. Detachment is fundamental to overcoming anxiety and embracing every aspect of ourselves—everything we are, no fear, only love. We become at one with ourselves, feeling compassion for our fellow human beings and finding peace within.

Whilst visiting Chenrezig, the Tibetan Buddhist Study Centre and Meditation Retreat, I bought a small book and CD from the Dharma Shop entitled:

'Always Maintain a Joyful Mind.' Author Pema Chodron.

The author reminds us that we have a limited identity and will age. We shouldn't become obsessed with trying to stop our bodies from falling apart. Instead, we should embrace pain, endure it, and allow our hearts to soften, thereby awakening. Today, I write these words:

LIFE is a gradual letting go. Accept willingly that you can no longer achieve the feats you accomplished when you were younger. Rather than waging a battle against time, striving endlessly to maintain a fitness level that is no longer attainable, embrace a gentle acceptance of what is. A loving embrace. The final detachment.

ROSE QUARTZ CRYSTAL

N*ew Year 2016*
For two months, I've been carrying a 23kg Rose Quartz Crystal in the boot of my car. Good friends in South Australia asked me to bring it back to NSW, as they plan to sell it later this year at the Lismore Gem Festival. I hadn't considered buying it because I couldn't afford it. Then, I realised that the money I saved from teaching and giving Reiki was the perfect way to invest in Rosie.

I rearranged my meditation room, placing the unique rose quartz crystal in the centre of my altar alongside a selenite wand I bought when I visited Adelaide last year.

Saturday 23rd January 2016.

This morning, I tuned in and downloaded three dispensations offered via 'The Sirius Library,' which connects to the 'One Heart Portal.' The voices and chanting moved me into meditation, loving it as I spiralled into a purple, swirling flame, lifting my vibrations and pulsing 'The Light' into my Crown Chakra. I channelled this illumination throughout my body, through each chakra, connecting down into Mother Earth. Placing my hands upon the Rose Quartz Crystal, I repeated the words...

Bless you and thank you, bless you and thank you, bless you and thank you. We are One with All, and All is One. We, the Emissaries of the One Heart, give thanks for the privilege of serving in this sacred portal. Connect www.thesiriuslibrary.com[1]

---

1.   http://www.thesiriuslibrary.com/

FRUSTRATIONS & JOY

Today, the full moon in Virgo feels incredibly powerful for me since I was born under the zodiac sign of Virgo. It's also the Chinese Year of the Monkey, and I am a Monkey! I'm having trouble sleeping, as I often do around the Full Moon.

Last night, I had a dream. Baz woke me up, saying I was thrashing about. Colin had been on my mind. I recounted the dream during breakfast, recalling the details as I spoke.

Elanora Heights, NSW, the home we once owned in the 70s, was built high on a cliff overlooking Narrabeen Beach. Colin was sitting on the lounge room side of the servery, while Baz and I were facing him on the kitchen side. Colin held a mug in his hand, beige with brown writing on it, a favourite of mine. He was hitting the rim with something, and I said to him, 'What are you doing?' He handed it back laughing, having chipped the top of the drinking rim. It upset me. Colin then handed me another mug, the same colour, but with a hole in one side near the handle. I cannot understand why he thinks it's funny. The feelings I have in the dream are of extreme frustration, yet, realising Colin has passed over, I am overjoyed to see him, hugging and clinging onto him.

The insight I gain when translating this dream to Baz is one of frustration and joy. As a child, Col's pranks drove me to no end of frustration. I have dedicated April Fools' Day to my beloved brother. There was never a way I was the winner or perpetrator. As a small girl growing up, he always had the upper hand when it came to playing tricks, much to his delight. I had buried those annoyances and forgotten about them.

In this dream, they emerged, and I acted out their rage. Without any control, I was always the little sister, the butt of the joke, and he was the trickster, challenging me to laugh and let go.

Thank you for visiting me last night, Col. Even though it caused intense frustration, it's all part of the healing, letting go of control.

Whilst reading...

'Beyond Doorways: The Mysteries Revealed' Author Alexis Cartwright.

Alexis tells me..._At the time of my birth, **'Chiron',** the Planet of Healing, was in the astrological sign of Virgo._

I learn..._I came into this lifetime with 'control' as my core wounding._

Alexis says...

"You like to be in control, and you are usually a perfectionist...

The key term 'I Heal' is to 'lighten up', feel the joy."

My dearest brother, I absolutely adore your cheeky smile! As I write these words, I can still see your laughing eyes.

VALIDATION

April 9, 2016
          The most significant day of my life.
'The Voice of the Silence' by H.R. Blavatsky jumped off the shelf of my bookcase once again. Recommended to me when I was 32, it opened today to pages 21-2, and I read:

Behold! Thou hast become the 'Light'
Thou hast become the Sound
Thou art thy Master & thy God
Thou art Thyself, the object of Thy search
The Voice unbroken that resounds
throughout eternities
Exempt from change, from Sin exempt.
The seven sounds in one,
The Voice of the Silence
Om Tat Sat

WOW! My heart wept with joy and gratitude. The cycle is complete. I have reached the pinnacle of my life, as validated by the text I was shown today. It has taken 40 years, from the age of 32 to 72.

"Om Tat Sat is the most effective purification tool and the supreme awakening."

Lord Krisna Wikipedia

KRIYA

Over the years, during meditation, I've noticed involuntary bodily movements. The spiralling, pulsing of 'The Light', pendulum body swinging from side to side, balancing. Someone called them 'Kriya.' I Googled the word and found:

Wikipedia: "KRIYA, a Sanskrit word.

The outward physical manifestation of awakened Kundalini includes spontaneous body movements associated with the flow of Kundalini.

Initially, there were erratic jerks in different parts of my body. As the years have progressed, I realise my body flows smoothly into meditation. By surrendering to my 'highest self', 'kriya' transpires without any conscious decision from the mind or body. Down, down, spiralling down. The right and left hemispheres of my brain come into balance, swinging like a pendulum, then spiralling up, up, up through my Crown Chakra, neck extended, head elevated. Experiencing rapturous states of 'bliss' in an ecstatic, expanded consciousness. Absent from my earthly body, my brain 'explodes' in light; I am One with 'The 'Light', I am Light' in an overwhelming luminescent space, surrounded by pure love, tears of joy, at peace....

Perfect harmony, the 'Golden Mean Ratio - Phi.'

In the description in 'Autobiography of a Yogi', Paramahansa Yogananda says Kriya is: "The secret key used to escape into 'Spirit'.

It is the Ultimate Gift! My Life is full of Gratitude.

WESAK 2016

It is the eve of Wesak, the most sacred day in the spiritual calendar. Yesterday, I attended Temple Byron to participate in a community service event. Temple Byron is a high-frequency portal that invokes Ascended Masters, Angels, and Archangels. It is a healing space where we provide hands-on healing, sing mantras, and play harmonic crystal bowls for approximately 75 participants or more who arrive each Wednesday night.

Before leaving for the Temple this morning, I look at a photograph Colin took many years ago—a black-and-white study of a spider's web, dripping with morning dew. Col was a talented photographer. While meditating, the spider's web surfaces in my mind. At the end of the meditation, I listen to Ave Maria in Latin. In my ultimate joyful connection with the Divine, my thoughts flash to Mama. I have achieved everything she ever wanted me to achieve; all she ever prayed for has come to pass. Maybe not in the precise 'Catholic' manner she desired, but the peaceful serenity that surrendering to the 'All That Is' brings is mine to behold. I am attending the 'Oneness Blessing' at the Red Yoga Tent in Byron Bay tonight, NSW. The 'Golden Orb Meditation' envelops me in bliss, guiding me into 'The Light', and tears of joy flow.

WESAK dawns. I picked up Kate, my friend from Byron Bay. We arrive in the picturesque town of Mullumbimby, greeted on the road by the majestic sight of Mount Chincogan, towering 309m above the little town. With the help of her iPhone, Kate directs the way. After a left-hand turn, we begin the ascent. The mountain road deteriorates, turning into a track. The Golf Turbo GT is struggling for traction, as it's not built for Aussie mountain roads. Much happier on a German autobahn. Urgh! Loose stones, OMG! At the top, as I step out of the car, I take a deep breath, releasing the tension that had been building up.

We settle into a large circle outside, introducing ourselves and stating our relevance to one another. I tell the group that El'mara (the Hostess), Kate, Carlos, and I are part of the Divine University Healing team at Temple Byron, where we provide community service each Wednesday night. Everyone is welcome.

The property boasts breathtakingly spectacular views. El'mara is playing a Crystal Bowl within the Meditation Circle of Light. The following ceremony unites us, directing us to face North, South, East, and West as we watch the sun set behind the mountain range. Trancing into deep meditation, my silhouette becomes the focus for visualisation. In my mind's eye, I see an amazing crystalline image sitting in a meditation pose directly in front of me, recognising it as my own Ethereal Angelic Self.

After the ceremony, we share food, coming together to exchange experiences of synchronicity and magic with like-minded folks. 'Souls in Synch.' I feel an increasing awareness of the necessity to form circles to raise consciousness and enhance 'The Light' on this little planet we call Earth.

Not looking forward to descending the mountain in the dark, say to Carlos:

"I will follow you!" he replies

"I was going to follow you!"

"OK, I will take it slowly!".

Trusting, I send my fears up to the Universe. It's easier to travel downhill. I can't see the dangerous drop-offs, which is a crucial factor that significantly influences my attitude. All is good.

NUMEROLOGY

Wikipedia Numerology meaning:
Numerology: The Ancient Mystical Study of Numbers Offering Understanding and Insight Into Oneself, Others, and Situations.

Today, Kate, a Numerologist, and I did an 'Energy Exchange.' I taught her Reiki, and she gave me a Numerology Reading.

There is so much more to Numerology than I ever imagined. The frequencies and numbers shift each time, for instance, when I changed my name from my maiden name to my married name, and then again when I adopted Christa as my spiritual name. Kate read my blueprint for each name, validating my life as it had unfolded. Each name represents a 3. Three threes. Wow!! Those 3s are present in my life again!

Afterwards, as we drive to Temple Byron, Kate inputs Baz's numbers into her phone. Baz has two sets of 11 and 66 and is considered a "Master" in Numerology. Wow! That's interesting. Baz is a 'Master.'

When Baz and I met in 1961, we were both in a six vibration; I was in 6, and Baz was in 66, which explains the attraction. Kate says:

"You were always meant to be together!"

EQUINOX ~ Full Moon In Pisces

M ercury, my ruling planet, has been in retrograde for three weeks. 'Communication Breakdown!' (there's an old song of that name!). Now, being aware of this fact, I have indeed been experiencing a communication breakdown. My computer is causing me grief, and I had an argument with Baz. He is usually calm, but he stormed out of the room in anger.

Bev De Vere has suspended the monthly Full Moon Meditations without providing an explanation. I will miss the meditations tremendously if they come to an end. Bev is a fantastic facilitator, and the group's energy is divine. It elevates me to great heights and allows me to fully integrate with my Highest Self.

I sit on my meditation stool in lotus position (as much as I can these days, with the stiffness of old age in my bones) in front of the altar, appreciating the beauty and peacefulness of my sanctuary. The picture window opens up to the garden beyond and the clear blue sky. I pick up each of my small crystals, hold them, examine them, and marvel at them. Then, I play 'Hari Om Tat Sat' and sing the chorus, which is my way of celebrating this special spiritual day. I would like to express my gratitude for the assistance I received last week, which enabled me to complete the children's Yogi book I plan to give to my daughter for Christmas, entitled 'Yogi ~ The Most Famous Dog in the World'.

My friend Anita read the book yesterday. As she read, she laughed and shed a few tears. Wow! That was such a great reaction. Anita mentioned she loved giving me honest feedback, which was truly encouraging.

My daughter Naomi has bred Hungarian Vizsla dogs for most of her adult life. Yogi was the gift she received in recognition of her dedication and devotion. Yogi won the ultimate prize: 'Crufts' 2010 - UK, the world's most prestigious Dog Show. That is another story.

VIRGO ABUNDANCE

After service tonight, Kaliana, Illumina, and I walk together to the gardens, where we meet Paul, the founder of Temple Byron. I note that the four of us are all Virgos. Paul, referring to the beauty surrounding us, says: "Well, you all relate to this."

Temple Byron spans 3 acres of a tropical paradise, encircled by sublime, Zen-inspired gardens, crystals, and sacred geometry. Truly magical.

Then Shri'amaia, one of the other Healers, arrives. Paul jokingly says: "This is a Virgo-only meeting!"

Paul comments that 'Chiron' is the ruling planet of Virgo.

As I drive into Byron Bay to meet the other Healers at a favourite café for Rama's birthday celebration, my brain goes into 'monkey mind chatter.'

Chiron Again! Will this ever end? How can this be! It is unbelievable.

This morning, I Googled:

'Chiron the True Ruler of Virgo' and print off the findings:

'Clearly, Chiron has an affinity with Virgo. Indeed, in many ways, it appears to be redefining Virgo and helps clarify some intense characteristics of this sign that Mercury, the traditional ruler, does not satisfactorily explain:

The focus, the dedication to service, the passion for teaching and healing, the depth of intelligence, the long-term commitment, and above all, the revolutionary spirit that seems to pour forth from Virgo...

You exemplify someone I've met many times who embodies this Chiron aspect of Virgo. Some of the most revolutionary women I've known, alongside some of the greatest healers, possess strong Virgo signatures.

Chiron appears to integrate these traits and qualities quite well; however, we must not overlook the Mary/Isis aspect of Virgo, the Goddess.

SPIRALLING TO THE LIGHT

This information gives me a deeper understanding of the metaphysical connection between my teenage love, Chiron, and me, and why we were drawn to each other all those years ago.

Quotes.www.planetwaves.net/cainer/archive/003530.php[1]http://cainer.com/ericfrancis/ aug5.htm-Astrology Secrets Revealed by Eric Francis

---

1.   http://www.planetwaves.net/cainer/archive/003530.php

RE-BIRTH

N *ew Year 2017*
        The birth of another year. Naomi, Andrew, and Aleisha arrive for a holiday. They have been living in Mumbai, India, since October 2015, when Naomi accepted a career promotion. It was lovely to see them; there were plenty of hugs.

The weather has been very hot and humid. They're staying in our caravan, parked in the driveway. Aleisha thinks it's a big cubby house, which is exciting! I reckon they may have regretted that decision, as there hasn't been a breeze, making it very difficult to sleep since there's no air conditioning in the caravan. They left today to stay at a resort on the Gold Coast, Queensland, and we will join them for two nights before they fly back to India.

This morning, I awoke with a vivid memory of a very realistic dream. I gave birth to a newborn baby painlessly and joyfully in water. After birthing,
Holding him close, feeling his little body next to mine.
"You are a boy!"
So vivid. So Magical. So Symbolic.

MEDITATIONS

The Divine University, Teaching Pillar, 'Yummy Studios' at Byron Bay, is holding a series of 22 meditations. I attend regularly when I'm not travelling, recording my thoughts and feelings.

The Facilitator: 'Ra'Shiym Christos, Mentor and Teacher, Divine University & Counsellor of Light.' The first in the series tonight is entitled... 'LOVE.'

The greatest vibration. Sheer power. Our manifestation into this human. vehicle is driven by desires, needs, and wants to love and be loved. It is the emotion that drives us as Humans.

I will give Reiki to my friend Jenny two days after this meditation.

Jenny enjoys reading the 'Spirit Oracle' cards. After the session, these two cards jump out.

"Love can transform and change our lives; all it requires is faith, which gives love power."

"There is a flame within your heart, a light that stems from the dawn of time. Ancient love and ancient knowledge are being rekindled. Close your eyes and feel the love inside you. Allow it to flow into your life and watch all transform to light."

WISDOM

The second Meditation in the series is titled *'WISDOM.'*
People form a circle, with some lying down, while others sit in a meditation pose or on chairs. Ra'Shiym's voice carries me away into deep meditation, spiralling me into 'The Light', connecting totally with his words, afterwards I write:

"Ancient Wisdom. Knowing. Clarity. Alignment is the Key. All these things I am, for I am the Manifestation of these spoken words. Divine Oneness."

Why, I ask myself, have I been given this powerful gift? Why not? Comes the answer from my higher voice: You are a conduit through which this Power, this Love, this Light flows, grounding it into Mother Gaia. A realisation when Ra'Shiym says:

"There is a Master before you."

The prayer I write down and place under the Rose Quartz Crystal on the altar is...

"That Master is I."

I express my gratitude for total alignment, ancient knowledge, wisdom, and inner knowing. Last night's meditation indelibly imprinted on my psyche.

I am my Master. I am my Divinity.

DIVINITY

Third Meditation in the series Ra'shiym says:
"Get comfortable, it will be full on tonight."
I hear my inner voice give assurance: 'it's ok, it's you, it's what you do!'
The meditation connects with a small, innocent child. No! I have no connection. There's a sense of nothingness, no feelings at all.

After the meditation, I reflected on my abandonment and forgiveness issues concerning my father. I found myself, in a way, always searching for him, recalling little from before I turned seven. The emotions were more evocative then. I had a strict, domineering mother. If anyone asked about my father, I was to reply:

"I lost my father in the War." My Mother did not see this as a lie.

Mama was right, though this statement suggests he was killed in the War when, in fact, he abandoned us for another woman—divorce and separation are taboo subjects, rarely spoken about.

Over the years, Reiki energy has connected me to my heart centre on a profound level. Emotionally, spiritually, and physically, it brings pain and hurt to the surface, facilitating healing and growth. I no longer wish to connect with a child, whether for the sake of innocence, security, or any other reason. I realised this was why I initially stepped back; the meditation clarified this.

I have placed my trust in the Universe, the Higher Force. I am now at peace... where I need to be at this stage of my life.

ONE with Divinity.

FAITH

A small group of dedicated meditators gathers at Yummy Studios each week to listen to and engage in meditations that cover all the essential aspects of life. Tonight, we meditate on 'FAITH.' Faith transcribes for me:

Surrendering to 'The Light', trusting in Source, the energy, highest self, oneness, and God within. Knowing uniqueness, beauty, and divinity.

FAITH to Know: 'We are part of a Greater Plan within the Universe.'

FAITH as described in...

'Gateway to The Divine Tarot' Ciro Marchetti's *Major Arcana Card is an evocative depiction of Faith. Four religious figures face the golden light of the Divine, seeking union through worship:*

A Tibetan Monk

A Jewish Rabbi

A Catholic Pope

A Muslim Imam

"Too often throughout history, these differences have been a cause of conflict, prejudice, and war... Despite these variations, the central column of light is the source of their worship.

Their FAITH shines through as the common denominator of all. Uniting All as One."

Paraphrased from Gateway to the Divine Tarot Copyright © 2009 Ciro Marchetti Llewellyn Publications.

SERVICE

Tonight's Meditation is based on...
    'SERVICE.'
I've found that when our hearts and souls overflow, we naturally step into serving others.

As I kneel and place my Reiki hands on those receiving healing on the floor of Temple Byron to provide service, the gratitude from which I draw breath daily pours forth.

I recall the words from the first 'Rune Reading' given on December 26, 1998...

"After the nourishment of your soul comes the possibility of nourishing others, not out of need but from overflowing. Only then can an equal exchange of energy take place."

'Zen Rune Copyright © Element Books 1998 Text © Maria Letizia Renzulli 1998

COMMUNION

Tonight's meditation at Yummy Studios, Byron Bay is entitled: *'COMMUNION.'*

It is the sixth in the series.

Tuning into meditation, I feel a potent, powerful energy rippling through my body, accompanied by intense pressure behind my third eye.

Throughout the ninety minutes, spiralling, balancing, pulsing in and out of 'The Light', I find myself in a euphoric, tearful, blissful mood, acknowledging...

Total Communion with...
Highest Self.
Communion with All.
Oneness.
Compassion.
Gratitude.

CHARITY

Today, Ra'shiym hands each of us a $5.00 note, telling us to ... "Sit with it, hold it, imbue energy into it. Then go forth, give it to someone in need." Memories come flooding into my brain.

Reminiscing... When I was ten, the ship stopped at Ceylon (now Sri Lanka) on my way to Australia from England. My mother had befriended a Salvation Army family member on board who had a daughter the same age as me. The family had visited before and escorted us around the city of Colombo. As tourists, small children surrounded us, running alongside and begging for money. I see them now in my mind's eye as I write these words, sixty-odd years later. Skinny legs and arms, gaunt little faces, big eyes looking at me. The Salvation Army friend says:

'Do not give them money.' I can't understand why.

We visited a Buddhist temple, stooping to remove our shoes before entering. The Buddhist monks bowed, handing me white and yellow fragrant flowers from the altar. They are Frangipanis. I have not seen them before, but I love them. They have held a special place in my heart, becoming the flowers of my wedding bouquet years later.

During my 20s (around the mid-to-late 60s), a massive charitable campaign unfolded in Sydney, Australia. I believe it was 'Freedom from Hunger', though I'm not entirely sure—TV advertising, door-to-door visits, and so on. I donated money, thinking it would aid the starving millions, only to discover later that the campaign's proceeds had been embezzled. The funds were used to build a mansion at Harbord, near Manly Beach, in the northern suburbs of Sydney. I closed my heart, refusing to give to charity for many years.

In the early 1980s, I attended a sales conference in Bali. I had been shopping and holding onto notes after just purchasing some clothes.

A skinny older man sat cross-legged on the footpath with a rag in front of him, holding a few coins. My heart went out to him. As I walked past, I dropped a note (probably $10.00 AUS), looking back to smile at him. I will never forget the look on his face. He was euphoric. I received a special gift that day: the gift of happiness. It was the best $10.00 I ever spent, a reminder of the joy of giving.

In 2013, Baz and I celebrated our 50th Wedding Anniversary by visiting Shanghai, China. I focus on giving to people in need. A man sitting on the sidewalk has been horrendously burned and disfigured. I hug him and give him money, treasuring the smile he gives me in return. Baz says:

"You can't give to everyone!"

Ra'Shiym's $5 note, carefully tucked in a separate compartment of my wallet, held special significance. I was always mindful of its intended purpose. One day, as I drove around the roundabout on my town's main street, I spotted two young buskers, one with a plaster cast on his arm.

As I parked the car, the song finished. Smiling, I asked them to keep singing and playing the guitar for me. After we chatted, one of them mentioned he needed money for a bus fare home to Sydney. I shared the story of being given a $5.00 note for someone in need, telling him he was that person. The three of us hugged, and I walked away with a smile. Thank you, Ra'Shiym.

NEED to GROUND

This morning, I emailed the Divine University Healing Team to advise them that I will arrive later than usual. I need to receive healing instead of giving it due to a fall I had on Monday. I'm feeling a bit scattered. The doctor advised that I have melanoma on my shoulder; I've been burying my head in the sand. Paul at Temple Byron mentioned that he also experienced a fall on Monday, hurting his leg, and he heard of several others who fell on the same day. I recount the story of these coincidences to Rama, another healer. Rama explains:

'You need to ground. Monday was full moon, and the energy was very forceful.'

Kylama, one of the Divine University healers, asks me:

"Why did you fall?"

I tell him about the melanoma biopsy. He places his hands on me while I lie on the floor, giving myself Reiki. Kylama's light language resonates with Reiki 'Dai Ko Mio'—our spirits blend. After the healing session, Kylama informs me that he has:

"cleared the blockage in my head."

I can't sleep, which annoys Baz as I get out of bed, my inner voice says:

'Google Melanoma to learn the statistics if the Doctor returns with a positive result.' I've been resisting my natural tendency to research. Instead, I try to block it out. No wonder I've fallen. This is counteracting the healing Kylama gave me. When I print the information, I feel better and more capable, standing in my POWER again. Wow! There are always more lessons to learn. The biopsy results prove to be benign.

INNOCENCE

On the way to Yummy Studios, tonight's meditation is titled *'INNOCENCE.'*

Thoughts of my teenage years skitter around. Times, venues, people, places. Pictures so real I say out loud:

"OMG! All these years later, and you are still there!"

I thought to myself, "How incredible is our brain? It is a storehouse of images, available on impulse—it is better than a computer!"

I dedicated this meditation to Chiron, my first love, as he is part of the images that came to mind while driving here. We have travelled this journey together and apart. Apart for most of our lives in this lifetime; as much as I try to block memories, they emerge uninvited and unaided. It is a love from another time, another place—two spiritual souls recognising each other from infinity. A mystical, magical place. A love and hurt that needed to be healed, brought out into the light, and set free.

During the meditation, I had a vision...

Remembering a time with Chiron... a luminous full moon, ripples of moonlight reflecting on a lake, a stolen kiss, a period of total idyllic, innocent young Love.

Thank you, Chiron, for being part of my soul family and returning briefly to illuminate the missing pieces of my life. You allowed my soul to soar free, elevated my healing to a new level, and enabled my transformation into a teacher.

EXPANSION

Thursday, 1 June 2017

On the first day of winter in Australia, I am rugged up in a warm scarf and gloves as I drive to Byron Bay for tonight's meditation, *'Expansion.'*

As Ra'shiym guides us through the meditation, my mind flits back to that first day, seventeen years ago, when I sat in a meditation circle on my camp chair at the motorhome rally in Warragul, Victoria. I once again experience a feeling of expansion from within, followed by the spiralling of my body as I am transported into Light, Love, and total Bliss.

For me, expansion epitomises the catalyst and the beginning of my spiritual journey. After that, I find myself seeking answers and wondering: "What happened to me on that day?" "Why did it happen?"

Now I've been given the answers to my questions. The words I write at the end of tonight's meditation are:

The Remembrance. The Recognition.
The Re-Connection. The Knowing.
I am the Divine Light, Divine Energy.
I am a conduit connecting the source to Mother Gaia
I am All I Need to Be. Blessed Be, Blessed Be, Blessed Be.

ASTROLOGY ~ NATAL CHART

Temple Byron's Sacred Space for Spiritual Practices and Personal Transformation'

On 13 April, I visited Paul Margolin, the Founder and Consulting Astrologer at Temple Byron in Byron Bay.

'Paul combines Western Astrology with Ancient Vedic Astrology using a unique method of incorporating very different forms to give a comprehensive and deep interpretation of the birth chart, life cycles, and future transits.'

Paul and I 'Exchange Energy.' Paul reads my Natal Chart in exchange for me giving him Reiki in the tranquil Meditation and Healing Space at Temple Byron.

Synopsis:

SUN, JUPITER – The best!

Paul tells me...

'Many astrologers would love to have your chart!'

With 6 Virgo planets in the 12th House—the House of Spirit and self-undoing—you carry the mark of an old soul. After lifetimes of healing yourself, now is the time to heal others. You are exactly where you're meant to be, as you've intentionally placed yourself there for a good reason.

Your Vedic and Western charts share a similar nature. Service.

In this life, I have been entrusted with the sacred duty of looking after Baz's soul. He cared for me in a past lifetime, and now it's my turn to reciprocate.

Karma balances the energies of the past and helps you step up spiritually, more than you ever thought possible. The powerful Uranus Energy will work in your unique way. There will be...

RECOGNITION, JOY, BLISS, PURPOSE.

These are the gifts from my spiritual journey, the rewards of my growth. Paul writes me a testimonial...

My name is Paul Margolin. I own and run Temple Byron, a healing centre in Byron Bay.

I have had many healing sessions with practitioners over the last two decades.

Christa Fleming stands out as an incredibly talented healer in many ways. She is a beautiful, heart-centred person whose main motive is to help others, and she has dedicated her life to doing so.

I found her sessions to be very powerful and even life-changing.

I would always recommend a session with Christa to anyone genuinely interested in healing.

Regards, Paul Margolin

templebyron@icloud.com - www.templebyron.com[1]

---

1.   *http://www.templebyron.com*

LESSON LEARNT

While sitting in the autumn sunshine, sipping a cup of tea, my mobile phone rings inside the house. I jump from the chair, tangling my feet around the legs of the table, crashing down onto the tiles, twisting my knee.

In excruciating pain, I get on the medical roundabout: an MRI, a physiotherapist, an osteopath, and I spend weeks on crutches. The diagnosis? A torn meniscus in my left knee for the second time. This time, I didn't rush to the hospital for an arthroscopy or consider a knee replacement. Instead, I embarked on an intensive exercise programme to strengthen and repair damaged muscles and tendons. I now experience less knee pain than I have in 16 years.

The pattern repeats, and the cycle continues. The lesson learnt is that healing is not always a linear journey. It often involves setbacks and challenges; however, these present opportunities for growth and learning. Each time I encounter a new obstacle, I am reminded of the resilience and strength I have developed on my spiritual path.

GOODBYE VAL

This week marks the Full Moon, a significant event at Byron Temple, where the energy reaches its peak and the space is filled with nearly 100 people. I doubt we can fit anyone else in. This event occupies a special place in my spiritual journey, and I always look forward to the powerful experiences it offers.

Val, my friend the clairvoyant, and Eve, the lady who drives her to Temple Byron, sit on chairs as usual. I reconnected with them both before the ceremony, saying, 'I've missed you,' as they had been absent for the last few weeks. Val's insightful readings have been a guiding light in my journey. She says she is moving to Grafton to live. After the healing, Val approaches, excitedly telling me:

"When you came to me, there was a powerful white light, and something big will happen to you soon!"

We exchanged mobile phone numbers and hugged one more time.

I will miss her presence, her insights, her clairvoyance.

RECOGNITION

Today is a close friend's birthday, and the six of us are celebrating with lunch at Ballina Golf Club. It is also the anniversary of Mama's funeral, which was twelve years ago.

Later in the day, when I attended Byron Temple, I walked from the car park, soaking in the tranquil beauty of the gardens, the crystals, the many statues, and the lights in the trees. I feel happy, bending to remove my shoes as I enter this sacred space.

Before the altar, with raised arms, I call forth the Masters, surrendering; euphoria overflows. I choose to meet and greet, welcoming everyone as they enter through the door. There are plenty of hugs and familiar faces. The incredible ecstasy continues.

Anna is 81 years old and a regular. She recently had a fall and tells me she has been in a lot of pain.

"You touched me in all the places where I had pain, my knees, feet, and chest! Thank you."

Lelama, one of the Healers, comes after the session, telling me she will be away until December and saying:

"You are amazing, I looked at you walking around bringing 'Light' to everyone. Thank you."

I think Lelama is amazing; she has had a significant influence on my life. Many years ago, I had the privilege of attending her sound workshops, where her angelic voice resonated in the Lotus Temple, inspiring me deeply. This experience was profound, and I held her in the highest regard. Now, she is thanking me, a moment of unexpected validation.

I recall Paul Margolin's words when he read my Astrological Natal Chart, saying:

"They will recognise you for the work you do."

SPIRALLING TO THE LIGHT

Today, I stand acknowledged and validated by someone I deeply respect and admire. I express my gratitude to the Universe for guiding me to this point, for shaping me into this divine conduit, this vessel. Driving home on the freeway, I am on a spiritual high, embracing the happiness that fills me with a sense of contentment. Then, there arises a mild apprehension and a fluttering thought. I'm not sure; I cannot grasp it. As soon as I walk through the door, I know! I get the look from Baz. He is angry. I ask if he has eaten. In reply to my question -

"No! I haven't eaten, I expected you home for tea!"

Last week I told my friend Shri'amaia:

'Baz is over all the anger.'

The Gods heard me boasting again. When am I going to learn?!!!

My elation is destroyed, gone in an instant. I choose not to explode, holding my peace, and just reply:

"It doesn't finish until 7.30 pm."

I am left depleted. One second euphoric, next empty. How can that be?

Later, I say to him in a calm voice:

"No one has the right to destroy another person's happiness."

BIRTHDAY REFLECTIONS

It is Thursday, the morning of 31st August 2017, my birthday. I wake up to the sound of the old clock in the vestibule striking five bells. Today marks my 73rd birthday. I get up to go to the loo; my knees and back are stiff and reluctant to move quickly. I snuggle back down into the warmth of my comfortable bed. I lie there reflecting on the previous evening. I had attended Temple Byron to provide service and healing, after which the Healing team drove a short distance to 'Yummy Studios' in the Byron Industrial Estate for a birthday dinner for Kaliana and me. A delicious meal follows: dahl, rice, date chutney, yoghurt, and coriander. A dozen of us sit around chatting, enjoying the food and each other's company. I sit next to Rama; he isn't feeling too well and thinks he's coming down with the flu, so he lay down on the Temple floor earlier tonight to receive. I attended to him first. He told me:

"Your healing is profound!"

After the main meal, Rama enters the room from the kitchen, carrying two small plates—one for Kaliana and one for me—each adorned with Lara's yummy homemade cake topped with a candle. She sings, "Happy Birthday." Rama then says:

"What do we love about Christa?" then says

"We love her healing hands." Others join in calling out:

"We love her kindness, the love she gives, her dedication to the Divine University, her youthfulness."

Shr'iamaia says

"Compassion and light she gives to everyone."

Ra'Shiym called

"Her knowing and wisdom." Our eyes held momentarily within that knowing.

I can't remember everything that was said, as I was overwhelmed with emotion. Expressing my sentiments, I'm grateful to be here with them all as 'spirits in synch.' This doesn't always apply to the rest of my daily life.

Shr'iamaia says:

"You are the go-between two worlds, showing others your Light."

It is a magical night, very Special.

THE FUR MUFF

It is 3:45 am. Baz is snoring; when I ask him to turn over, he sighs. I count the hours I've slept. Like him, I had fallen asleep in the armchair last night, which is a regular occurrence for Baz, but not for me. I struggle to keep my eyes open, drifting in and out of sleep, then drifting off again. Nothing is riveting on television until I finally rise stiffly from the chair. The clock in the entry vestibule strikes 9 pm as I snuggle into the warmth of my cosy bed. Upon estimating, I counted my sleep in the armchair and figured I'd slept about seven hours. It is still early, not yet daybreak. I pull the doona around my shoulders, sinking in and breathing deeply, my mind relinquishing and drifting into a meditative state from somewhere in my subconscious. I hear the words 'Chandos Park'. Where did they come from? I haven't remembered that name since I was a child. I'm taken back to when I was ten years old, back to the Muff.

My eyes are wide open now, and I hurry to get out of the warm bed. The urge is there; I must write the words flooding my brain before they disappear into the ether. I scribble on a notepad, bring the computer to life, make a cup of tea, and prepare some raisin toast.

Chandos Park is located in Stanmore, Middlesex, England, where I lived before moving to Australia in 1955. I Google it: There it is! Visions on the screen. However, there's a missing component—no image of the steps with small columns on either side. I can see them now in my mind's eye as I walk on them. As a little girl, it was a happy place—a place I enjoyed visiting with cousins, friends, and sometimes by myself. Memories flood back to me...

It is late afternoon in winter, with bare trees, a chill in the air, and a grey sky. I walk with my mother and another little girl, about the same age, who is walking alongside us—a friend's daughter. My mother stops me at the steps; her voice carries intensity. The other child skips ahead. My mother talks about my muff. I feel the softness of its fur and the warmth enveloping my small hands as I wiggle my fingers inside, experiencing a sense of protection. She cajoles me, enticing me to part with my beloved muff.

"She's poor, you won't need it in Australia!"

My mother and I walk up the steps to join her. The loss hits immediately. As I pull off the muff, my hands feel the icy cold air. I plunge them deep into the pockets of my coat. Oh, wow! I feel that loss as I write these words, sixty-three years later, also recalling the joy and happiness on her face as I handed the muff to her. It's strange; I do not remember her name.

I reflect... We were never wealthy in monetary terms. Was it a feeling my mother instilled in my psyche at the tender age of ten? She gifted me a rich spirit to carry throughout my life. Wow! Another piece of the puzzle falls into place.

The steps are symbolic...

*On that day, I ascended the steps between
the columns, through the Portal –
'As I Give, I Also Receive.'*

NIGHTMARE TRIP

Octber 2017
Another year is flying by. Baz and I had been away in the caravan, visiting our son, his family, and our grandchildren in Adelaide. I can only describe it as a disastrous trip. So many things went wrong. We purchased an old Holden Jackaroo four-wheel drive to tow the caravan, having previously used our son-in-law's Land Rover, which he had left with us while living in India for several years. In hindsight, driving halfway around Australia in an old vehicle we had just bought was foolish, especially since we didn't know its capabilities. On the first day out, towing a fully laden caravan up The Great Dividing Range, we encountered mechanical issues and reached Glen Innes, where a stressed mechanic told us: 'Get rid of it!'

He fitted a new fuel filter, and we continued our journey to Adelaide instead of turning back. Old Jack handles flat roads well; it's the climbs he dislikes. It reminds me of myself when I try to tackle hills or climb too many stairs. I get breathless and start panting, slowing down more and more as I ascend. Well, we made it to Adelaide. It was the return trip that truly put the icing on the cake. There was a steep uphill climb out of Adelaide, and we immediately ran into trouble. In Tailem Bend, I scrapped all plans for a sightseeing trip around South Australia. Ballina and home looked more appealing by the minute. The maps came out! Which route would involve the least climbing to get back over the Great Dividing Range, a mountain range spanning 3,500 km, the whole length of the East Coast of Australia? The Golden Highway from Dubbo through Muswellbrook and the Hunter Valley Wine Region seemed the least problematic. En route, we passed through the small Victorian town of Underbool. We spotted a Holden Dealer, but we kept driving. I hear my inner voice saying:

"Might be a good idea to do a U-turn."

The third time I heard the voice, I reckon we were about 15 km past Underbool.

"Baz, it might be a good idea to do a U-turn!!"

We spend three days by the roadside at a free camp while a mechanic works on the old Jackaroo. During that time, I shed a few tears. I still miss my dearest brother's counsel, wise words, and presence. He would have made me feel better. I share these feelings with Baz, and he replies:

"You do that for me, you are the strong one."

In exasperation, I reply:

"Who does it for me? Who do I turn to?"

In my heart is the answer to that question. My trust is in the Universe: I only need to ask.

Leaving Underbool three days later, we experienced a blowout on the caravan's tyre within two hours. We contacted Victorian Roadside Assist, and then three days later, the other tyre blew out. It was Sunday morning, and we were now in New South Wales, miles from anywhere. Fortunately, my mobile phone worked, so we waited two hours for NRMA Roadside Assist. All this stress had been making us both unhappy. I say:

"It is inconsequential; we are stressing and making ourselves unhappy about a car, a caravan, and a holiday. People are starving and dying in war-torn countries throughout the world. Other people are being diagnosed with life-threatening health problems, so in the whole scheme of things, it is all about nothing!"

Seeking, worrying, fearing, and being concerned about 'trivial' matters are all part of our 'human experience'. Our 'Quest' is to throw it up to the Universe, surrender, and trust. To sit in the eye of the storm and be at peace...

NOURISH YOUR SOUL, RECONNECT WITH YOUR TRUE ESSENCE

N *ew Year 2018*
I am invited to attend the 'Starlight Wellbeing Festival', Bangalow, as a Presenter, Lecturer, and Reiki Healer. My brochure reads:
'Nourish Your Soul & Reconnect with Your True Essence.'
Reiki 'Universal Life Force' ~ Spirit of Healing Energy.
Learn a Simple Hands-On Technique.
I give lectures on Thursdays and Sundays while also engaging in 'hands-on' Reiki healing sessions at the booth. After the lectures, I received positive feedback from many attendees, with several expressing interest in learning Reiki. A young couple from New Zealand expressed their gratitude for the lecture, saying:
"You are an inspiration."
Thank you. I express gratitude to the Universe. I am truly blessed. I feel incredibly rewarded when I see recognition and understanding in people's eyes and faces, and my words resonate within their souls, allowing them to suddenly 'get it.' It is so gratifying.
At the end of each session, I give out a lucky door prize: 'Free Reiki Hands on Healing Session.' The winner, a young man in his 20s, tells me that he decided that if he won the lucky door prize, he would book in and learn Reiki level 1.
Luca attends my 'Teaching Sanctuary' the following Thursday for private tuition.
Reiki Workshop:
'A Spiritual Journey to Self-Empowerment'

- **Become a Certified REIKI Practitioner.**

- Become Initiated & Attuned to REIKI Level I Energy
- Simple, easy 'hands-on' techniques
- Learn REIKI ethics
- Learn how to do a complete REIKI treatment
- Discover & Explore the benefits of Self-healing
- Immediately after the workshop, you can help friends and loved ones.
- Receive REIKI Level 1 Certificate
- Teaching and reference booklet

Luca and I had a wonderful day together. I taught Luca Reiki, initiating him with Level 1 Reiki Attunements and suggested he...

'Go Forth & Heal.'

'Your Work is to discover your World & then with all your heart give yourself to it.'

~ Buddha

NAMASTE

O n Sunday, as the 'Starlight Festival' winds down, I socialise with other stallholders, chatting and giving Reiki to Nicolas, a Spiritual Healer and Clairvoyant. He tells me:

This is your last lifetime. I'm being told you need to open up even more than you are!

OK, I fulfil that by baring my soul and writing this book.

Whilst browsing, I purchased a mystical set of Oracle cards entitled: 'NAMASTE, I see you. Oracle Cards & Guidebook.'

On January 11th, while I was meditating and giving thanks for my life, I randomly drew a card from the pack. Number 3! Since I was ten, threes have played an integral role in my life, particularly the number 33.

The card reads: 3 Leadership Namaste.

I see you drawing on your wisdom and communicating the seeds of love with others. 'Stop and look back upon the path you have journeyed; you have been through much and have become wiser and stronger because of it. This card calls you to step out and share your words of wisdom. You are a strong, protective leader who can shelter others during the storm. The Universe calls for you to shine your light so others may find their path. Shine with all the stars in heaven!'

Thank you; I hope to 'shine my light' by sharing the written words of this Book.

These beautiful words form the farewell song sung by the Divine University Healing Team to participants as they prepare to leave the Sound, Healing, and Blessing night, held each week at Temple Byron, Byron Bay, NSW, Australia.

'NAMASTE'

'Namaste, beautiful ones,
Blessed be your day
Blessed be your journey as you travel on your way
May you be protected and nurtured on your way
Surrounded by the love light to guide and light your way.
Ooh ooh beautiful ones, we sing you Namaste
Blessed be your journeys, blessed be your days,
Blessed be the love-light that guides and lights your way
Oh, Oh, beautiful ones
We sing you Namaste.

Copyright © 'Namaste' - Words channelled by 'Kaliana Raphael Rose'

ANALYSE CHARACTER

Finally, I'm reading a book that discusses energy, colours, and the expanded state of consciousness I experience. The author validates many aspects of my life. The book is entitled...

'Hands of Light' by Barbara Ann Brennan.

The book clarified and verbalised my life purpose, explaining why I chose my father to be my biological and absent father in this incarnation. Barbara Ann Brennan invites the reader to take part and discover their own:

Character Analysis and Defence Mechanisms. By examining the dynamics of five major categories, we reveal the blockages in the energy systems that lead to disease and illness.

Barbara Ann Brennan tells us that we can find the key to heal ourselves. I highly recommend reading this book if you're on a journey to discover your soul.

I define my central character:

My father's rejection of me in childhood is a contributing factor. Externally, everything seems perfect, but there's a sense that something is missing in life. How true that is! As I delve deeper into my character analysis, I'm told that eventually, a crisis will shatter my deepest convictions. The death of my beloved brother was meant to be this crisis.

I found it exciting to psychoanalyse my character this way and realise that I am on the right path. I am on the journey to knowing and loving my 'Higher Self,' the true me. The Author tells me about my Higher Self and my life's pathway...

'I have a deep connection to all, am one with all, and can enjoy life to the full.'

Meeting and marrying my husband as a teenager, we have stayed together. We have two wonderful, loving, successful adult children, three grandchildren, and two grandchildren adopted through marriage. We've travelled the world, enjoying many countries, living dreams, and loving life, which doesn't mean it was always idyllic. I spent years regretting the business decisions I made, living with those choices, often to the detriment of my health, and learning from them.

The worst period of my life was undoubtedly the loss of my brother, who represented not just my big brother, but also filled the role of my absent father. My brother's patience, knowledge, and willingness to share time with his little sister were remarkable. There was never a question I asked that he didn't answer thoroughly. I still miss his presence and wisdom.

My journey has brought me fulfilment, peace, joy, and a profound understanding of who I am and where I belong in the universe. This clarity allows me to recognise the wrongs in the world, often enabling me to see both sides of the story.

My heart goes out, and compassion flows for those who need love and care.

Paraphrased Reference & Knowledge gained from 'Hands of Light' Copyright © Barbara A. Brennan

LEARNING & KNOWLEDGE ~ 2018

This marked a period of renewed learning and growth for me. Early in the year, I signed up for several courses at Byron Bay Community College.

The first course I embarked on was 'MIND BODY BOOK,' a unique opportunity to unleash my inner storyteller and bring my book to life. Authors, Teachers Christina Larmer and Louise Sommer.

Once I enrolled and paid, I was motivated to finish my book. This course taught me the importance of time management, structure, and technique. I realised I still had a long way to go before the final page.

Followed by:

'SELF-PUBLISH YOUR BOOKS WITH AMAZON.'

"A DIY course on self-publishing online as an e-book and paperback." Author, Teacher Christina Larmer.

This course brought me closer to the realisation that my manuscript might one day become a reality. I applied the skills and knowledge I had learned. All the available time in my life is now dedicated to writing. I've concluded that writing 'the story' is the easy part. There is much more involved, including copyright permissions, bibliography, acknowledgements, and so on.

Further study: I regularly attend.

SOPHIA - The Byron Sofia Philosophical Study and Discussion Group, where I've lectured and taken part in group discussions.

AMITAYUS (Meaning: The Buddha of Limitless Life) – 'A Home Hospice Service: Last Aid – Caring for the Dying at Home.'

Earlier this year, I reached out to Byron College to express my interest in attending this course. Set to begin in October, it is expected to conclude in early 2019. I aspire to become an Amitayus Hospice Service Volunteer and contribute to the community by offering respite to carers of individuals who choose to die at home. The brochure reads...

"Practical, compassionate care and support for those who are palliative and wanting to die at home." As quoted from the AMITAYUS leaflet.

THE EYE OF THE STORM

F*ebruary 26, 2019*
   Today, my good health has faded away. I was diagnosed with an autoimmune condition...

'Giant Cell Arteritis or Temporal Arteritis,' an inflammation of the Carotid artery to the brain, with complications being...

Blindness. Stroke.

Ten days ago, I struck my right temple on an open kitchen cupboard door. The following day, bruising and swelling appeared, along with a slight headache. Expecting the pain to subside, it didn't. I considered going to Ballina Hospital the next Sunday, but the thought of sitting in a hospital waiting room for hours didn't appeal to me. I gave Reiki to my friend Jenny on Monday, and it was a fairly typical day.

On Tuesday morning, while sitting on the stool having breakfast, my head was extremely tender and incredibly sore to touch, and I couldn't even brush my hair. My right ear was so painful that I couldn't lie down on a pillow. Realising I needed to see a doctor, I rang hoping for an emergency appointment, but my doctor was fully booked.

"I have to see someone!"

The doctor I saw was young, telling him the kitchen cupboard story, he said:

"That's a furphy! The blow did not cause this!"

I thought, OMG! Am I imagining these symptoms?

Printing information from the computer, handing it to me, he said...

"You have Temporal Arteritis, inflammation of the main artery to the brain. Please obtain the prescription for Prednisolone 50mg and take it today. I will book you in for blood tests and contact a Vascular Surgeon for a biopsy."

I replied: "No! I am not taking that drug!"

I explained to the doctor that my brother died at 56 years old from liver and kidney failure after taking a similar drug.

"I would like to wait for the blood tests and biopsy results first."

"No, you could go blind! You could wake up tomorrow with no sight."

It gave me no choice; if this drug could save my sight, I had to take it. Blood tests and ultrasound confirm the diagnosis within days, and I climb onto the 'Medical Roundabout.' I realised almost immediately that the Universe was looking after me again. The blow to my temple from the open kitchen cupboard door led me to seek medical help, which protected me. I could have just gone blind, having no symptoms.

This is a long-term treatment using steroid drugs to relieve inflammation for two to three years, possibly until I die.

How blessed and grateful I am! I could have lost my sight, but instead, I find myself in a deep state of gratitude for the lessons this experience has taught me.

Here I sit in the eye of the storm.

Chaos surrounds me, yet it doesn't penetrate my consciousness. Despite the turmoil, I find myself in a state of calm. I'm at peace, with a complete acceptance of the situation and a deep trust in the journey ahead.

Shortly after the diagnosis, an email arrived in my inbox. The message it imparted to me...

When a person who has cultivated their spiritual awareness and understanding becomes comfortable, their world often collapses on one or more levels. Physically, mentally, emotionally, and spiritually, this represents the dissolution of that person's old illusory belief system. Remember that nothing is ever lost; it only changes form. That which seems to have disappeared will reappear in a higher form if it is part of one's consciousness and wholeness.

Paraphrased from Email 'The Arcturians'

My physical, mental, and emotional world had truly collapsed. I clung to my spiritual realm, drawing strength from it. The gods had seen me blissfully sitting in the 'Light'; now this battle would become the next part of my journey.

At the beginning of this quest in Warragul, Victoria, I had connected with my departed brother's spirit. We had crossed over to the 'other side' together in a small boat. While searching for answers, I struggled to comprehend the words I read in the spiritual shop in Adelaide.

"An Expanded State of Consciousness."

Now, before me was the answer:

'The mind has the potential to find peace, to let go of grievances, and to feel expanded.'

I added the words...

'To feel reverence, awe, wonder, and gratitude knowing...

I am in the presence of Spirit.'

PURPOSE, JOY & BLISS

May 2025

M It has been six years since my diagnosis of Giant Cell Arteritis. Within weeks of receiving this devastating news, my life as I knew it began to crumble. I was forced to jump onto the roundabout, with no alternative given by the medical professionals. The roundabout has been a constant, dizzying experience, riding a rollercoaster of highs and lows.

The medication strips away who I am. The person I see in the mirror is no longer there; someone else stares back at me. My small, elfin face has vanished, replaced by a bloated version. It's hard to come to terms with the changes to my face and body and my loss of identity.

I am one of only 7% worldwide who do not respond favourably to the massive daily doses of steroid medication I am forced to take to prevent going blind, having a stroke, and possibly facing death in the process—the side effects I find intolerable. Sleep eludes me, as I get only a few hours here and there. Mentally, I confront my demons. I discovered that no research has been conducted in fifty years on the multiple adverse side effects I am experiencing. That knowledge does nothing to foster a positive outlook; I am on this drug for the long haul—initially told it would take two to three years, but it has now turned into four and a half years. Once a patient is diagnosed and prescribed high-dose steroids, the only way off this medication is through a slow process of gradually decreasing the daily dose. Several times during this process, my body relapsed, forcing me to increase the dose again. Constant blood tests determine this; I shudder to think of the number of blood tests I've endured over four and a half years. That's another story! I am currently in remission.

A year after receiving my life-changing diagnosis, in February 2020, the world faced a devastating blow to its very core. The diagnosis for the world was a viral pandemic of global magnitude, known as COVID-19.

Fear and panic ensued. Supermarket shelves were stripped bare. Borders between states and across the country were closed, preventing people from visiting loved ones, hospitals, doctors, or workplaces. Small businesses went under due to a lack of customers and struggled to meet their financial commitments. Weddings and family gatherings were cancelled. We were advised against dancing, singing, or hugging and instructed to keep a distance of 1.5 metres apart. Face masks became the norm. Funerals were also affected, with church doors closed to parishioners. Worst of all, family members were not allowed to be with loved ones who were dying.

The virus spread across the globe.

COVID-19 was insidious; it frequently targeted the elderly, sick, and vulnerable, often resulting in fatal consequences. I became one of the 'vulnerable' after the medication had suppressed my immune system.

For many years, I have held the view:

One shouldn't 'stop living' in fear of death, as death is our ultimate realisation. Life should be embraced to the fullest, minute by minute, day by day, year by year.

The fear of death and disease has overwhelmed the psyche of the world en masse, leading to lockdowns. This mindset cannot be sustained; while it may save lives in the short term, in the long run, it is detrimental to one's health. There's a conundrum: the world is desperately holding on, putting lives on hold and hoping against hope for a 'cure'. This isn't in our best interests as human beings who desire freedom, love, joy, and happiness. The need for care, compassion, and empathy has never been stronger. The world will never be the same again. May we all unite as ONE in our power, support each other, and face the consequences. Some will not survive; that's nature's way, but others will grow stronger in the face of adversity.

I gained insights into why I had been diagnosed with GCA and realised the fragility of the human psyche when faced with adversity. The mental state of the world was precarious. The streets were teeming with angry people protesting the loss of their freedoms. The world was in chaos!

I was willing to let the world pass by, enjoying my solitude and finding peace in the sanctuary of my home. I revel in my thoughts, quite content to sit at my computer and write, record, and reminisce about my life. I've realised that being happy and content without needing external interaction is a gift.

Having said all that, I've survived! That was THEN. This is NOW.

In my eightieth year, I'm back teaching and have taken on a voluntary role as a lecturer at U3A (University of the Third Age). I titled the course...

'Loving Yourself: A Chakra Journey to Discover Your Inner Divine Self.'

This is a 'Self-Help, Self-Healing' workshop that incorporates....

'Relaxation, Mindfulness and Meditation through the Seven Main Chakras ~

The Energy Portals to Our Inner Being.'

About a dozen people come each week. I've received heartfelt hugs and gratitude from them, and I know I'm exactly where I need to be in my life. Serving others, sharing spiritual knowledge, and ancient wisdom bring me immense joy and bliss.

EPILOGUE

One year before my brother's death, the core beliefs of the Theosophical Society that resonated with me are now an integral part of my being. Below are those exact words my heart recognised and embraced...

I believe in the utmost truth. I believe that all of us living on this little planet we call Earth are ONE. All races, all religions, all creeds, all sexes, we are all EQUAL. I believe certain laws govern the Universe and that its forces do not operate by chance; we are all part of that Universal Law. I believe God, whoever or whatever one perceives Them to be, abides in each of us, and we are all Divine beings. Theosophy means the 'Wisdom of God.' It is a statement of the modes of action of the Divine Mind. The questions that humanity has always asked have found some satisfying answers in an understanding of "God's Plan, Evolution." This understanding is the heritage of every soul. One will possess it only as one learns to be a brother to all that lives, for Loving action is the Divine Wisdom at work, and whoever acts lovingly will inevitably come to this Wisdom. In possession of the Divine Wisdom, they know the truth which sets men free. Paraphrased from The Theosophical Society in Australia, C. Jinarajadasa. Vital Questions Answeredwww.austheos.org.au

After spending two-thirds of my life in a spiritually unconscious state, I found myself pondering this question: Why did he have to die?

The pain, grief, and loss I felt after my brother's death awakened me, providing insight into the meaning and true purpose of my life. The reason he died became clear when I received the Ultimate Gift, the gift of 'Light', which transformed my life from chaos. I have been called to offer my service, act as a conduit, and pass on ancient knowledge and wisdom. I do so with honour and privilege.

My brother's death taught me to embrace the spiritual aspect of my life, recognising the divine soul I already am. When we greet the mystical with reverence and gratitude, we uncover immense peace. This gift is bestowed upon a soul that is ready.

THE END

What does 'The End' mean? Where does it end?

When my brother passed away, I discovered on this journey that there is no end, only physical death; the spirit is eternal.

May all who embark on this sacred journey be encompassed by...

'The Light.'

Blessed Be, Blessed Be, Blessed Be.

Light, Love, Laughter & Healing.'

Christa

'Who looks outside dreams
Who looks inside awakens.'
Carl Jung

MEDITATIONS & TEACHINGS

THE COSMIC CONSCIOUSNESS WORKSHOP
This workshop had a significant impact on me. It was inspiring, clarified my thoughts, and encouraged me to incorporate the following ceremony into my daily practice.

UNCONSCIOUS
Grasping at life as it passes. Desiring possessions, material wealth, in the mistaken belief that possessions and wealth bring happiness.

Until something happens in our lifetime to awaken us to our spiritual nature, we die! It is a needless pursuit; ' there are no pockets in our last suit.'

CONSCIOUS
Realising life has a deeper meaning for us. Beginning to ask the questions. This realisation moves us to become aware of our:

SUB-CONSCIOUS
To dwell in our subconscious is to meditate and become 'still.'

Aware. Tuned into our inner being, enabling us to merge with our:

HIGHER CONSCIOUSNESS
A blessed state of being. Connected to our own Divine Higher Self. 'Tuned' into Nature to a greater degree. Seeing the beauty surrounding us.

Moving away from negativity into acceptance.

We are on the journey to Unity.

Unity with All. Unity with the Divine.

Elevated to become:

COSMICALLY CONSCIOUS
Connected to the Cosmos. Connected to the Cosmic Aum.

Mother Earth, GAIA, leading to the 'Ultimate State of Being'

DIVINE CONSCIOUSNESS
'True Awakening.'

Compassionate to every living being.
Wise. The Wisdom of the 'Knowing.'
Filled with the joy of just 'Living,' content.
No longer craving material wealth & possessions.
At Peace.
Being Love.
Full to Overflowing.

My true awakening to Divine Consciousness led me to know I have achieved the ultimate realisation, there is no higher state for me, I am

ONE with ALL & ALL is ONE

SPIRALLING TO THE LIGHT

DAILY CEREMONY

A simple ceremony to start each day:

Stand with your feet apart, in line with your shoulders, and extend both arms out to the side from the hips. Bring your focus to your nostrils, feeling the air as you breathe in, and become aware of your breathing. Breathe slowly down to your navel. Place the tip of your tongue behind your upper teeth and relax your jaw. Close your eyes and gaze upwards, behind your forehead. Create a circle of breath from your nostrils to your navel and back, relaxing...

Lifting arms slightly, fingers pointing down – say...

Unconscious

Lifting arms to hip level, say...

Conscious

Outstretched arms to heart level say...

Sub-Conscious

Raising arms further to shoulder height, fingers pointing up, say...

Higher-Consciousness

Arms open, fully elevated in surrender, say...

Cosmically Conscious

Arms fully elevated, bring your palms into a prayer position, and say...

Divine Consciousness

Bring your prayer hands down until they rest on your heart. As you breathe into your heart, envision it expanding into the cosmos. Gradually lower your hands to just below the navel, the centre of your being (Dan Tiem, or Hara), and place your hands there. Left over right or right over left. Breathe deeply into this area, relax, and let your hands go.

Enjoy.

THE ART OF MEDITATION

Meditation is a state of being where we connect with our inner essence.

Meditation brings peace, calm, joy, and love not only to ourselves but also flows through to our friends and loved ones.

Meditation is the key to enlightenment, teaching us the true meaning of life. It represents conscious mindfulness that aligns you with universal force, universal energy, your highest self, your God presence, and spiritual awareness, however you may describe it.

While meditating, you often gain clarity on a situation, see things more clearly, and understand the underlying reasons.

Generally, you will experience greater physical well-being, increased energy, relaxation, and alertness, as meditation teaches us to focus and concentrate, which is the opposite of when we are stressed; our thoughts are scattered. We learn to become still, to listen to the silence, and to go within.

The ability to meditate is not taught as such; guidelines are provided, and meditation comes when the soul is ready.

These guidelines will help you stop 'monkey chatter' and calm your mind from being constantly overloaded.

The first step to halt that internal chaos of thought...

Honour yourself, give yourself time to BE, and be who you truly are. If you haven't found that person, meditation will take you there. Become conscious of giving yourself time—5 to 10 minutes, if that's all you have. Once you get used to giving yourself time, you can even meditate in a shopping queue.

An hour or half an hour is ideal. Turn off your phone, TV, computer, and radio.

Please close the door of the room you're in.

Even put up a sign: 'Please Do Not Disturb – Meditation in Progress.'

Then, your partner and family will also adjust to allowing you some time off.

Ideally, creating a 'sacred space' doesn't need to be large; it can be as small as a corner of a room in your home or even a table or desk. Decorate it to your liking, perhaps with crystals, flowers, candles, special keepsakes, sacred symbols, or religious statues—whatever represents YOU!

Choose a time of day that suits you. As you get used to allowing yourself time and space, it will become a priority in your life. Don't get caught up in the everyday drama of your life today. Let it go.

Choose loose-fitting clothes. Get comfy and relax.

I suggest you listen to some soft meditation music, as there are plenty of options available. One of my favourites is Robert Haig Coxon's "The Silent Path."

If you haven't done so already, close your eyes, take a deep, relaxing breath, and sigh if you feel like it; then release and allow yourself to unwind. Thoughts flow harmlessly through your mind; acknowledge them. Then let them go into the Universe and set them free.

Focus on your breath, noticing the cool air as you inhale through your nostrils. Think about your navel. Carry your breath deep down into your navel, then create a circle of air, bringing the air back up and exhaling through your nostrils.

Relax. Repeat. Bring your thoughts back to your breath, the air you breathe, your life breath.

If you're working with Guides or Angels, it's time to call on them.

Each morning, I call forth Archangels to bless my day...

I call upon Quan Yin, the God and Goddess of Compassion, wishing her 'Good Morning.'

Calling on Archangel Michael to 'Protect me on the journey of this Lifetime.'

Calling upon Archangel Gabriel, may I always walk in your light.

Calling upon Archangel Raphael to 'Guide me in Healing Spirit.'

Calling upon Archangel Ariel to 'Fill my life with peace, joy and love.'

Calling upon Lord Metatron to 'Surround me with Electromagnetic Light.'

I call upon my Highest Divine Self to 'Guide me through this day.'

Imagine you're standing in a shimmering column of 'Light'...

Above your head is a pure white flower of your choosing.

Maybe a rose, daisy, or lotus blossom—you decide.

As each petal opens, radiant white 'Light' shines throughout your body.

Bringing to you, Self-Powering Energy.

This 'Light' envelops you with extraordinary joy and peace.

315

'The Light' is engulfing you in Love.

'The Light' is above your head, illuminating your face.

Smile. Imagine... 'The Light' around your shoulders.

'The Light' gently circles each of your vertebrae, moving slowly, round and down, round and down, round and down to the base of your spine.

If you experience any physical or emotional pain, pause and take a moment to acknowledge it. Take a breath, breathe 'Light' into the pain, accepting its presence, releasing it, and letting it go out into the Universe.

Carry 'The Light' into your thighs, your knees, your calves, your ankles, and into the soles of your feet. Become aware of the soles of your feet as they connect with Mother Earth.

In this ethereal column of 'Light', draw it deep into the Earth, grounding yourself in Mother Gaia.

Now bring 'The Light' up through your toes, into your ankles, calves, knees, and thighs, and up into your pelvic region, pausing just below your navel:

The centre of your being, your core, your 'Hara.' Breathe easily and deeply into your navel.

Imagine the energy travelling up, down and around your whole body.

Releasing, relaxing, giving breath to your entire system.

Carry 'The Light' and energy into your waist, into your Solar Plexus, in front of your rib cage. Breathe in 'The Light' to release any emotional hurt you may hold in your Solar Plexus.

Breathing deeply into your Heart, expand your heart with Love....

Loving you, cherishing you. 🖤

Carry 'The Light' into your throat; may you always speak your truth and be your truth.

Then let it flow into your shoulders. Sigh, releasing your burdens.

Imagine 'The Light' flowing along your arms, through your elbows, wrists, hands, palms, and fingers.

Extend your arms, bringing your hands into a prayer position above your head. Hold for a moment, then move your hands down the length of your body to rest below your navel, with your right hand over your left or your left over your right. Imagine the petals of the flower closing.

SPIRALLING TO THE LIGHT

Separate your hands, take a gentle deep breath, and release. Welcome back. Blessed be.

⁓◎

CHAKRA HEALING MEDITATION

Chakras are our wheels of energy. I like to describe them as...
'portals to our inner being.'

It is time. 🖤

Sit or lie down. Make yourself comfortable. Close your eyes and take a deep breath. Just Let Go!

Focus on your nostrils and feel the cool air as you breathe. Breathe in a circle down to your navel and then back up to your nostrils. Release and relax, then repeat. Thoughts drift harmlessly through your mind. Acknowledge them, let them go, and return your attention to your breath. Always return to your breath. Silently tell yourself...

'What do I need to come into my life right now?'

(It may be good health, love, happiness, security, peace.)

Whatever you need, set your intention now. Then release your intention into the Universe to manifest for you in divine timing.

'It is as it is, as it was meant to be.'

Now place your hands over your eyes, with your palms resting on your cheekbones and fingers pointing upwards, crossing over the Brow Chakra, your third eye, located in the middle of your forehead. Your eyes are shrouded in darkness. The Chakra's colour is a deep indigo purple; it serves as the gateway to your soul, intuition, knowledge, and inspiration. This third eye distributes light throughout your entire body and radiates your light into the world.

Now, place your hands above your ears with your fingers pointing upwards and meeting at the centre of your head – your Crown Chakra. The colour of this Chakra is pale lilac. It represents the connection to the Divine Source of the Universe, balancing the left and right sides of the brain while aligning both sides of your body. This Chakra embodies intuition and intellect, as well as masculinity and femininity, light and dark, and activity and passivity – all dualities that bring true clarity of thought.

To achieve Oneness.

Now, place your hands at the back of your head where your neck meets the base of your skull. Your fingers can point upwards, or you can put your hands side by side across the back of your head. This position is relaxing and soothing, promoting deep peace, connecting with ancient parts of yourself, and allowing for past life knowledge and recall.

Now, gently place your hands over your throat, with one hand positioned slightly higher than the other to cover your entire throat. The colour of the chakra is blue, which represents self-expression.

'I have great value, I am worthy. I am aligned with my highest truth.'

Now, place your hands on your heart, in the centre of your chest, with your left hand over your right or your right hand over your left. The colour of the chakra is green. This represents your emotional connection, opening to love, peace, and contentment.

I walk my path with ease and grace. I radiate Love.

Now place your hands over your rib cage, side by side or on each side of your body, at your Solar Plexus Chakra. The colour of the Chakra is yellow. This represents your Life Force, your Power Centre.

I'm connected to the abundant flow of the Universe.

I am one with Divine will and easily manifest my dreams.'

Position your hands below your waist, resting on either side of your body, with your fingers pointing down and touching at the centre. This represents your Sacral Chakra, which is orange in colour and is associated with creativity and sexuality.

'I love all dimensions of myself, weaving and creating the tapestry that is my life.'

Now, place your hands over your pubic bone, either right over left or left over right, or you can rest your hands with your fingers pointing down on each side of your body. This is your base chakra. The colour of the chakra is red. This chakra represents your basic instinct to survive.

I am connected to the Energy of Mother Earth.

My body, mind and spirit are grounded and purified.'

If you're experiencing any pain or discomfort in your body, whether physical or emotional, place your hands on that area for as long as it feels comfortable, then release and relax. Breathe into that area and let go.

Congratulations! You've spent time getting to know yourself, healing, and achieving wholeness and oneness.

Take Care. Love Yourself.

Namaste.

LOVE THE HIGHEST VIBRATION~BLISS
Love is the highest vibration of energy that is possible.
It is Bliss.
The 'gift' is the ability to access the bliss, love, and peace...

I am Blessed.
I am One with my God... Divine Consciousness
I am One with Gaia
I am One with Humanity
I am the Unified Light
You also are the Unified Light
You are One with Humanity
You are One with Gaia. You are One with your God
We are all Blessed.
'NAMASTE, the God in me sees and honours the God in You.'

SPIRALLING TO THE LIGHT

'LIGHT BODY' INTEGRATION ~ BECOMING 'THE LIGHT'

The following instructions lead me to 'The Light', a state of spiritual enlightenment and bliss that is the ultimate goal of this meditation.

I hope you find the same sense of bliss.

Concentrate on breathing through your nostrils, acknowledging the cool air as it enters your body. The breath of life. Your life. Lips slightly parted, take a deep breath into the navel, the core of your being, 'Hara.' Create a circle of breath, nostrils to navel, navel to nostrils. The tip of your tongue gently rests on the palate behind your top teeth—slow, rhythmic breathing. The neck extends, and the head rises, like a puppet on a string.

Relax and release your thoughts. When unnecessary thoughts surface, acknowledge them, then let them go into 'The Universe.' Focus back on your nostrils and return to breathing.

Now, looking upwards behind closed eyelids, focus on your Crown Chakra, and slowly the spiralling begins. Relax, go with it! Let it happen. The body is physically spiralling down, around, down around, down around. Repeat the words to yourself, down and around, down and around, down and around. Now, swing like a pendulum. Left to right, right to left, left to right. Repeat the words in your mind from left to right, right to left, and right to right. A perfect balance between the right and left brain. Correspondingly, both sides of the body are balanced: masculine and feminine, active and passive, yin and yang, light and dark, and intellectual and intuitive minds.

Visualise the sign of 'The Infinity' (a sideways figure 8), balancing from left to right and right to left. Picture this symbol in your mind's eye, and as you do, feel a sense of balance and harmony washing over you, spiralling down, down, into the earth, into Mother Gaia. Then, visualise it spiralling up the spine, around each vertebra, up, up, into the Crown and beyond, into The Cosmos. The 'LIGHT' explodes into the core of your being.

As your breathing slows, a sense of tranquillity envelops you. The spiralling becomes faster, your eyelids flutter, and the light flickers. Stay there, go with the spiral, go with the spontaneous energy. Peace... Nothing else! This blending of energies brings true clarity of thought, allowing you to enter into Oneness with your Divine Highest Self. Divine communication with the energy source. Total 'Light body' integration. Being 'The Light.' The Ultimate Experience. BLISS! The Greatest Gift.

Gently bring yourself back. Wiggle your toes, your fingers.
Feel your body on the floor or chair. Take a deep breath.

Visualise the roots of a magnificent tree grounding you into Mother Earth. Open your eyes.

Welcome back.

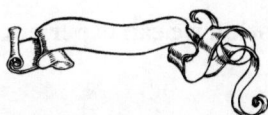

I am The Light
I am One with Divine Consciousness.
I am the Mountain
I am the Rock
I am the Lake
I am the Tree
I am the Eagle
I am Peace
I am Love
I am Bliss
My Eagle Soars.
I am One with All & All is One.
May all beings on beautiful Mother Gaia become one.

My Buddha has awakened. I am honoured, grateful, and privileged to give 'Divine Service' for the nourishment of others.

I am 'Full to Overflowing.'

You may feel 'Full to Overflowing' as you conclude your meditation. This is the feeling of being spiritually nourished and complete, a testament to the power of the meditation process.

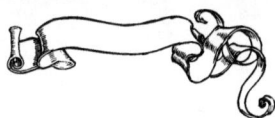

Enjoy the Journey! Blessed Be.
Namaste

"The most beautiful & most profound emotion we can experience is the sensation of the Mystical..."
Albert Einstein (1879-1955)

As the Sufi Aphorism goes....
   'When the heart weeps for what it has lost.
   The Spirit laughs for what it has found.'
   This profound wisdom has guided me through my spiritual journey, helping me find joy in sorrow.

SOURCE NOTES
Sir Thomas Aquinas. Quote Adapted. *"For Those Who Know"*
Laurel Atherton. *"I've Been Thinking About My Brother"* Copyright 1989 by Blue Mountain Arts, Inc. All rights reserved. Reprinted by permission.
'Theosophy Core Beliefs' - The Theosophical Society Brochure *'Vital Questions Answered'* C Jinarajadasa
'Rune Awakening' -© Maria Letizia Renzulli. *"Zen Runes"* © Element Books Limited. 1998 The Text © Maria Letizia Renzulli
Death by Fire... - Warrandyte Historical Society - Based on Research by the late Bruce Bence
Vegetarian - The Awareness Institute – *"The Healing Art of Reiki'*
'Inner Peace for World Peace'- Swamiji. *"Be the Change You Want to See, Inner Peace for World Peace"*
'Wesak'- *www.wesak.com.au*[1]
Oxford University Press, 1999 -Aboriginal. Refugee.
'Spiritual Support' - *"You Are the Wind Beneath My Wings"*
'Karuna® Master's Degree'- Laurelle Shanti Gaia *"The Book on Karuna Reiki* ®, *Advanced Healing Energy for our Evolving World"* Infinite Light Healing Studies Centre, Inc. 2001
Theme From Time'- David Soames
'Archetypal Reiki'- Dorothy May *'Archetypal Reiki'* Journey Editions. 2000 ISBN 1-885203-90-X
'The U Turn' - Dorothy May *'Archetypal Reiki'* 20. *The Mountain: Spiritual Attainment.*
'Asking for Guidance – Dorothy May *'Archetypal Reiki'* The Mountain.
"Pure Thoughts, Pure Mind, Pure Body' - James Allen *"As A Man Thinketh"* First Published 1903. (Wikipedia)
'Lost & Now Found'- *'Sometimes we Need Grace' Author Unknown.*
'The U Turn'- Sogyal Rinpoche *"The Tibetan Book of Living & Dying"* Harper San Francisco 1992. Copyright ® Rigpa Fellowship 1992
'The Living Practice & Creating a Routine. 'Dorothy *May 'Archetypal Reiki*
'Surrender in Love' - Brenda Sutherland *"Meeting in Love"* 'Living Now' December 2004
'Journey Continues' *'Evanescence' My Immortal"*
'Reiki Magic & Insights'- Richard Flanagan *'The Sound of One Hand Clapping'* Pan MacMillan 1997
'Conscious Not Cautious'- Osho International Foundation *'Everyday Osho'* Fair Winds Press 2002
'Special Day' - Venerable Thubten Lhundrup *"Practical Meditation with Buddhist Principles'* Hinkler Books Pty. Ltd. 2006
'Relaxation & Meditation' - Lama Surya Das *"Awakening The Buddha Within"* Bantam 1997 Copyright © Lama Surya Das 1997
'Deep Trance Meditation- Golden Mean Ratio' Advanced Esoteric Science www.merkaba.co.il/home[2]

1.   *http://www.wesak.com.au*

'Breathwork Mastery' - Alakh Analda www.rebirthing.com.au[3]

'The Alpha Plan' - Louis Proto *"The Alpha Plan"* Penguin Books 1989

'Recognising Divinity' *"Kryon Lifting the Veil"* Book 11 The Kryon Writings.Inc. Copyright© 2007-Lee Carroll www.kryon.com

'Reiki & Writing' - Matt Shooting Star *"Journey Over Mountains"* www.spiritsongflutes.com.au[4]

'Reiki & Writing' - Jain *"Vedic Maths with Jain"* www.jainmathemagics.com[5]

'Why? Answers Validated - Sogyal Rinpoche *"The Tibetan Book of Living &Dying"* Harper San Francisco 1992. Copyright © Rigpa Fellowship

'Joyce is Waiting' – St. Teresa of Avila *"May there be peace within"*

'Ignite Your Divine Voice' - *"Ishtar"* www.orderwhitemoon.org/goddess/Ishtar[6]

Character Analysis - Barbara Ann Brennan *"Hands of Light"* Copyright © 1987 Bantam Books 1988 ISBN 978-0-553-34539-

'The Legacy of Love' - Sayings of the Buddha *"To Mourn Too Long"*

'When Your Soul is Singing' - Paul Hoogendyk *"Eagles Don't Fly in Flocks"* www.ancientpathways.com.au[7]

Marianne Williamson, *"Our Greatest Fear"* A Return to Love Reflections on the Principles of A Course in Miracles HarperCollins Publishers 1992

Raym Richards *"Alchemy of Crystals"*© Raym 2000,2003,2007 & 2008 www.global-healing.com[8] Global Healing 2000 ISBN 0957793529

'Grace Within' - Ian Gawler. Chandrika Gibson, ND *"Warrior Spirit"* Nova Holistic Journal April 2010

'Spirit Re-Visits' - Quote Author Unknown *"I will not be far away, for Life Goes on"*

'The Unknown Job' - Qala www.qalasriama.com/qala.plp[9]

Universal Balance – Google *tarot and numerology – futurepointindia.com*

'Chenrezig Institute' - *'Guns N' Roses'* Song & Lyrics *"Civil War"*. You tube

'Declan Galbriath' Song & Lyrics *"Tell Me Why"* YouTube

'Follow Your Heart' - Toni Carmine Salerno *'Spirit Oracle' Cards* Copyright © 2005 Published by Blue Angel Gallery, Australia ISBN: 978-0-9579149-2-6

'Simple Abundance' - Sarah Ban Breathnach *"Simple Abundance"* Headline Group A Hodder & Stoughton Book 1996 ISBN 0 7336 0404 8

'Full Circle' - Madam Helena Petrovna Blavatsky "H.P.B" *"The Voice of the Silence"* Theosophical University Press 1889 ISBN 0-911500-04-9

---

2.   http://www.merkaba.co.il/home

3.   http://www.rebirthing.com.au

4.   http://www.spiritsongflutes.com.au

5.   http://www.jainmathemagics.com

6.   *http://www.orderwhitemoon.org/goddess/Ishtar*

7.   http://www.ancientpathways.com.au

8.   http://www.global-healing.com

9.   http://www.qalasriama.com/qala.plp

'Oneness Conference' - *"Zen Koan"* Buddhism - Buddhist quote - *"What have you gained from Meditation?....."*

'Chiron The Healer' *"Healing the Ancient Wound – The Journey of Chiron."www.stevers.com/ancientwound/myth.htm*[10]

'Chiron is a comet...www.cometastrology.com

'Chiron The Healer' - James Allen Born 1864-1912 *"The Wisdom of James Allen"* Published early 1900s

'Chiron The Healer' - Alexis Cartwright *"Transference Healing Animal Magic"* Transference Healing Pty. Ltd. 2005 www.transferencehealing.com[11] ISBN 0-9750628-2-4

'Frustrations & Joy' – Alexis Cartwright *"Beyond Doorways The Mysteries Revealed"* Transference Healing Pty. Ltd. 2005 www.transferencehealing.com[12] ISBN 978-0-9750628-1-4

Henry Scott Holland - *Carmelite Monastery, Tallow, Waterford. "There is No Death"*

'Spirit Oracle Cards' - Toni Carmine Salerno *"Spirit Oracle"* Cards Copyright © 2005 Published by Blue Angel Gallery, Australia ISBN 978-0-9579149-2-6

'Symbolic Return' - Lonely Planet Publications Pty. Ltd., *"An Ancient Magic."* www.media.lonelyplanet.com/scotland-6-orkney[13]

'Emotional Endings' – *A mind stretched to new dimensions...*adapted from a quote by U.S. author & Physician Oliver Wendell Holmes (1809-1894)

'Thoughts in Conflict' - *"Deja Blues"* Copyright 2000 Open Channel Sound Company (BMI) *"Stevenhalpern Inner Peace Music" www.stevenhalpern.com*[14]

'Contrasts & Differences' - Ciro Marchetti *"Gateway to the Divine Tarot"* Llewellyn Publications 2000

'It Is As It Is, As It Was Meant To Be' *Tao Te Ching* Lao-Tzu

'The Power of the Universe' - Alexis Cartwright *"Transference Healing Animal Magic"* Copyright © owned, published, and distributed by Transference Healing ® Pty. Ltd 2005 www.transferencehealing.com[15] ISBN 0-9750628-2-4

'Detachment' - Pema Chodron Copyright 2003, 2006 *"Always Maintain a Joyful Mind"* Shambhala Publications, Inc. www.shambhala.com[16] ISBN 978-1-59030-460-0

'Validation' - Madam Helena Petrovna Blavatsky "H.P.B" *"The Voice of the Silence"* Theosophical University Press 1889 ISBN 0-911500-04-9

'Kriya' - Wikipedia

'Kriya' – Paramanhansa Yogananda *"Autobiography of a Yogi"* December 1946 Philosophical Library

'Numerology' - Wikipedia

10.   http://www.stevers.com/ancientwound/myth.htm

11.   http://www.transferencehealing.com

12.   http://www.transferencehealing.com

13.   http://www.media.lonelyplanet.com/scotland-6-orkney

14.   http://www.stevenhalpern.com

15.   http://www.transferencehealing.com

16.   http://www.shambhala.com

'Equinox' - Full Moon in Pisces' –

"*Yogi – The Greatest & Most Famous Dog in the World*", Brenda Fleming, Unpublished, 2018.

'Virgo Abundance' - Eric Francis "*Astrology Secrets Revealed*" www.planetwaves.net/cainer/archive/003530.phphttp://cainer.com/ericfrancis/aug5.htm[17]

'Meditations' - Toni Carmine Salerno "*Spirit Oracle Cards*" Copyright © 2005 Published by Blue Angel Gallery, Australia ISBN: 978-0-9579149-2-6

'Astrology-Natal Chart' Paul Margolin www.templebyron.com[18]

'The Elohim Gateway' - Laurelle Shanti Gaia, copyright 2001 Infinite Light Healing Studios Centre, Inc.. "Karuna Reiki ® *Advanced Healing Energy for Our Evolving World*" ISBN 0-9678721-2-X

"Nourish Your Soul & Reconnect with Your True Essence" Starlight Festival.

'Namaste' Channelled by Kaliana Raphael Rose '*Namaste Beautiful Ones, Blessed* Be *Your Day*" Copyright © www.roseofraphael.com.au

'Namaste' - Lee-anne Caulkett & Francie Griffin "*Namaste, I see you Oracle Cards*" www.lee-annecaulkett.com[19], www.franciegriffin.com[20].

'Learning and Knowledge' *Amitayus* Leaflet, *Last Aid: Caring for the Dying at Home.* (1879-1955)www.quotes.net[21].

'Epilogue' - The Theosophical Society ~ C. Jinaraladasa "*Vital Questions Answered*" www.austheos.org.au

'Zen Runes' © Element Books This Text © Maria Letizia Renzulli 1998

'The End' - Carl Gustav Jung (1865-1961) "*Who looks outside dreams......*"

'The Silent Path' Robert Haig Coxon

Albert Einstein (1879-1955) "*The most beautiful...* "

Sufi Aphorism. *When the heart weeps......*

---

17.   http://www.planetwaves.net/cainer/archive/003530.phphttp://cainer.com/ericfrancis/aug5.htm

18.   http://www.templebyron.com

19.   http://www.lee-annecaulkett.com

20.   http://www.franciegriffin.com

21.   http://www.quotes.net

ABOUT THE AUTHOR - Brenda Christa Fleming

Brenda lives between the Great Dividing Range Hinterland and the Pacific Ocean in New South Wales, Australia, known as the Ballina/Byron Bay Gateway, and is locally referred to as 'Paradise.'

After the death of her beloved brother, Brenda asks, "Why?" Why did he have to die? That question leads her down a pathway of spiritual experiences, more questions, and more answers, which ultimately change her life.

At the time of her brother's death, she focused on the material aspects of this world: making money and pursuing possessions with the belief that they bring happiness. His death helped her realise there's another way.

This is a diary of my spiritual journey. I documented each occurrence on the date it happened. The words flowed from my thoughts, tumbling from my brain and appearing on paper, then later onto my laptop, handed to me in

various ways—sometimes by Tarot or Spirit Oracle Cards, and other times by my inner voice inspiring me with insights and wisdom, guided, I know, by my dearest departed brother, Colin.

The mysticism of Tarot, Runes, and Spirit has long fascinated me. It runs in my blood, my genes, and my DNA. The first stirrings of my life in this lifetime began on planet Earth, deep in the recesses of my mother's womb, on a remote island named Flotta, a stronghold for the British Naval Base during World War I and II. Flotta is located north of mainland Scotland, marking the point where the Atlantic Ocean and the North Sea meet. It is one of the mystical islands of 'Orkney', older than the Egyptian Pyramids and Stonehenge. The island is also home to Viking Norse warriors, Celtic nobles, shamans, and soothsayers.

My life journey has taken me in a circle, to where I am now, 'in service' to my fellow man as a spiritual teacher, practitioner healer, lecturer, writer, and author."

www.ingramcontent.com/pod-product-compliance
Lightning Source LLC
LaVergne TN
LVHW051110080426
835510LV00018B/1975